The
Maudlin
Impression

ReFormations

MEDIEVAL AND EARLY MODERN

Series Editors:
David Aers, Sarah Beckwith, and James Simpson

The
Maudlin
Impression

English Literary Images of

Mary Magdalene,

1550–1700

PATRICIA BADIR

University of Notre Dame Press

Notre Dame, Indiana

Manufactured in the United States of America

Library of Congress Cataloging-in-Publication Data

Some portions of chapters 1 and 3, revised and adapted for this volume, were
originally published in "'To allure vnto their loue': Iconoclasm and Striptease in
Lewis Wager's *The Life and Repentaunce of Marie Magdalene*," *Theatre Journal* 51:1
(1999), copyright © 1999 The Johns Hopkins University Press; and in "Medieval
Poetics and Protestant Magdalenes," in *Reading the Medieval in Early Modern
England*, edited by Gordon McMullan and David Matthews (Cambridge: Cambridge
University Press, 2007), copyright © 2007 Cambridge University Press.

Badir, Patricia, 1976–
The Maudlin impression : English literary images of
Mary Magdalene, 1550/1700 / Patricia Badir.
p.   cm. — (ReFormations: medieval and early modern)
Includes bibliographical references and index.
ISBN-13: 978-0-268-02215-0 (pbk. : alk. paper)
ISBN-10: 0-268-02215-1 (pbk. : alk. paper)
1. English literature—Early modern, 1500–1700—History and criticism.
2. Christian literature, English—History and criticism.   3. Mary Magdalene,
Saint—In literature.   4. Idols and images in literature.   5. Iconoclasm in literature.
6. Christianity and literature—Great Britain—History—16th century.
7. Christianity and literature—Great Britain—History—17th century.   I. Title.
PR428.C48B33   2009
820.9'351—dc22

2009027702

FOR MY

Parents

CONTENTS

FIGURES

NOTE ON EDITIONS, SPELLINGS, AND PUNCTUATION

I have used scholarly editions of medieval and early modern material when available. If a modern edition was not available I turned, in most cases, to the earliest printed text. I have left spelling and punctuation untouched in these instances. I realize that this produces a rather odd effect, making the edited texts read, rather artificially, as more modern than their unedited contemporaries. I have, however, opted for consistency over readability and am hoping that the pleasures of the text are not radically diminished as a consequence.

ACKNOWLEDGMENTS

My research for this book has been assisted by many library and gallery professionals. In particular, I want to acknowledge the help of Vivien Adams at the National Gallery in London; Matthew Percival at the Witt Library in London; Dr. Jane Cunningham, Librarian, at the Courtauld Institute of Art in London; Louisa Dare at the Courtauld Gallery; Helen Trompeteler and Erika Ingham at the National Portrait Gallery in London; Lucy Fenwick at Sotheby's in London; Alastair Laing at the National Trust; Lidia Fisher of the Royal Commission on the Ancient and Historical Monuments of Scotland; Karen Limper, Curator of British Printed Collections 1501–1800 at the British Library; Sikelela Owen at the British Museum; Sue Grinols of the Fine Arts Museums of San Francisco; Erica Nordmeier at the Bancroft Library, University of California, Berkeley; Stephen Tabor at the Huntington Library; Rachel Howarth, Curator of the Harry Elkins Widener Collection at the Houghton Library of the Harvard College Library; Anne Guillemet-Lebofsky at the Isabella Stewart Gardner Museum in Boston; Sergio Guarino, Curator of the Pinacoteca Capitolina in Florence; Elena Obuhovich at the State Hermitage Museum in St. Petersburg; Florian Kugler at Kunsthistorisches Museum in Wein; and Andrew Mussell, Archivist, Lincoln College, Oxford.

I would also like to thank John Thorold of Marston Hall, Grantham, for permission to reproduce his portrait of Elizabeth, Countess

of Orkney; and Ryan Smith for taking the picture of the reclining Magdalene at Launceston.

Portions of chapter 1 and chapter 3 were originally published in *Theatre Journal* and in *Reading the Medieval in Early Modern England*.[1] I would like to thank Johns Hopkins University Press and Cambridge University Press for granting permission to reproduce selections here.

This project would have been impossible without the financial assistance of the Social Sciences and Humanities Research Council of Canada, the Killam Trusts, and the University of British Columbia. Likewise, I want to thank Shirley Neuman, Alan Tully, Sherrill Grace, Gernot Wieland, and Dennis Danielson for providing the necessary institutional support.

More important than money and time is the moral and intellectual support of colleagues and friends. First and foremost a deep curtsey to three dear wise women: Miranda Burgess, Siân Echard, and Judy Segal, who know that it is best to write in good shoes. I also nod to the fine early modernists of the fifth floor: Mark Vessey, Stephen Guy-Bray, Vin Nardizzi, and Elizabeth Hodgson. And, of course, fond gratitude is due to Anthony Dawson and Sandra Tomc, who read every word I write, and who keep pushing me further. Paul Yachnin, thank you for the collaborative diversions, and Julie Crofts and Roger Luckhurst, thank you for the London excursions.

I owe much to my students and particularly to my research assistants: Gretchen Minton, who was there at the very beginning; Katherine Willems, Camilla Pickard, Brent Whitted, Sheila Christi, and Gavin Paul, who helped along the way; and, finally, Amanda Lewis, who was there, so patiently, at the very end.

Theresa Coletti, Katherine Jansen, Erika Lin, Gordon McMullan, and David Matthews, as well as the Re-Formations: Medieval to Early Modern series editors, David Aers, James Simpson, and Sarah Beckwith (to whom, in particular, I owe so much), have thrown their support behind this project at different stages. This is a much better book than it might have been thanks to their careful attention. Margo Shearman is to be thanked for the superb copyediting. And I must thank Barbara Hanrahan at the University of Notre Dame Press for thinking that the world needs another book on Mary Magdalene.

Though at risk of being read as maudlin, I thank my friends who are now my family: Elana Zysblat, Claudio Ance, and Ombù Ance; Laura Quilici, Scott Massey, and Lola Massey; Theresa Lam-Hawes, Richard Hawes, Nathan Hawes, and Devan Hawes. Nancy Wacho-wich, thank you for reminding me, on a weekly basis, of my prairie soul. And, finally, the denizens of 885 Union Street: Erik Price, Lucie Price, and Jacob—I thank you most of all.

INTRODUCTION

Creeping After the Cart

Verely I say vnto you, wheresoeuer this Gospel shall bee preached throughout all the worlde, there shall also this that shee hath done, be spoken of for a memoriall of her.

—Matthew 26:13 (Geneva edition)

John Marbeck was an unremarkable Tudor Protestant. In the 1530s he was an early supporter of John Calvin; in 1543 he was arrested and charged with contempt for the mass, and his papers, including an unfinished Bible concordance, were confiscated. Under Edward VI, Marbeck rose to minor prominence, publishing, in 1550, *The booke of Common praier noted* for the use of cathedrals and collegiate choirs. In 1574, despite his advanced age, he was still writing of his desire "to labour in the Lordes haruest" as vigorously as possible, good health permitting. And yet, despite his enthusiastic support for the English Church, Marbeck felt that some aspects of pre-Reformation religious culture had been left behind in the perhaps overly exuberant forward-reaching spirit of reform. As he would explain to his patron,

Lord Burghley, his purpose now was to "softly creepe after the Carte, picking vp such scattered corne, as is fallen out by the waye in the Lordes fielde." It is difficult, however, to figure out precisely what Marbeck thought he was picking up. The work that follows the dedication to Burghley is just what it purports to be: the *Lyues of holy Sainctes, Prophetes, Patriarches and others, contayned in holye Scripture . . . Collected and gathered into an Alphabeticall order, to the greate commoditie of the Chrystian Reader.* But biblical figures were never cast from the cart of the Protestant reform; they didn't suffer the dire fate of medieval saints whose *vitae* were derived from superstitious legends and outmoded apocrypha. In fact, one could even argue that the evangelical tendencies of the new theology assured the *dramatis personae* of the Old and New Testaments even greater prominence after the Reformation. And yet, in Marbeck's mind, these lives, "to good to bee lost, or trodden under foote," were endangered and in need of his "simple iudgement to bee sorted into sheaues."[1] Moreover, the prefatory epistle to Marbeck's *Lyues,* signed only "RN," registers a slight tinge of uneasiness by insisting that the book "is of God, and his holy Saintes, and therefore to be reuerencd: collected out of Scripture, and therefore no vaine fable."[2] This budding anxiety can be explained only by shifting attention from the content of the book to its form. While it is the case that Marbeck's decision to contemplate the Scriptures is entirely orthodox, the business of gathering the lives of biblical figures into an elaborate book is not. The compendium of saints' lives is a distinctly medieval, distinctly Catholic genre. In choosing to emulate it, Marbeck makes his fondness for imaginative narration and compilation unmistakable and, in 1574, in need of some defending. It isn't the corn that matters, in other words; it's the gathering of it into sheaves.

Marbeck's concern with the material and aesthetic pleasures of collecting and reformulating saints' lives provides an important way of understanding the phenomenon I address in this book: the lively early modern history of Mary Magdalene. The Magdalene is a figure whose embeddings in the medieval imagination help us to think across the rupture between old and new forms of writing that made Marbeck, and his anonymous commentator, uncomfortable. Over the course of the English Reformation, the cult of the saints came under siege. Church dedications were curtailed, images and icons were destroyed, and the medieval legends were debunked.[3] Things changed in Catholic circles as well: in response to the inroads made by Protestants, the twenty-fifth session of the Council of Trent (1563) called for the eradication of all superstition, "all filthy quest for gain," and "all lasciviousness" associated with the medieval cult of the saints.[4] And yet Mary Magdalene, because of her scriptural vitality, retained her centrality as a model saint for a modern world. In England, literary reproduction of the Magdalene story never ceased; in fact, it may have intensified. More than one hundred poems, biographies, homilies, sermons, and one play on the subject of the "blessed sinner" were published in English between 1550 and 1700. Many more texts were circulating in manuscript form, and this count does not even begin to consider the prolific references to the saint in works that were not wholly dedicated to the Magdalene story.

In these texts Mary Magdalene is not, as some late modern proponents of her cult would contend, a vessel for a Christian lineage—a living Holy Grail—nor is she an uncomplicated metonymic sign for competing definitions of *Ecclesia*. She is, rather, a complex and evolving attempt to give aesthetic shape to religious experience in an age in which the form and function of religious art are uncertain. Her relationship to the medieval past is also complicated. She is not a hermetic vessel used to store forever the iconic and sacramental practices and experiences of a banished culture that might otherwise be forgotten. While she does preserve many treasured images and valued conceits, she is always available to be refashioned in new terms, under new historical conditions. In this sense, she is what Pierre Nora describes as a *lieu de mémoire*, or a site of memory, which protects the past while also reimagining it, giving it new life in the present.[5] In the following chapters, I argue that English writers "gathered" (to return to Marbeck's terminology) the bits and pieces of the medieval Magdalene and used them, within the unfolding drama of the Reformation, as sanctioned resources for thinking about the commemorative form and mnemonic function of religious art. Here the Magdalene stood in the middle of controversies over likeness and presence—that is, amidst a precarious and uncertain polemic on the nature and power of illustration and image—and in this tentative location she served, precisely as Nora suggests, "to resurrect old meanings and generate new ones along with new and unforeseeable connections."[6]

This book traces these meanings from the middle of the sixteenth century to the end of the seventeenth century. I show how the figure of Mary Magdalene serves, initially, as a constellation of imagistic memory reconceived to formulate the look and feel of English Protestantism. The Magdalene is used, in this formulation, to express a shared concern for the Christian future brought about by the loss— for better or for worse—of embodied ways of encountering Christ's invisible presence. Here, she helps to articulate representational practices that mitigate the agony of that loss and that assuage uncertain circumstances by giving the Scriptures appreciable aesthetic form. In this new context, the Magdalene becomes the model for a new generation of poetic portraits commemorating English Christians in terms that accentuate not only their extraordinary piety but also the haunted "look" of genuine love.

As this poetics takes shape over time, Magdalene writing becomes more erudite and more mannered, and eventually its potency is understood as lying less in its ability to illustrate the emotional affect of the Word than in its capacity to render some sense of the ineffable magnificence of the Christian experience. And yet at the same time the image becomes ubiquitous, circulating through bookshops and print stalls in poetry, sermons, and printed pictures. As if in anticipation of her decadence and eventual demise at the hand of history, some writers begin to position the Magdalene against this unbridled proliferation; however, by the end of the seventeenth century examples of the image make evident the enormous gap that separates the Middle Ages from the Restoration. Only in rare instances does Mary Magdalene serve, once again, as a site of memory—connecting the present to the past and to a time when the woman with the alabaster jar was inseparable from the beauty of holiness.

Scattered Corn

The Magdalene found between "Mary, mother of John" and "Mardocheus" in Marbeck's *Lyues* is just what the author promises: a life delivered out of the Scriptures.[7] Mary Magdalene is a "sinfull woman" from Bethany who, in token of her great repentance, brings costly oils to Jesus at the Pharisee's house. There, she falls to her knees, washes Christ's feet with her tears, dries them with her hair, and anoints them with oils. Christ forgives her sins and she devotes her life to him. Martha, Mary's sister, disapproves of Mary's silent devotion, but Mary proves her fidelity by listening tirelessly to Jesus' preaching. She attends the crucifixion and the sepulcher, and she mourns the disappearance of Christ's body. She is the first to see Jesus standing in the garden, but she does not recognize him until he addresses her. She reaches toward him, once again to kiss his feet, but he rebukes her and tells her that she must inform his brethren that he is to ascend to his father.[8] Marbeck's Mary is the Magdalene of the Renaissance, rooted in Scriptures and stripped of the legendary apparatus associated with her medieval cult. However, Marbeck's practice—the stitching together of scriptural fragments to form one compelling story—introduces the topic of the Magdalene's medieval legacy.

The Magdalenes of the Middle Ages were generally conflations of Mary, sister of Martha and Lazarus (Luke 10 and John 11); Mary Magdalene, from whom Christ expels seven devils (Luke 8) and who attends the sepulcher (Matt. 27; Mark 15–16; Luke 23–24; John 19–20); "the woman" who anoints Christ's head (Matt. 26; Mark 14; John 12); and Luke's "sinner," who bathes Christ's feet in the home of Simon the Pharisee (Luke 7).[9] The composite figure was first conceptualized by Gregory the Great. The story was further embellished by a collection of attendant legends that were rendered popular by the *Legenda aurea*.[10] The Magdalene became known as a courtesan of noble descent, one who relinquishes a past tainted by luxury in favor of a contemplative life of ascetic devotion to Christ. This latter portion of the *vita* seems to have been derived from scattered scriptural references linking Mary with the wealthy town of el Mejdel (Magdalini in Greek); with precious oils; and possibly with other New Testament women, including the woman taken in adultery and the Virgin Mary. Other legends were also woven into the biblical tissue: the eleventh-century story of the sea journey that brought Mary Magdalene (along with Lazarus and Maximus) to Vézelay; and the earlier legend (probably Italian) about the penitential life of Mary of Egypt who lived out her days in a cave in the desert, covered only in hair and ascending to heaven seven times a day (at the seven canonical hours).[11] This saint's relics (including a skull marked with the print of Christ's finger) were found in a cave at Sainte-Baume near Marseilles where they continue to be venerated today.

Medieval English Christians dedicated 1 college, 63 hospitals, and 172 parish churches to St. Mary Magdalene.[12] They painted her tending Christ's feet, weeping at the cross and the sepulcher, preaching to the masses, and meditating (or reading) in the desert. Her image graced church windows and illuminated manuscripts and prayer books. She was the subject of plays, miracle accounts, biographies, sermons and homilies, hymns, and poems. She was, with the exception of the Virgin Mary, the most important figure in the English cult of the saints. We know a lot more now about the medieval Magdalene than we did a decade ago largely due to the recent efforts of Victor Saxer, Susan Haskins, Katherine Jansen, and Theresa Coletti.[13] Each of these scholars has worked to define what Debora Shuger calls Mary's "sacred eroticism" by illustrating how centuries of popular devotion and exegetical debate articulated the saint's nearness to Jesus' body, both during his life and after his death.[14] The Magdalene's tender ministrations model a penitential practice premised upon physical understanding. Her profound and lugubrious mourning at the cross and at the sepulcher, coupled with her extraordinary encounter with Christ after his death, constitute an original experience of sacramental presence. Finally, her most privileged status as preacher of the resurrection makes her a mesmeric and politically charged icon for the authority of women within institutional religion. Coletti's groundbreaking assertion that medieval literature dedicated to the saint conducts sustained cultural dialogue about the contributions of "feminine spiritual experience, authority and corporeality to late medieval theology and religious practice" is now assumed wisdom. For those of us who study these fields, Mary is an "organizing symbol" who presides over our dialogue, "exposing its assumptions and risks, bearing witness, through her own semiotic multivalence, to the contested, overdetermined symbolic systems of late medieval religions."[15]

Marbeck was obviously trying to leave this potentially explosive figure on the other side of the Reformation where she clearly belonged, instead favoring a figure derived exclusively from scriptural sources. And yet, even the much reduced Magdalene that Marbeck preserves in his *Lyues* had come under attack as early as 1518 when Jacques Lefèvre d'Étaples, in a treatise entitled *De Marie Magdalena*, revived the opinions of some church fathers by arguing for the presence of three distinct women in the Gospels: Mary Magdalene, from whom Christ expelled seven devils and who attended the sepulcher; Mary, sister of Martha and Lazarus; and the woman, a nameless sinner, who anointed Christ with oil upon several occasions.[16] Of the composite Magdalene, Lefèvre wrote:

> Strong, I admit, are the authors, and their number is great, but the gospel is stronger than any number of authors. Strong too is an ancient custom, even a false one, and it often claims for itself, although erroneously, the Church's authority. Yet the truth is stronger still.[17]

The tremors resulting from Lefèvre's proposal were registered in England in three conservative tracts written in 1519 by John Fisher, bishop of Rochester and chancellor of Cambridge University. Fisher's response to Lefèvre would prove to be what Anselm Hufstader calls "the training ground" for his controversy with Luther and for his opposition to Henry VIII's divorce. For Fisher, the stakes were very high indeed:

> I immediately thought of how many difficulties would confront the whole Church if Lefèvre's opinion were ever to be accepted. How many authors would have to be rejected, how many books would have to be changed, how many sermons formerly preached

to the people would now have to be revoked! And then, how much uneasiness would arise among the faithful, how many occasions of loss of faith. They will soon doubt other books and narratives, and finally the mother of us all, the Church, who for so many centuries has sung and taught the same thing.[18]

Coletti has argued that the saint's infamous sexuality was at the heart of early humanist critiques of the single Magdalene. Lefèvre and his followers were, accordingly, motivated by the belief "that perfection in holiness is consonant with ethical perfection." They did not dispute Jesus' justification of the sinner in Luke 7 but rather maintained that superior holiness, "'the realized image of God' in humankind, was not something that could emerge, as the vita of a single Magdalene would have it, in one sudden transformative act."[19] While this assessment is certainly accurate, Fisher's response to Lefèvre also suggests that the issues congregating around Mary Magdalene take one to the very core of Christian representational practice. Lefèvre thought that the church needed to be liberated from the fictions generated not by God, but by theologians, artists, writers, and historians—and Fisher knew what effecting such liberation would mean.[20]

Crucial to my own argument is the fact that Lefèvre and Fisher locate the figure of the Magdalene at the center of a debate that sought to articulate the possibilities and limitations of religious art. The critical question for both writers was just how much one could supplement the truth of the Gospels with story or with illustration. While Lefèvre was denounced by the church for his views, the events of the next two decades would reveal that his principles were the same as those guiding Protestant reform and that the habits he sought to denounce constituted the practices—the "ancient customs"—that latter-day historians would identify as the imaginative (the fictive, the affective, the emotional, the image-making) qualities of medieval art and literature.

In his incisive discussion of the postmedieval construction of the Middle Ages, James Simpson argues that the imagination was fingered, by iconoclastic church reformers, as precisely the thing that threatened to "block access to abstract reason and to invest the material with idolatrous desire." It was thus also "the boundary line between the popular and the learned, between image and the word," and it ultimately served to "divide historical eras," positing superstition on one side of a paradigm shift and rationalizing faith on the other. The Magdalene's resilience to the history-making energies of reform thus becomes an index of the enduring importance of the imagination to early modern religious culture. When the Magdalene appears in Marbeck's *Lyues*, for instance, she may be a stripped-down version of her former self, but her life remains a tissue woven from the very threads that humanist scholars tried to pick apart. Her appeal continues to reside in the composite, or rather composed, nature of her story, proving, as Simpson suggests, that despite the attempt to consign the imagination to the realm of history, it would continue to inform present reason "by feeling its way back into the body of the past, across massive historical ruptures."[21]

The Magdalene that resurfaces in the chapters that follow is the place to which writers like Marbeck return, gathering up, along the way, the inspired narratives that might have disappeared had anyone actually adhered to Lefèvre's sense of the Gospels' certainty. Moreover, the composite Magdalene recuperated from the vault of idolatrous icons is more than illustrative of a tenacious attachment to culturally significant stories; she actually speaks to the necessity of making such stories and provides an anthology of aesthetic strategies and creative possibilities to do so. The key passage from the Gospels, in this respect, is Matthew 26:6–13:

And when Iesus was in Bethania, in the house of Simon the leper, There came vnto him a woman, which had a boxe of very costly oyntment, and powred it on his head, as he sate at the table. And when his disciples sawe it, they had indignation, saying, What needed this waste? For this oyntment might haue bene solde for much, and bene giuen to the poore. And Iesus knowing it, sayde vnto them, Why trouble yee the woman? for shee hath wrought a good woorke vpon me. For yee haue the poore always with you, but me shall yee not haue alwaies. For in that shee powred this oyntment on my bodie, shee did it to burie me. Verely I say vnto you, wheresoeuer this Gospel shall bee preached throughout all the worlde, there shall also this that shee hath done, be spoken of for a memoriall of her.[22]

This passage is often at the core of theological debate on the subject of Christ's vanishing presence—from discussion on the form and substance of the Eucharist to learned engagements with pneumatology.[23] These complex issues are beyond the scope of this book; however, some attempt to articulate the Magdalene's centrality to the subject of Christ's presence is indeed called for.

Matthew 26 was used, first by the church fathers and later by the defenders of Catholicism, to argue that the admittedly extravagant gestures of Mary Magdalene were the iconic equivalent of costly gestures bestowed upon Christ through the vehicle of the church. The medieval compendium of patristic glosses, the *Glossa Ordinaria*, turns Christ's statement ("me shall yee not haue alwaies") into confirmation of his enduring corporeal presence ("Ecce ego vobiscum sum omnibus diebus usque ad consummationem saeculi") as anticipated by the sacramental sensuality of Mary's act. Mary's oil is the physical supplement, the very "odour of faith" (fidei odorem) for which Christ sheds his blood (pro qua mox fusurus sum sanguinem) and which remedies the annihilation of his death (Officium est sepulturae quod vos perditionem esse putatis).[24]

This traditional reading of Matthew 26 would survive the Reformation in the Catholic annotations of the Rheims-Douay Bible published in 1586 "for the better understanding of the text, and specially for the discouerie of the Corrvptions of diuers late translations, and for cleering the Controversies in religion, of these daies." The note accompanying verses 6–13 describes Protestant readings of the passage as "simple lost, or lesse meritorious" and compares them to the disciples who found the cost of the oils bestowed upon Christ's body to be "fruitless." Here the proximity of Mary's act to the account of the Last Supper allows it to be linked to the doctrine of transubstantiation, and though the reading acknowledges that "we haue him not in visible maner as he conuersed on the earth with his disciples," it makes a claim for the real presence made possible by Communion.

"We haue him after an other sort," claims the gloss, "in the B. Sacrament, and yet haue him truly and really the self same body."[25]

For Protestant exegetes, the passage provides an opportunity to consider the inevitable loss of Christ's humanity—the central theological problem facing post-Reformation English Christians. Calvin insists that the prescription for ritual, found in the Catholic gloss of Matthew 26, fails to recognize the specificity of the original event: "Though Christ desired not the vse of oyntment . . . yet in respect of the circumstance, this anointing pleased him." Calvin's commentary argues that Mary's exceptional qualities—her special grace as made apparent by "a secreat motion of the spirite"—are the key elements on display. Thoughtless repetition of an original gesture does not indicate like grace in others, for Mary's singular act is memorable only because it makes her predestination evident. Thus, "there was no commandement which enioyned Mary to this annoynting, neither was it needeful that there should haue beene a law set downe for one worke." Calvin continues:

> Christ doth not simply defend the anoynting, that we shuld follow the same: but declareth that there was a cause wherfore it was acceptable to god. It is conuenient [that] this should be wisely obserued, least, that togither with the papists, we should preposterously deuise sumptuous rites for the worshipping of God: for when they heard that Christ would that Mary should anoynt him, they imagined that he was delited with incense, waxe candles, magnificall ornaments, and such like pomps. For this cause they had at their glorious ceremonies, & they thought that they could not worship God aright, if they should not lash out into great charges.[26]

Calvin concurs with Lefèvre and Lefèvre's supporters when he locates the image of Mary Magdalene at the heart of theological debate over the integrity of sacramental culture. And he would not be the last to weigh in on a passage whose meaning would continue to be debated for several more generations. Even as late as 1646, amidst the turmoil of the Civil War, preachers like Richard Ward were using Matthew 26 as proof of Christ's bodily departure to heaven where he remains "till his comming againe."[27] The passage is frequently linked to Mary's presence at Christ's grave (Matt. 28; Mark 16; Luke 24; John 20), suggesting that, even before the crucifixion, she anticipates that Christ will not always be available in human form. From this perspective, the Magdalene's anointing becomes important to a developing Protestant poetics because it prefigures Christ's physical departure and recognizes that his memory will need to be constituted in imaginative work.

Protestant commentators also acknowledge that Christian memory is an affective experience. Despite Calvin's stalwartly rational mandate, for instance, the odoriferous sensuality of the *Glossa Ordinaria* reverberates through his reading of Matthew 26:

> For Christ sayth that he shal not be alwaies with vs, to be worshipped with outward pomps. We know assuredly & by experience of faith we fele that he is present with vs by spiritual power & grace: but he is not visibly conuersant amongst vs to receiue earthly honors at our hands. So they are outragious obstinat, which doe thrust vpon him fantastical charges against his will. . . . Therefore Iohn praiseth Mary, because that she had reserued that oyntment for the day of his burial. But after that the perfecte truth of his figure appeared, & Christ come out of the graue, he did not only perfume one house but all the worlde with the comfortable quickening sauour of his death.[28]

The key phrase comes at the end of the passage as Calvin broaches the subject of what Mary sees after the resurrection. Calvin stops sounding like Calvin as he grapples with "the perfecte truth" of a figure. What is this presence? Is it a lifelike specter, an image, or a *figura?* The only way Calvin can explain the moment is to describe its affect—what it looks like, how it feels, how it smells, and even how it tastes. The presence seems to be a spiritual triumph, knowable through the "experience of faith" and accountable only through the iteration and commemoration of Mary's profoundly physical act. While knowledge of Christ does not lie in the empty mimicry of scriptural events, Calvin comes very close to admitting that the reading of the Gospel alone is insufficient without an "idea" of Mary Magdalene to show us just how real the spiritual encounter can be.

Calvin's reading of the Magdalene as a passionate register of the experience of the Holy Spirit echoes through other early modern glosses on Matthew. For instance, while maintaining that Mary's gesture was "sweetly ordered by Almighty God in his secret counsel, and by his fatherly providence, to excellent ends," John Trapp remarks that she will be remembered because "Maries name now smels as sweet in all Gods house, as ever her oyntment did."[29] Wherever one finds the Bible, it seems, one also finds Mary, who makes it known that reading Scripture should be an emotional exercise deeply invested in an epistemology of the senses.

It is Erasmus's paraphrase of Matthew 26, however, that provides the most provocative reading of the Magdalene's special know-how:

> And because he should reuyue and ryse agayne, before that his frendes should do hym this honoure, he suffered this pompe of buryall to be bestowed vpon him before his death: to the intent he mighte imprint by manye meanes in his disciples myndes the mencion of his death, and by honoure, to mitigate the horrybleness thereof.

Apparently mediating between tradition and revision, Erasmus writes that Christ tolerates Mary's act to pre-emptively impress the memory of his death upon the minds of his followers and in so doing ease their horror. Mary's function is to supplement or "mitigate" the ghastly truth told in the Gospels with a memory that Christ understands, at least in Erasmus's paraphrase, as preventing the emptiness that death creates:

> Therefore depraue not her godlynes, whiche is so acceptable vnto God, that whereas the gospell of my death shall be preached through out all the worlde, this woman also shall be mencioned, whiche with a godly and holy duety, hath preuented my sepulcure.[30]

Erasmus's point is that Mary Magdalene's commemorative function is different from that of the Gospels, which undertake the scriptural mission of recording Christ's Word: she draws the Word into the world, making the connections between it and the lived lives of those who follow it. If Erasmus's gospel of death serves as what Christopher Collins has argued is typical of scriptural writing in general, if it is "a writing down" that strives to "preserve contact with the authorial voice of God despite the passage of time and the vicissitudes of history," then the Magdalene's gesture is a kind of "poiesis," or a "making-up" that brings scriptural writing forward and allows it to begin to take appreciable shape.[31]

The chapters that follow will show that Erasmus was not alone in his allusion to a supplementary symbolic act, intimately associated with the Magdalene, which softens the sadness of the Christ's death and departure and even prevents him from vanishing entirely. However, before turning to the imaginative work the Magdalene enables, I want to return briefly to Lefèvre, who, in one of his final volleys in the debates of 1519, recalls a pilgrimage to Sainte-Baume. Lefèvre asks his traveling companion, who has just finished saying his prayers to the Magdalene's relics, what he thinks his devotions will accomplish. The friend replies:

> I do not put my faith in the (relics) which are presented. I take little interest in them, but I do not scorn them, for Christ does not require that I put my faith in these things. I rather keep my faith in the events, which are narrated, to me, most of all in those, which I know the Church to celebrate. Then I raise my mind to heaven, to the exemplars of those visible things, lying open to the eyes of the mind, not to those of the body—this, or something like it, is what I turn over in my mind.[32]

Lefèvre's friend, likely expressing the views of Lefèvre himself, seems to be saying that his faith is supplemented by the contemplation of the Magdalene—an exemplar of visible things able to give imaginative form to the events central to Christian culture. I want to suggest that early modern theologians, despite their differences of opinion, do not seem to be at odds on the subject of Mary Magdalene. While their writing bears witness to the idealism, the fanaticism, and the spiritual disillusionment that is inevitable at moments of cultural transformation, it also reminds us, as Marbeck does, that at the center of religious history there is "also this"—the Magdalene—a site of memory that works to "inhibit forgetting, to fix a state of things, to immortalize death, and to materialize the immaterial," lending familiar, appreciable shape to the experience of faith.[33]

A Memorial of Her

Shuger has trenchantly argued that, in Renaissance practice, biblical narratives retained "a certain (if limited) flexibility: not necessarily a theological flexibility but a sort of extradogmatic surplus of undetermined meaning—or rather meaning capable of being determined in various ways." These "determinations," she continues, "should not be reduced to theological positioning (although they have theological implications); they take shape at the intersection between the biblical text and other cultural materials."[34] This book takes a deeper look at one of these points of intersection. I consider how literary glosses of the Gospel-based Magdalene stretch backward into the medieval past in order to recuperate and protect a range of image-making practices; I also consider how these practices, in turn, lend material, tangible form to the Bible of the Reformation. I argue that, in the wake of the Protestant Reformation, the Magdalene story did not tumble disregarded to the wayside. Rather, it was gathered up by English writers and retold in a bewildering array of literary genres. At a very basic level, the purpose of this book is to test the Magdalene's flexibility, to register her range of possible meanings as her rich medieval legacy comes into contact with the push and pull of religious reform. But more importantly, this book shows how devotional writers of the sixteenth and seventeenth centuries used the Magdalene to articulate the possibility of describing religious experience in a literature that could elide the controversial, embodied character of art while it continued to explore the potency and appeal of beautiful things. This book thus enters into dialogue with other early modernists who have studied the translation and publication history of the Bible in early modern England.[35] It is also aligned with scholarship that seeks to recognize a visual poetics born of iconoclasm, and it speaks to renewed interest, in Renaissance studies generally, in the Catholic past as well as to recent attempts to register the marks of that past within the annals of Renaissance literary history.[36] More pointedly, this book contributes to literary history published in the wake of Louis Martz's *The Poetry of Meditation* and Barbara Lewalski's *Protestant Poetics.*[37] This body of scholarship continues to conceptualize a bewildering mass of writing practices all loosely gathered under the rubric of early modern religious literature. Some of this work is more invested in the range of subject positions made possible by literary culture, while some concentrates, as I do, more specifically on formal debts, contributions, and innovations.[38]

The first chapter of this book ("The Look of Love") considers the most sensational facet of the medieval saint's biography: her association with vanity and luxury, and hence with iconic visuality. I will show how the resplendent lady of Magdala, articulated but underplayed in works such as the *Legenda aurea*, *The Old English Martyrology*, *Legendys of hooly wummen*, and the Digby *Saint Mary Magdalen* play, dominates Protestant allegorical literature as the sign of the decadent precursor to the One True Church. The chapter looks at early modern treatments of Luke 7 (in which Mary washes Christ's feet in the home of Simon the Pharisee), in particular Lewis Wager's morality drama, *The Life and Repentaunce of Mary Magdalene* (1566), where the iconic Magdalene, figured as the ornate and covetous Roman Church, devolves into the penitent Mary who is the embodiment of a stripped-down, modest piety founded in the Scriptures. In Wager's play, as in the other postmedieval treatments of Luke, attention to Mary's life with Jesus brings the saint's preconversion state into focus. However, at the moment of her conversion, Mary's sinful sexuality transforms into a surprisingly nostalgic physical intimacy with Christ that is first and foremost something to behold. Central to the work that follows, then, is the saint's location in the middle of the fractious dialectic between sober Protestant words and gaudy Catholic icons woven into much of the religious writing of the early modern period. The Magdalene's post-Reformation afterlife proves, as W. J. T. Mitchell contends, that "the history of culture is in part the story of a protracted struggle for dominance between pictorial and linguistic signs, each claiming for itself certain proprietary rights on the 'nature' to which it only has access." However, rather than contributing to our knowledge of early modern iconoclasm—rather than showing that the various stages of the English Reformation were either more or less invested in the plastic image than hitherto imagined—postmedieval memorials of the Magdalene coalesce into a poetics that challenges the completeness of any piety premised entirely upon the reading of the Scriptures or entirely on the physical veneration of images and icons. The early modern recuperation of the medieval Magdalene reveals that the opposition between words and pictures is, as Mitchell concludes, misleading, as text and image are, at least with respect to the Passion narrative, epistemologically inseparable.[39]

Chapter 2 ("Touch Me Not") turns from Simon's house to the sepulcher and *hortulanus* scenes (John 20) that dwell on Mary's lamentations for the loss of Christ's body in order to formulate new ways of contemplating his presence in the world. The chapter traces the afterlives of a twelfth-century homily, *De beata maria magdalena*, in the meditative prose and poetry of Catholic (Henry Constable, Robert Southwell, Richard Verstegan, William Alabaster) and Conformist (Thomas Walkington, Gervase Markham) writers. All of these writers saw, as the homilist did, Mary's singularity as residing in her ability to see Christ when no one else could. While she fixates on the absence of Christ's body she is blind; when she learns to find Christ's presence within the "sepulcher of her heart" she can not only see and feel him, she also has the means to describe him. Christ becomes a shadow in these texts—an affect that is felt in words that disturb and disorient the Magdalene's senses. And the narratives, like ghost stories, represent and constitute absent presence, not by describing that presence itself but rather by describing the effect it has upon its most privileged and clairvoyant seer. The chapter concludes with the suggestion that postmedieval writers ultimately understand Mary as a haunting figure of meditation in her own right, to be acknowledged not only for her exceptional insight, but also for her ability to inspire a religious poetics that reflects, as precisely as possible, what it means to remember Christ.

Chapter 3 ("The Task of Beauty") returns to the sepulcher scene in order to reconsider the Magdalene's vision in the light of her "choice" (Luke 10) to listen to Christ's words rather than to act, as her sister Martha does, in his service. The chapter engages poetic portraits of three aristocratic, early modern Magdalenes: Mary Sidney, Countess of Pembroke; Margaret Russell, Countess of Cumberland; and Lady Magdalen Herbert. It is the Magdalene's calm attentiveness to the Scriptures that appeals to the poets (Nicholas Breton, Aemilia Lanyer, and John Donne) who pay homage to these noble women. Like Mary of Bethany—a figure whose contemplative posture is imaginatively linked to the medieval Magdalene's legendary life as a desert hermit—these models of Protestant piety are mystical visionaries able to comprehend meaning beyond ordinary understanding. As such, these latter-day Magdalenes serve as ghostly tutors that stir tormented writers into action, inspiring a devotional poetics for an age that had left the religious icon behind.

Counter-Reformation aesthetics draw the medieval Magdalene's stunning visuality into relief once again—an observation made manifest most blatantly in the paintings of the Continental Renaissance: the Magdalenes of Titian, Correggio, Tintoretto, and Rubens. Chapter 4 ("Penance in a Sheet") considers the Magdalene portrait, in painting and in print, in order to explore increasingly sophisticated renderings of the beauty of her holiness. The chapter begins with a discussion of Lancelot Andrewes's sermons in order to show how Laudian religious sensibilities, and the English revitalization of Counter-Reformation art, create an aesthetically conditioned spirituality (or perhaps a spiritually conditioned aesthetic—it is difficult to distinguish one from the other) that appealed to an increasingly erudite audience. The chapter then turns to George Herbert's "Marie Magdalene" in the context of an evolving taste for dense, compressed epigrammatic treatments of religious subjects. Devotional writing, in this context, is brought into contact with the art market (in particular with printed reproductions of famous paintings), and, as the proximity between art and literature becomes more appreciable, I argue that Magdalene poetry becomes more self-conscious and more concerned with execution than with content. With this observation in mind, the chapter concludes with the Magdalene poems of Robert Herrick, Henry Vaughan, and Richard Crashaw, which approach *ekphrasis* in their exploration of the Magdalene's "art." These poems, while deeply invested in plastic visuality, are also aware of the perils of making words indistinguishable from pictures. Thus, just as printed images of the Magdalene were becoming more ubiquitous in English culture, the Magdalene poetry can be read as re-establishing age-old tensions between visual and literary art.

Chapter 5 ("She's a Nice Piece of Work") turns to the Restoration and to Aphra Behn's *The Rover*. My reading of Behn's play draws attention to the strategic deployment of portraits of the courtesan figure Angellica Bianca. I suggest that there is evidence to consider these portraits alongside those of the mistresses of Charles II, some of which feature their subjects *à la Madeleine*. I show how these Magdalene portraits participate in the reinvigoration of the medieval saint's worldliness—a subject that is taken up in contemporary sermons and pamphlet literature as well. The vulgarization of the Magdalene in Restoration culture in general, and the demise of the person of Angellica at the hands of an English Royalist in particular, suggest that English consumers of art and literature no longer acknowledged (or needed) the forms of remembrance and commemoration that the post-medieval Magdalene once embodied. And yet, I argue that Behn's own portrait of Angellica discloses a tenacious attachment to the sinner-saint of the New Testament Gospels who haunts the play as her former self, marking the loss that comes with historical rupture while simultaneously imparting a sense of sanctity and grace to those special few who still have vision and insight.

The Maudlin Impression is neither a social history nor a history of religion. It is a literary history of imitation and invention. In other words, while this book participates in what Ken Jackson and Arthur Marotti have called the "turn to religion" in early modern studies, it does so selectively, nudging aside (although never away) both the fine points of theology and the vicissitudes of religious history in order to explore the resilience of a single topos across time, across belief systems, and across subject positions.[40] Readers will notice that, as my narrative moves through history, pre-Reformation material is less conspicuous as the Restoration divests the medieval Magdalene of most of her mnemonic resources. However, taking my cue from the editors of this new series, I want to argue that the Magdalene's presence in literature published between 1550 and 1700 suggests an alternative to the habit of seeing the medieval and the early modern periods as two separate, almost incommensurate realms. I say this not because the Magdalene survives the Reformation untarnished or unchanged, but because by the end of the seventeenth century the figure continues to function as she did in the Middle Ages: she is the avatar of a cultural poetics in which the affective interplay between loss and recollection provides a rich source of figurative language—a language of love that registers something of the past by turning the mind toward the contemplation of beautiful things.

The Look of Love

And beholde, a woman in the citie, which was a sinner, when she knewe

that Iesus sate at table in the Pharises house, shee brought a boxe of

oyntment, and shee stoode at his feete behinde him weeping, and began

to wash his feete with teares, and did wipe them with the heares of her

head, and kissed his feete and anoynted them with the oyntment.

—Luke 7:37–38 (Geneva edition)

In 1618 Harim White, bachelor of divinity and chaplain to James I, wrote a sermon called *The Ready Way to Trve Repentance*, and he dedicated it to his mother, Dorothey Dalby. The sermon is a meditation on the seventh chapter of the Gospel of Luke, cited in the epigraph above. In accordance with long-standing tradition, White conflates Luke's "woman in the citie" with Mary Magdalene and ties the success of the saint's penance to her preconversion notoriety:

She was the very filth of sinne, *Sentina malorum*, one that set her selfe to sale, *prostibulum inter gentes*; an insatiable Woman, *Que prostituit se omnibus*, hauing her Chastity at command for money, the by-word of the people, one pointed at, the very scumme and scoffe of the world, it should seeme a sinner aboue measure, and such a one was *Mary Magdalen.*[1]

For the Protestant Magdalene, as for her Catholic predecessor, the *a priori* condition for salvation is sin; and the greater the sin, the more extraordinary the salvation.[2] That this aspect of the sinner-saint's biography would survive the Reformation is not surprising. More jarring, however, is White's retention of, and elaboration upon, the dramatic nature of Mary's repentance:

> The demonstratiue absolution, and remission from sinne is Pub-like, and requireth *externa testimonia operum*, to make manifest this conuersion; and therefore our Sauiour turnes him to the Phari-sie, rehearsing the loue and workes of *Mary*, as sequels, and fruits of her faith, namely her washing, anoynting, wiping and kissing, &c. . . . And so doth *Mary Magdalene* here, giue testimony of the remission of her sinnes before God by faith, before the world, by loue. The remission of sinne is such a thing as without it *none can be saued*, and once hauing obteined it, none such can perish.[3]

This passage points, in a recognizably Protestant fashion, to the importance of grace bestowed upon sinners by Christ alone, but it is also preceded by an account of the "rites and ceremonies" expressing the saint's true repentance:

> To knock our hard and stony hearts with the Publican. Luke 18.
> To smite thy thigh. Ier. 31.18.
> To teare the haire. Sam. 13.
> To wring and smite the hands. Ezech. 21.
> To rent the garments. Esay. 37.
> To frequent solitary places. Esay. 2.
> To lye vpon the ground. Dan. 10.
> To put on a Sackcloth. Ionah 3.
> To Strewe Ashes. Iob 42.

To proclaim solemne & publike fasts. Io. 2.
Ieiunare, to fast. Ier. 14.
Vlulare, to howle. Ier. 15.[4]

Inward sorrow is made manifest in a histrionic performance of contrition, one that seems, despite the biblical invocations, out of place in a sanctioned sermon by a sober court divine. And yet, the text is understood by its author to be a reaction against "dissembled, Popish, *perfunctory* hypocrisie," alluding instead to an apparently acceptable form of devotion modeled specifically upon Luke's example.[5]

White's rather frenzied view of penance is, in fact, moderate in comparison with another contemporary treatment of the same scriptural event: Thomas Robinson's *The Life and Death of Mary Magdalene* (1620).[6] Robinson's epic poem begins in Aphrodite's palace with an account of the luxuries and pleasures found therein. Aphrodite is attended by an array of vice figures (Flattery, Wantonness, et al.), including a most wicked Mary Magdalene. This Magdalene beguiles and deceives her lovers, luring them into her prurient bower of bliss. Disgusted with her behavior, God dispatches a messenger, the prick of conscience, Syneide, whose invocation goes unheeded. Instead, Mary follows a witch, Archeron, to the depths of hell where she mixes and mingles with famous lovers (Pyramus and Thisbe, Antony and Cleopatra, et al.) and with other archfiends, the likes of Melancholy and Nemesis, who drive her to madness:

> Thus (ah poore soule!) shee's tossed too and fro:
> The deadly feinds, y^r furious will obtaine:
> And nowe her body headlonge downe they throughe,
> Into ye brinish waters of ye maine;
> And nowe in fiery flames shee's allmost slaine:
> > Sometimes shee liues in dens and hollowe caues,
> > Sometimes shee has her dwellinge in ye graues,
> And sometimes on ye top of ragged rockes shee raues.[7]

Like White, Robinson emphasizes the degree to which the Magdalene's penitential affect is intensified by the depth of her former depravity. Christ witnesses Mary's melodramatic display of emotion and appears before her as a courtly lover to a distraught lady. She falls at his feet, amazed and short of breath, to be pardoned. Now prepared to encounter Wisdom and Repentance, she finds the "pourtract of [her] outward frame" reflected in a pool of her own tears:

Thees haires, y^t modestly should haue been ty'd
(For modesty's a maydes best ornament)
Layd out in tresses, haue declar'd my pride:
Thees eyes were made to viewe ye firmament,
And giue Him glory, y^t such glory lent.
    But (woe is mee!) they haue ye glassee beene,
    Where folly lookd, and wantonnesse was seene,
Soe ioyfull to attend vpon the Cyprian Queene.

Thees cheekes should blush at sin with crimson die,
But they to lewdnesse cheefely doe inuite,
With smiles deceiuinge ye behoulders eye:
Thees lippes were made to prayse, and pray arright,
Not to delude ye soone-deluded sight:
    This tongue should singe out Halleluiahs,
    Not accent vaine lasciuious essayes:
Hands, feet, heart, all were made to speake y^r makers prayse.[8]

Both texts are astonishing elaborations of Scripture that justify their extravagances by proclaiming the pedagogic value of the theatrical display of penance. "The profites that from Poetry arrise," writes Robinson in his dedication to Henry Clifford, "Where each thinge, truly acted, we may see, / As in a theatre."[9] The same logic underpins Nehemiah Rogers's prose meditation, *The Penitent Citizen* (1640), wherein the spectacular properties of public penance are once again praised in order to emphasize the value of seeing a performance of the Scriptures: "Many *Penitents* are brought upon the *Stage of Christianitie* in holy Scriptures, acting their parts before a world of *Spectators* ... to what purpose if they be not seene?" In the theater, Rogers argues, a good actor is at the center of the image, for he "weepes in good earnest, fights in good earnest, forgives in good earnest &c." The good actor "*acts* to the life, as doth the *Penitent.*" Stressing the public duty implicit in the performance of penance, Rogers notes that the worthy actor is "the strongest *motive of Affection*" and the most likely inspiration to potential converts. "*Behold this woman,*" he concludes, "and you that are heere present with *your Bodies*, bee present with *your mindes.*" Mary's visible display gives rise to feelings that linger long after her play has finished. Likewise, when latter-day Christians are called to the stage to perform their own contrition, they too must intimately engage their audiences:

> Before your Conversion no regard was had, you were then (like an Actor) within the *Tyring-house*, where you were *Rampant* and swoare oathes that you never cond [*sic*]: But now you are upon the *Stage* and none had more need be wary of *words and actions.*
>
> You know that no ordinary blemish, scratch nor spot is regarded in a *Table*, before an *Image* bee drawne upon it; But after the *Image* or *Effigies* is portraited, every little spot is observed in it: Such is the difference of spots in Christians before Conversion and after. Therefore have care that your well *ordered life* shews a well *ordered heart.*[10]

The exposure is risky but the payoff is high, for penance must be seen—and felt—to be believed. The Magdalene's secret is that she bares all, subjecting both body and soul to the exhaustive scrutiny of a stern and pitiless crowd.

These writers were not oblivious to the political and theological tensions that made religion and theater uncomfortable bedfellows. Elsewhere in his text, Rogers polices a fine border between the testimony provided by biblical images of penance (and latter-day imitations of the same) and the idolatrous kisses lavished on Christ's picture by papists.[11] And the possibility that Mary's example might carry with it the putrid fragrance of Romish decadence was evident to Robinson, who writes in his dedication,

> The brazen age is nowe return'd agen,
> And hath defac'd the Poets Siluer pen;
> Whereas in former time, the greatest men
> Were not asham'd to be call'd Poets then.[12]

The obvious way to mitigate the controversy would be to bind Mary's theatrical affect to her sinfulness. But despite their recognition of the pitfalls of visual pleasure, these treatments of the conversion scene beg readers to cast an appreciative eye upon their heroine even after she has met with reform. At the end of Robinson's epic, for instance, the poem's speaker cannot tear himself from the Magdalene's spectacle of contrition:

> Mee thinkes, I see ye Damsell at her worke,
> While shee embalmes his feet with odours rare;
> With modest blush, howe shee hath learnt to lurke,
> And kisse his feet, his marble feet, so faire,
> And then to wipe them with her carelesse haire:
> Often her hands, often her lippes, came near[e];
> Oft wipes shee of ye oyntement, y^t I feare,
> The oyntement wanted sweet, his feet perfumed weare.[13]

The effect that the sinner's rueful form and meek gestures have upon those who watch her is, finally, the most striking feature of these post-medieval adaptations of Luke 7.

This chapter considers how reformulations of Luke's sinner were used to conceptualize the difference between the Catholic past and the Protestant present. In keeping with James Simpson's claim that the official programs of iconoclasm instituted between 1536 and 1550 worked "to distance the past from the present as rapidly and decisively as possible either by demolishing the medieval, or, more enduringly perhaps, by creating the very concept of the medieval as a site of ruin," I argue that ancient constructions of the luxurious and loquacious Magdalene are revitalized in Protestant writing in order to align her with a degenerate and decadent faith that would be fortuitously demolished by the providential forces of Protestantism.[14] The resplendent Magdalene idol is naturally replaced by the new church's model recruit, a stripped-down and piously silent embodiment of reformed piety; but because no one can resist making the point that the Magdalene looks as exquisite in repentance as she did in sin, she retains the "look of love" extolled by White and Robinson and inadvertently reinstates the power of the very image she was designed to repudiate. These recastings of Luke 7 are self-contradictory and often unsuccessful. And yet, I argue that they organize the Magdalene as a repository of imagistic memory, or a *lieu de mémoire*, drawn out of the body of a demonized past, which helps to formulate the substance and shape of post-Reformation devotional literature.

The chapter takes as its centerpiece Lewis Wager's Edwardian morality play *The Life and Repentaunce of Mary Magdalene* (1566).[15] The play is important to the postmedieval history of the sinner-saint, and warrants our detailed attention because it is the most explicit and self-consciously theatrical reformation of the figure available for present consideration. As observed by Laura King, Wager's reworking of Mary Magdalene's conversion narrative dramatizes the Reformation by means of "the topos of the transfer from Old Law to New Law" and, as such, the Magdalene effectively becomes the Reformation Everyman.[16] The first section of the chapter probes Wager's use of Mary's medieval history in order to show how *Life and Repentaunce* follows the Magdalene from her prepenitent status as a gaudy, outmoded icon of Catholic idolatry, through to her conversion into a model female reader flanked by the loquacious presence of the personified Gospel. The second section presses at this reading of Wager's play in order to argue that the morality plot cannot sustain the theological principles that it teaches because the theatricalized retelling of Luke 7 also replays the eucharistic enactment of the word made flesh. The third section shows how Wager's reading of Luke further depends upon a Gregorian gloss that understands the sensual display of penance, the washing of Christ's feet with tears and hair so central to Robinson's portrait, as *physical* evidence of salvation. That is, Mary's conversion from a state of sin to a state of grace is conceptualized as a reformation of body parts. Eyes, lips, hair, and hands that once served the self are revitalized, in a blazon of contrition, to serve Christ. In this posture Mary becomes an index of Christ's humanity, certainly, but she also becomes a subject of formal aesthetic interest, a protobaroque portrait of religious subjectivity, in her own right. Wager's penchant for portraiture poses an obvious problem for a man who promises, from the onset, to privilege the Gospel story "written in the .vii. of Luke with wordes playne" (53–54, 60). However, in the final section of this chapter, I will turn to four later examples—J. C.'s *Saint Marie Magdalens Conversion* (1603), Thomas Collins's *The Penitent Pvblican* (1610), William Drummond's sonnet "For the Magdalene" (1630), and Joseph Sweetnam's *S. Mary Magdalens Pilgrimage to Paradise* (1617)—in order to think about how the aesthetics of looking, awkwardly deployed by Wager's Reformation play, acquire the florid facility of Robinson's epic.

Once a Sinner, Always a Sinner

From its onset, *The Life and Repentaunce of Mary Magdalene* assumes that the agendas of Protestantism and of the theater are not necessarily incompatible, as the heroic drama of the Reformation is staged by means of the *vita* of Mary Magdalene.[17] Never acquiescing to the scourge of the antitheatricalist pen that apparently marked the play as "spitefully despised," the play's prologue insists that the work encourages manly virtue, praises God with unyielding vehemence, and teaches true, stalwart devotion to the king. "There was neuer thyng inuented," one is informed, "more worth, for mans solace to be frequented" (12, 36–37). *Life and Repentaunce* assures that the Magdalene's exquisitely dressed, prepenitent body reflects not only the dangerous entrapments of femininity but also the pitfalls of perverse piety and, by extension, the decadence and degeneracy of the Catholic Church. Wager's manipulation of the psychomachia plot initially establishes his protagonist as a representative of the unreformed church: Mary's encounters with Infidelitie and his minions, Carnall Concupiscence, Cupiditie, and Pride of Life, dressed as Catholic clergy, illustrate both the depravity of the institution and the pusillanimity of its concomitants.

When Wager's Magdalene walks modestly onto the English Reformation stage, she is understood to have shed this past. The reformed penitent leaves behind her history of decadence and sexual profligacy, here allegorized as both medieval and Catholic; but she also, allegedly, leaves behind a literary tradition, inherited from the late Middle Ages and from the saint's play genre in particular, in favor of a Magdalene bound more appropriately to the narrative recounted in the Gospels. Incompatible with Wager's explicitly Calvinist (and implicitly Pauline) ambitions is the long-standing tradition of representing the Magdalene as a preacher and contemplative. However, because Wager's mode is historiographic, and because he is writing an allegory of the Reformation, he can only extol the virtues of the present picture by formulating a pathology for the past. So while the excision of Mary's progress to France and to the desert in Egypt produces something that looks more like the New Testament story, Wager finds himself relying upon discredited nonscriptural accounts of the Magdalene's early life as an aristocratic whore.

The most comprehensive study of the medieval Magdalene as *beata peccatrix* is Katherine Jansen's *The Making of the Magdalen*. Jansen shows that preachers and moralists "invented a woman called Mary Magdalen in order to preach on the evils of vanity, *luxuria*, prostitution, and the frailties of women." Her study illustrates how the figure, from whom Christ expels seven devils (Luke 8:2), becomes conflated with Luke's unnamed "sinner" who bathes Christ's feet in the home of Simon the Pharisee. The account of the anointing of Christ's head at the home of Simon the Leper (Matt. 26:6–7; Mark 14:13) and John's account of the events in the home of Mary and Martha (John 12:1–3) are also added to this composite account. And finally Gregory, in the same sermon in which he famously conflates three distinct Gospel figures, consolidates the Magdalene's lascivious reputation by reconfiguring the seven devils from Luke 8 as the seven capital sins. Jansen writes:

In so doing, the pontiff transformed Mary of Magdala's demonic possession into a disease of the soul caused by sin. Consequently her physical symptoms become outward signs of the sinful sickness afflicting her soul. Henceforth she was known as *peccatrix*.

Once Mary Magdalene had been identified as Luke's sinner, Jansen shows that preachers and hagiographers, working in the wake of Gregory's influential sermon, attributed the usual female sins of vanity and *luxuria* to her, turning, in particular, to her youth in order to invent the history of her royal lineage and surrender to sin. And "once tainted by *luxuria* . . . all it took was a leap of the imagination to transform the female sinner (*peccatrix*) into a prostitute (*meretrix*)."[18]

The narrative strategies that Jansen describes are very close to the surface. The Magdalene story becomes a tale of transformation as the encounter with Christ at the home of the Pharisee clearly demarcates the end of ignorance and sin and the beginning of true knowledge and godliness. In Jacobus de Voragine's widely translated *Legenda aurea*, for example, the depravity of Mary's past must be established before the sanctity of her present can be recognized:

> Thenne whan magdalene habounded in rychesses / And by cause delyte is felawe to rychesses / And haboundaunce of thynges / And for so moche as she shone in beaute gretly and in rychesses so moche the more she submyssed her body to delyte / and therfore she lost her ryght name and was called customably a synner. (William Caxton's edition, 1483)

The ensuing plot, then, is a tale of progress that charts its heroine's conversion from the depths of sin to the heights of salvation, making it clear in the process that without the sinner there could be no saint. Crucially, the conversion is described as a complete transformation, effected by Christ's blessing, which puts an end to the Magdalene of the past and sends her antithesis blazing forward into the future. "And this," writes Jacobus, "is the she that same marie magdalene to whom our lord gaf so many grete ʒeftes. And shewed so many grete signes of loue / that he toke from her seuen deuyles / he enbraced her alle in his loue / and made her ryght famylyer."[19]

And yet, for all of its lurid potential, the Magdalene's past does not consume her medieval *vita*. Jacobus handles the before-and-after story efficiently, dedicating less than a quarter of his account to the saint's New Testament life. The English medieval texts also move quickly from sinful past to present penance in order to locate the Magdalene's saintly vocation as preacher and hermit at the center of the narrative. *The Old English Martyrology*, for instance, testifies that Mary's conversion renders her so dear to Christ that after his death "she could no longer look on any man" and she thus retires to the desert.[20] *The Northern Passion* amalgamates the passage from Luke with that from Matthew 26:13, noting nothing more than: "in haly writt of hir mene rede / þat Marie haued done a synfull dede."[21] *The Early South-English Legendary* introduces the Magdalene as wealthy and of aristocratic origin, and describes her as "sunful and for-lein" as well as fair of "bodie: and of fote and honed"; the text is, however, relatively brief on the subject of her demise, moving swiftly from sin to repentance in order to turn, once again, to her legendary mission.[22] Osbern Bokenham's tale of Mary Magdalene, featured in *Legendys of hooly wummen*, includes the confession "Y am a synnere, & of euery cryme / Wyth spottys defoulyd ful horrybylly . . ." but, once again, only as a prequel to the observation that her voice now serves the mendicant vocation.[23]

Likely because the saint's sinful past is so theatrically promising, the Digby Mary Magdalene play provides one of the most extensive descriptions of Mary's early life, both before and after her meeting with Christ, as Mary's sin is worked out allegorically upon the stages of "World" and "Flesh." The psychomachia plot is less than straightforward; here, one sees the roots of Wager's Reformation camp and Robinson's baroque spoof. Satan enters first, and bids World's King to draw Magdalene to him. World, in turn, summons his messenger, Sensuality, to call forth the King of Flesh. Flesh then calls upon his Lady Lechery, who proceeds, along with her fellows, the six remaining deadly sins, to woo the affections of the wealthy and therefore vulnerable Mary. They resort to a tavern where Mary falls in with the gallant Curiosity, with whom, much to Satan's delight, she returns to World's stage. She sleeps, only to be awakened by a good angel who encourages her to leave her evil ways. Mary vows to proceed to the home of Simon the Pharisee where she hopes to find the "Prophett wherso he be, / For he is þe welle of perfyth charyte."[24] And yet, despite the play's unapologetic indulgence in guilty pleasures, the emphasis falls squarely on Mary's later life of virtue. While a full third of the play is dedicated to Mary's time with Christ, only half of that section dwells on her temptation and her fall. The preconversion Magdalene is certainly an important feature of the play, but she is alluded to only briefly in order to lay the ground for her subsequent accomplishments as a convert.

The profligate prostitute character, who is the concern of over two-thirds of Wager's play, really comes into her own after the Reformation when imaginative energy turns away from the postresurrection biography, particularly Mary's later days as a minister and contemplative, and is redirected toward the manifestations of the Magdalene's penance as they are circumscribed by the Gospel of Luke. However, the emphasis does not shift from preaching to penance solely because the legendary apparatus is no longer available to the Protestant writer. The conversion narrative, in the light of the historical ruptures posted by the Reformation, essentially acquires a new vitality of its own.

Two glosses of Luke 7 would have been ready at hand for any writer remaking the Magdalene for Protestant England: the *Paraphrases* of Erasmus, and Calvin's commentaries on the Gospels. Erasmus does not conflate, after Gregory, Luke's "woman in the citie" with Mary Magdalene. And yet, while he leaves the sinner unnamed, she is nevertheless marked with some of the stigma of medieval precedent. In keeping with Gregory and Jacobus, Erasmus's woman is "a common harlotte . . . a woman of notorious vnchaste lyuing" whose eventual grace is in no way unrelated to her former state of misery. The importance of the woman's past is made clear for Erasmus in the parable of the creditor and the two debtors embedded in Luke's account of the meal at the Pharisee's home. Christ tells of two debtors, one who owed five hundred pence and the other fifty. The creditor forgives them both. Christ asks Simon which of the two debtors will love the creditor the most—the answer is the debtor owing the most. In Luke, Christ uses the parable to explain that because he has forgiven the woman's many sins, she will love him more than those, like Simon, who see themselves as following the path of righteousness. The woman's past misdoings determine the authenticity and extremity of her present conversion. The parable is crucial to Erasmus because it helps him to articulate an essential turning point: "she came hither a synner; but she was throughly made hole, as soone as she touched the physycian."[25] The woman who leaves Simon's house is not the woman who entered it.

Calvin, also espousing evangelical accuracy, attempts to disentangle Luke 7 from its association with the complex legend of Mary Magdalene, and yet he too retains the habit of reading the passage as a story of transformation in which the precondition of true piety is the disavowal of the past. He begins by recognizing the precision of Erasmus's grammar. Erasmus's invocation of the woman "which was" a sinner suggests, for Calvin, that while the woman had changed, "the infamy of her former life was not as yet extinguished amongst men." This woman, despite her conversion, cannot shed her past; in fact, it is the lingering memory of that past that makes her penance all the more poignant.[26] While shutting the door on the composite Magdalene, Calvin and Erasmus appear to leave open a window that Wager happily climbs through as he, likewise, reconnects sinner to saint and recycles the conversion narrative in order to prefigure the theological rift that would eventually distinguish the Catholic past from the Protestant present.

There is nothing particularly extraordinary about Wager's conceptual leap. Frances Dolan has comprehensively illustrated how Catholics were persistently linked, in post-Reformation political culture, to disorderly women.[27] And Rachel Weil has also noted the long-standing Protestant tradition of representing the Catholic Church as an "overmighty, sexually profligate and obscenely rich woman," and has further remarked that upon occasion "prostitution was itself imagined as an idolatrous religion: brothels were described as 'temples to Venus,' whores as 'nuns' or 'votaries of Venus,' sex as a sacrifice or act of worship."[28] As a prostitute figure with an aristocratic past of

decadence and licentiousness, the preconversion Magdalene of medieval legend lends itself well to this topos. Gregory Scott's *Brief Tretise*
of 1570, for example, is a rant against "certain errors of the Romish
Church," in particular the worship of saints like Magdalene, whom he
understands to be the patron saint of whores.[29] A more interesting
condemnation of the Magdalene is found in the Elizabethan "Homily
Against the Peril of Idolatry," which finds a correlation between the
preconversion saint and the distractions of images and icons:

> Thinke you, assoone as they turne their faces from the Preacher,
> and looke vpon the grauen bookes and painted Scripture of the
> glorious gilt images and idoles, all shining and glittering with
> mettall and stone, and couered with precious vestures, or else
> with Choerea in Terence, behold a paynted table, wherein is set
> foorth by the arte of the painter, an image with a nice and wanton
> apparell and countenance, more like to Venus or Flora, then Mary
> Magdalene, or if like to Mary Magdalene, it is when she played
> the harlot, rather then when she wept for her sinnes. When I say
> they turne about from the preacher, to these bookes and schoole-
> masters and painted scriptures: shal they not find them lying
> books? teaching other maner of lessons, of esteeming of riches,
> of pride, and vanity in apparell, of nicenesse and wantonnesse,
> and peraduenture of whoredome.[30]

Wager's play seizes upon this kind of iconoclastic language in
order to fashion Mary's body as a pregnable space of erotic possibility
into which an allegory of Reformation can be infused. She, the Catholic Church, becomes through pornographic reference a habitus of
vices, the devil's stable, the filthiest place in hell (400, 417–18). The
Magdalene is the whore of Babylon—an epithet Dolan describes as
"widely used to denounce the pope as the Antichrist and the Roman
church more generally," and which also "yokes together the familiar seduction and corruption of the unruly feminine and the more outland-
ish threat of the foreign, even fantastical."[31] Mary's easy seduction at
the hands of Infidelitie and company is represented as an erotic fan-

tasy of penetration: Infidelitie procures the lovers; Cupiditie opens
the gate; Carnall Concupiscence kindles a fire so that "she beginneth
to burn in carnall desyre" (368). Infidelitie promises a titillated Concupiscence that "I would haue hir cleaue vnto you so fast, / That she
shall not forsake you while her life doth last" (371–72); and Pride of
Life makes "an entrance" by Infidelitie's wicked craft, "So that we may
come into hir at pleasure, / Fillyng hir with wickednesse beyond all
measure" (374–76).[32] Mary's response to this innuendo is to greet
each vice character with a coy kiss, lending justification to Infidelitie's
remark, "The more closely that you kepe fyre, no doubt, / The more
feruent it is when it breaks out" (547–48). The lecherous bond between Mary and Infidelitie is secured by means of a punning match in
which Mary demonstrates her vulgar rhetorical skill. When asked if
she can play upon the virginals, she responds, "Yes swete heart . . .
There is no instrument but that handle I can, / I thynke as well as any
gentlewoman." At which point Infidelitie, picking up the pun, produces his recorder, noting, "Truely you haue not sene a more goodlie
pipe, / It is so bigge that your hand can it not gripe" (838–44). Mary's
inviting body and her bold, salacious words constitute, according to
the vices, a bewitching, predatorial form, an irresistible image of pun-
gent carnality that allures and entraps the most innocent and unsus-
pecting of prey.[33] Sexual innuendo intensifies as kissing and wordplay
give way to intimations of fornication. Mary narrates her encounter
with the mysterious man with the "flaxen beard," flirtatiously recounting her shock upon discovering him in her bed. She tells of her seduction, aided by smells of musk and civet, and concludes by defending
her fall as the result of natural feminine submission to the will of men.
Infidelitie confirms Mary's self-analysis by suggesting that she alone
is responsible for her insatiable sexuality:

> I beshrew your hearts, whore and thefe wer agreed
>   You knew the spirit wel inough before you cam there
> I am sure, that so honestly he had you feed,
>   That the reward dyd put away the feare.
>
>   (1105–8)

This Magdalene is different—at least in emphasis—from her medieval predecessor because she is being deployed to different ends. By recasting the Catholic past as a narrative of error, dominated by what Simpson calls the rule of imagination, Wager posits the necessity for new starts for both the individual and the church. And, as Simpson concludes, "new starts require iconoclasm"—that is, "a destructive passage through the imagination in order to recover the pure instantiation of God's Word in Scripture."[34]

Wager's Magdalene, casting lewd glances toward those too weak to look away, becomes the embodiment of the imaginative excess, the gaudy surplus of creative energy, which Protestant iconoclasts associated with religious art.[35] Wager's descriptions of Mary's form summon forth caustic reformist descriptions of the often lavish three-dimensional carvings, in wood or in stone, of saints whose veneration was also conceived of in ambiguously pornographic terms. Iconoclasts railed vociferously against these freestanding images thought to be "great puppets for old fooles, like children, to play the wicked play of idolatry before"—a statement remarkably similar in tone and sentiment to Wager's take on the Magdalene, as in both cases the tricks of "puppetry" slip both alliteratively and metaphorically into a lewd critique of "popery."[36] Pride of Life's command that the Magdalene let her "eies roll" (616–18, followed by the stage direction indicating that she does so) is, for instance, evocative of the most notorious of the old Catholic puppets, the Rood of Boxley, which apparently had movable eyes and lips.[37]

Wager is not concerned with just any form of holy image; he rails specifically against the statue. His concern is typical of early Reformist iconoclasm directed more pointedly toward the three-dimensional image, which, because it invited physical proximity and even direct contact, was thought to promote idolatrous attitudes with greater efficiency. Protestant anxiety arose, in part, from the knowledge that there is something fundamentally dangerous about a freestanding figure that offered itself up for fondling. In keeping with the Reformation subtext, and in preparation for the climactic stripping of the altars, the stage action of the entire first half of *Life and Repentaunce* becomes occupied with the dressing of the Magdalene. In the same way that devotees dressed and adorned the statues of popular saints with fine clothing, jewels, and incense, Wager has Infidelitie and his companions in vice decorate the body of their star pupil. The spectator is provided with a peep-show perspective as the dialogue suggests that the stage becomes a dressing-room mirror in which the performer is adorned for public consumption by her lecherous disciples. In the words of the Elizabethan homilist denouncing the practices of statue veneration, Mary becomes a "nice and welltrimmed harlot" who is, Wager confirms, "plesant to euery mans eye" (308).[38]

As laborious as it may seem, it is worth pondering the extraordinary detail of Mary's dressings, for the minutiae speak not only to the visual extravagance of Wager's iconoclasm—the oxymoronic condition that sets his play on the path to failure—but also to a developing obsession with Mary's body that far surpasses medieval precedent and fuels a burgeoning baroque aesthetic. Wager's words draw attention to the erotic possibilities of Mary's costume from her first entrance. Her problem, it seems, is that her tailor has sold her, at considerable expense, an ill-formed garment that does not show off what she deems to be a waist more proper than that of any gentlewoman in the land. Infidelitie takes his cue and notes that the garment cannot be mended ("it is past amendement, / Meddle with it, and you spyll it vtterly"), alerting the spectator to the seeping carnality of Mary's flesh (173–74). "Of taylers craft," Infidelitie, not surprisingly, has "some skill," and drawing upon both sartorial and pedagogic meanings of the verb "to dress," he proclaims:

> Shortly my ofspryng and I shall her so dresse,
> 　That neither law nor prophets she shall regard,
> 　No though the sonne of God to her them expresse.
> (179; 318–20)

It is Cupiditie who is elected responsible for Mary's fashion education, and he advises his pupil to ensure that her garments be of the "newest guise," while Pride of Life joins voices with Carnall Concupiscence to lecture Mary on the proper uses of "bodies geare" (623; 150). Mary proves a star pupil, responding to her teachers' fervor with "Your wordes do not onely prouoke my desire, / But in pleasure they set my heart on fyre" (686–87). She is shamelessly established as a highly sought-after article of desire within a depraved culture of relic consumption. Her physical appeal is more than a simple reiteration of the covetous Mary of medieval legend; she is pointedly figured as a three-dimensional object of erotic idolatry to be decorated, worshiped, and ravished by her bedazzled popish patrons.[39]

The use of costume as erotic accessory is made most clear in the vice figures' promotion of Mary's lingerie as luxurious finery that embodies not only the extravagance (and implicit physical discomfort) that was the demarcation of class status, but also the illicit allure of fetish gear.[40] Of Mary's breasts, Pride of Life suggests, "Your garments must be so worne alway, / That your white pappes may be seene if you may." Concupiscence concludes that

> Both damsels and wiues vse many such feates,
> I know them that will lay out their faire teates,
> Purposely men to allure vnto their loue,
> For it is a thyng that doth the heart greatly moue.
>
> (674–81)

Pointing once again to the centrality of artifice in the advancement of seduction, Infidelitie insists that Mary wear nothing over her bodice ("overbody") in order to display fully the contorted features of her refined figure. "Let your body be pent," he insists,

> and togither strained,
> As hard as may be, though therby you be pained. . . .
> Your nether garments must go by gymmes and ioynts
> Aboue your buttocks thei must be tied on with points.
>
> (690–701)

The recurring references to underwear determine that this is the business of exposure; the dialogue implies that the stage is a dressing-room mirror within which the spectator views, illicitly, the fleshy, corrupt body of the woman beneath the stays and joints.[41] For the Mary of *Life and Repentaunce*, transgression lies not only in her bedroom femininity, but particularly in the way in which her costume suggests the possibility of there being no costume at all—a prospect alluded to by Infidelitie early on in the play, when he suggests men would "liefer haue you naked, be not afrayde, / Then with your best holy day garment" (303–4). Interestingly, the flesh promised by the text is described as clean. Pride of Life calls Mary "a pretty wenche and a cleane" (358), and the vices' song refers to Mary as "so cleane, so swete, so fayre, so good, so freshe, so gay" (885). Cleanliness, in these instances, signals decadence and inattention to matters divine, an observation consistent with Keith Thomas's conclusion that "bathing, particularly in warm water, long retained undesirable associations with decadent Romans, brothels and sexuality."[42] Moreover, the makeup, the silks, and the satins, as well as the "wiers and houpes" (700) of Mary's prurient boudoir, amount to a mock inventory akin to the lengthy lists of the contents of shrines provided by the cranky commissioners of the Reformation. Of particular interest here are the combs, caps, shrouds, bodices, girdles, and sleeves, not to mention the teeth, locks of hair, and other miscellaneous body parts that filled parish reliquaries and fortified clerical coffers.[43] The Reformist scorn for the bodily materiality of idol veneration by means of perfume, incense, or candlelight is also reflected in Infidelitie's suggestion that Mary sprinkle her garments with rose water and use her civet, pomander, and musk so that "the odor of you a myle of, a man may smell" (770–74).

The idolatrous treatment of body parts and their coverings is behind Calvin's derogatory description of the revered head of Mary Magdalene allegedly located in Marseilles. "Men do make a treasure of her," Calvin writes disdainfully, "as it were a god descended from heaven."[44] Richard Layton's 1535 inventory of parish artifacts expresses similar suspicion of the abject corporeality of the cult of the saints when it notes "a great comb called St. Mary Magdalene's comb."[45] Calvin's and Layton's remarks alert one to the awareness, both before and after the Reformation, of the sensuous appeal of the Magdalene's hair—a luscious covering that, in Wager's play, seems to function as a sign for the practice of gilding statues in gold and precious metals. Cupiditie concludes of Mary's hair,

A craft you must haue, that yellow it may be made,
With some Goldsmyth you may your selfe acquaint,
Of whom you may haue water your haire for to paint.

$$(641-43)^{46}$$

Gilded hair, like the gilded statue, "yong men vnto your loue it will allure," while flowing curls articulate and accentuate (as does the *bon grace* upon her head) each of the Magdalene's physical features (639).[47] This scene is the play's centerfold, marking the turning point of the drama where the three-dimensional puppet will be replaced by the flattened, two-dimensional surfaces of the Word.

Striptease

The moment of conversion, in *Life and Repentaunce*, is incited by the appearance of the defiant figure, the Lawe, whose presence before the fallen Mary makes possible the entrance of the equally confident Knowledge of Sinne. These two robust figures battle valiantly against the lecherous and effeminate Infidelitie for control over the forlorn Ecclesia, and their success becomes a manly victory of reason over desire and of the future over the past—at least in theory. The triumph of Lawe and Knowledge drives Mary's eyes upward, away once and for all from the now tarnished appeal of the lurid Infidelitie (1160). This triumph is signaled by the presence of Christ himself, who exorcises the demons from Mary's now contrite body. It is at this jubilant moment that one notes a radical shift in the discussion of clothing and undress:

Auoide out of this woman thou Infidelitie,
With the .vii. diuels which haue hir possessed,
I banish you hence by the power of my diuinitie,
For to saluation I haue hir dressed.

(1385–88; emphasis mine)

When Mary next returns to the stage, she is described as "sadly apparelled" and carrying a jar of ointment (1765). Her body, now free of vice as Justification, Faith, and Repentaunce have taken the places of Pride of Life, Cupiditie, and Carnall Concupiscence, is no longer an abused icon. Mary is redressed, reformed, and properly pious.[48]

The play essentially becomes a dramatic re-enactment of the Edwardian Statute of 1550, which ordered that persons having "anye images of stone tymbre allebaster or earthe graven carved or paynted" shall "deface and destroye or cause to be defaced and destroyed the same images and everie of them."[49] Thomas Cranmer's catechism (1548), also roughly contemporary to Wager's play, works to the same purpose, ordering that "thou shalt not gylte [statues], and set them in costlye tabernacles, and decke theim with coates or shertes, thou shalt not sense them, make vowes or pilgremages to them, sette candelles before them, and offer vnto them, thou shalt not kysse their feete, & bowe downe vnto them." Visitation reports are replete with evidence suggesting that reformers did indeed go after the richly adorned statues in English parish churches. For example, one of Cromwell's agents stripped the shrine of St. Anne at Buxton of its "cruchys, schertes, and schetes, with wax offeryd," while Dr. London, writing to Sir Richard Rich, reports, "I have pullyd down the image of your lady at Caversham, with all trynkettes abowt the same, as schrowdes, candels, images of wexe, crowches, and brochys. . . . The image ys thorowly platyd over with sylver. I have putt her in a chest fast lockyd and naylede, and by the next bardge that comythe uppe it schall be browȝt to my lorde, with her cootes, cappe and here."[50]

The Reformation stripping of the altars makes divestment a profoundly moral act. Likewise, Wager's Mary Magdalene is spiritually transformed when she returns undressed, her eroticism absorbed in formidable Protestant polemic. The body of Wager's reformed penitent is no longer an altar of pornographic spectacle because she has been stripped of her excessive ornaments. What Wager's Magdalene is actually wearing when she returns to the stage is uncertain, though the directions appear to be alluding to the convention of performing public penance *en chemise* or in loose undergarments, released from the artificial scaffolding of corsets, from the trappings of a covetous and unnatural style, in order to convey a modest humility before God.[51] In this sense, Wager's compunctious Mary may be an allusion to the

ideal female penitent whose exemplary piety is demonstrated by extraordinary humility, devotion, and, most importantly, silence.[52] Her
entrance as penitent is followed by a conversion speech that, though
of considerable length (sixty-four lines), is the penitent's last significant contribution to the dialogue. She does not speak of herself as the
first of Christ's evangelists; following Paul, Mary's exemplary piety is
passive: "To all the worlde an example I may be, / In whom the mercy
of Christ is declared" (1769–72). Christ reiterates her passivity in a
reconfiguration of Matthew 26:13:

> Goe thy way forth with faith and repentance,
> To heare the Gospell of health be though diligent,
> And the wordes therof beare in thy remembrance.
>
> (1530–32)

If Mary carries with her the memory of the Gospel, it is not in her
speech but in her look.

On the other hand, given the frequency with which metaphors
of nakedness figure in Puritan rhetoric, the modestly dressed penitent may hold further significance for those who read or gaze upon
her. The above-cited iconoclastic injunctions reveal an appropriation
of the language of clothing, and subsequently of nudity, in order to
advocate the superiority of the naked truth. Judy Kronenfeld argues
that this kind of slippage proves that the rhetoric of religious controversy did not systematically place the concept of nudity in binary
opposition to that of "decent and comely apparel." Nudity could just
as easily be associated with the "naked truth." Within the framework
of Renaissance Christian cultural expectations, the assumption that
"clothing is a good if the alternative is a shameful or uncomely nakedness" operates in conjunction with the assumption that "clothing is
not a good if the alternative is the naked truth."[53] A similar case could
be made for Wager's Mary, who in the tradition of the Magdalene
nude is metaphorically stripped down in order to embody the purity
of the church she represents and yet on stage remains sadly dressed,
conveying a comely modesty appropriate to her penitential status before God.[54]

By this point in the play the stage picture is, at least in theory, radically different from what it was. Mary's tending of Christ's feet is managed and contained by the stage directions that ask Mary to "creepe vnder the table, abyding there a certayne space behynd . . . as it is specified in the Gospell" (between 1828 and 1829). This instruction may well be theatrical shorthand, but the authoritative reference to Luke, as well as the implication that Mary does in fact retreat behind a table, would direct readers' as well as spectators' attention to the Gospels, here represented by the long, sobering speeches of Justification and Love. As in John Bale's *Thre Lawes*, where the resolutely two-dimensional virtues demand what Ritchie Kendall describes as "critical detachment" rather than the all-too-playful "emotional spontaneity" encouraged by the artful vice figures, the dialogue of *Life and Repentaunce* reconfigures the act of gazing itself.[55] Described on the title page as "very delectable for those which shall heare or reade the same," *Life and Repentaunce* appropriates Reformation "ways of seeing" in which lookers are conceived of as readers and listeners.[56] Having denounced the empty visuality of Catholic stagecraft, Wager will now convey, to those who care to hear, "what is true beleue, / Wherof the Apostles of Christ do largely write" (53–54). Hearing and reading become privileged epistemologies as the visual representation of the new faith is flanked and flattened by words and by text. As the almost verbatim transcription of Calvin's *Institutes* in Faith's long speech suggests, Wager's finale conceives of the stage as book, the figures upon it as sermonizers, and the action behind it, the washing of Christ's feet, as appropriately controlled illustration.[57]

For the Protestant preacher, images were not necessarily demonic, particularly if one could look upon them as one "looketh upon a book."[58] For Wager, as for Bale and the other Reformation playwrights, a reformed theater would ideally stage pictures that resolved into text and perform images that stood as signs of the Word. This particularly Protestant way of thinking about the relationship between images and words is nicely illustrated by Joseph Leo Koerner in his reading of a Lutheran altarpiece in Schweinfurt (executed in the 1590s) which serves, Koerner argues, as a "scaffold for writing": "Its images stand, as it were, between quotation marks. Twice removed, they picture words, and behind these what words, when read, would picture."[59] Likewise, Wager's spectator is supposed to see a picture of words, and behind these words, that which the words, when read, would picture—Mary Magdalene bathing Christ's feet. The image is a startling example of Christ's bidding in Matthew 26:13. The Gospel is being read and, on the stage, just behind the Word, is a recollection or memory of "that which she hath done." Wager's work is at this moment the closest to his purpose of speaking "figuratively" of Mary's repentance. However, the moment is also incontestably real and thus invites the intrusion of the imagination.[60] When Mary turns her attention to Christ's feet, washes them with her penitential tears, and dries them with her loosened hair, the performed gesture demands intimate physical interaction and thus threatens to undercut the intended textuality of the stage image by allowing the audience to remember and even ponder Mary's erotic past. Despite Wager's best intentions, the exchange between Christ and the penitent Magdalene is palpably sexy, a fact that is intensified when Christ directs attention to the tactility of his own body. "Touche any partes, / Of my body," he says, as if in deliberate contrast to the *noli me tangere* sequence that illustrates the transformation of corporeal to divine love at the moment of the resurrection (1871–72). Text and body compete for supremacy in a moment of riveting theatricality, a moment fully engaging what Elizabeth Harvey has called a "history of tactility" that "simultaneously signals the dangers of erotic touch and the possibility of contact with divinity."[61]

Mary's physical knowledge of Christ supports Debora Shuger's conclusion that representations of the Magdalene are partly concerned with "the *body* of Christ, that is, the real presence," and as such they are "eucharistic as well as erotic—or, rather both at once."[62] But, more precisely, Wager can't avoid Mary's physical affect because the sight of her penance, her look of love, is central to the Gospel story he wants to tell. Erasmus certainly recognizes this to be the case in his gloss of Luke 7, which draws attention to the Magdalene's spectacle:

> Dooest thou not see hir all full of wepyng, with hir heare lying about hir shoulders, makyng lauasse of hir precious perfumed

oynctemente, liberall and more then liberall of hir kisses, geuyng to my fete, lying prostrate aforeme. & ourtwadly she wing [*sic*] all the behaueour and vsing of hir body, a paterne and liuly exaumple of a repentaunte persone. These are manifeste tokens of a certain excedyng great loue towardes me. The more earnestely that she hateth hir self, so muche the more frankely she tendreth me and maketh of me.[63]

Here the reader, like Simon, is made to follow the gaze of the Pharisee as Erasmus describes precisely what is to be seen. Readers are compelled to dwell on the visual detail of the scene as the narrator concludes that the woman's many sins are forgiven not because she "hath muche fasted, not for that she hath vsed muche praier & contemplacion, not because she hath been a deuoute obseruer of many pharisaicall constitucions," but rather because she *shows* by her deed that she "hath loued much":

She had made no praiers in wordes, she had made no confession at all in wordes, but she dyd muche the more euidently confesse hirselfe by hir doynges, and muche the more effectually did she praie with hir teres. And this is to Christ the moste acceptable confession of all. And with this sorte of praiers is he the most soonest moued to shewe mercie.[64]

The woman's tactile tenderness is the proof of her devotion. The touching of Christ will take away a man's sins, and "if he cannot come to touche Iesus head, leat hym touche hym ye the fete. There is no parte of Iesus so basse, but y^t it maie make hym whole from al his synnes."[65]

Calvin was aware of the potential problems Luke 7 posed to the radically Protestant agenda. The *Harmonie* confers with Erasmus's articulation of the sinner's singularity, reading the penitential acts ministered upon Christ's body as "manifest signes of her righteousnes" that "testifie her thankfulnes." However, while Erasmus is eager to differentiate the woman's honest display of love (illustrative of the "feith of the ghospell") from the Pharisee's hypocritical acts of piety ("burnt sacrifices" and "washinges"),[66] Calvin worries that overstating the woman's actions might result in the idolatrous imitation he sees as characteristic of Catholic ritual:

> She came behynde Christ, and there threw her selfe downe at his feete, in which appeared her shamefastnes and humilitie: she brought her oyntment, and offered her selfe and all shee had in sacrifice to Christ. All these things are for vs to follow: but the sheading of the oyntment was a particular action which should be yll drawne into a general rule.[67]

If the problem posed by phenomenological presence is implicit in Luke 7, it is rendered absolutely explicit when Wager puts the story on the stage. Stripping cannot, in Wager's case, reveal the naked truth but mirrorlike draws further attention to artifice and imitation. Beneath Mary's sad costume, there lies, in fact, not the prurient sexuality of a woman, but the body of a boy actor.[68] Despite the fact that *Life and Repentaunce* is a play about the undressing of artifice, its success depends upon keeping some things artfully covered up. Crossdressing was, of course, one of the principle concerns of Puritan antitheatricalists, and it is worth remembering the Prologue's confession that some felt *Life and Repentaunce* ought to be "spitefully despised" regardless of its overtly Protestant theology. While Wager may have wanted his theater to discourage the leaps of the imagination associated with idolatrous worship, militant opponents may have surmised that those lured into loving the luxurious Magdalene would also gaze longingly at a "sadly dressed" boy. By dwelling upon the contours of the penitent's contrite body, Wager solicits the antitheatricalist fear that it is "art itself that effeminates."[69] Thinking back to Wager's representation of vice as bedecked figures whose "Catholic" antics captivate the spectator in the first half of the play, one gets the feeling that this fear is one that Wager shares as much as shuns. Wager's play promises, like the mirror, to reflect back the plain, simple, unadorned truth, freed from the tricks and trappings of an outmoded faith where every sign was thought to embody the truth it represented. But Wager's inadvertent encounter with the material pressures of the theatrical experience suggests that the iconoclastic staging of reform could by no means fully reform the fundamentally iconic stage. *Life and Repentaunce* ultimately beguiles and deceives by means of the very art it condemns.[70]

Body Parts

Wager's presentation of the new Magdalene's faith fully enacts the "dialectic between iconophilia and iconophobia," now recognized as integral to the propagation of Protestant culture.[71] As Wager organizes the Magdalene story around a narrative of rupture that seeks to confine the past to history by divesting it of its legitimacy, his Magdalene becomes a site of memory protecting the very remembrances that history seeks to alienate. While the cult of Mary Magdalene was no longer a part of daily devotional life, Wager makes the saint a residual sight of continuity within the unfolding drama of the Reformation, a place for registering experiences thought to be lost, in particular the intimate experience of Christ's presence. In *Life and Repentaunce*, the Magdalene escapes her intended meanings; she essentially "escapes history" by showing her audience how it feels to touch Christ; in so doing, she reinstates the commemorative function of religious art.[72] This reinstatement—this site of embodied memory—will, I argue, be developed, over the course of the next century, into a more or less coherent religious poetics that continued to think across historical rupture in order to retrieve and reinvent a useful strategy for finding Christ.[73]

The seeds of this poetics are most evident in Wager's play as emphasis shifts from Christ's body to Mary Magdalene's body. Consider again how Wager's Cupiditie sees his pupil:

> The haire of your head shyneth as the pure gold,
> Your eyes as gray as glasse and right amiable,
> Your smylyng countenance, so louely to behold,
> To vs all is moste pleasant and delectable,
> Of your commendations who can be wearie?

> Huffa mystresse Mary, I pray you be mery.
>   Your lyps as ruddy as the redde Rose,
> Your teeth as white as euer was the whales bone,
> So cleane, so swete, so fayre, so good, so freshe, so gay.
>   (877–85)[74]

And then note how Cupiditie's inventory of insidious body parts is re-made by Repentaunce, who looks upon the contrite Magdalene kneeling at Christ's feet:

> As thus, like as the eyes haue ben vaynly spent
>   Vpon worldly and carnall delectations,
> So henceforth to wepyng and teares must be bent,
>   And wholly giuen to godly contemplations.
>
> Likewise as the eares haue ben open alway
>   To here the blasphemyng of Gods holy name,
> And fylthy talkyng euermore night and day,
>   Nowe they must be turned away from the same.
> . . . .
> The tong which blasphemie hath spoken,
>   Yea and filthily, to the hurt of soule and body:
> Wherby the precepts of God haue ben broken,
>   Must hence forth praise God for his mercy daily.
>   (1441–56)

Mary herself participates in this blazon of contrition when she reverently insists

> But like as the parts of my body in tymes past,
>   I haue made seruants to all kynd of iniquitie,
> The same iniquitie away for euer I do cast,
>   And will make my body seruant to the veritie.
>   (1789–92)

All her worldly attributes, "through vnbelief of synne" deployed in acts of carnal pleasure, will henceforth help Christ alone, "and for his sake other innocents" (1818–20). While conceived with eyes diverted from earthly matters and with ears open to the Word, this representation eventually returns to the physicality of Mary Magdalene, itemizing her features (particularly eyes, ears, and hair) as penitential attributes.

This account of the sinner's supple body parts, as vigorous in conversion as they were deadly in sin, is an elaboration upon Gregory, who was the first to write of Mary's corporeal conversion:

> What she therefore displayed more scandalously, she was now offering to God in a more praiseworthy manner. She had coveted with earthly eyes, but now through penitence these are consumed with tears. She displayed her hair to set off her face, but now her hair dries her tears. She had spoken proud things with her mouth, but in kissing the Lord's feet, she now planted her mouth on the Redeemer's feet. For every delight, therefore, she had had in herself, she now immolated herself. She turned the mass of her crimes to virtues, in order to serve God entirely in penance, for as much as she had wrongly held God in contempt.[75]

Gregory sets in motion the idea that the contrite Magdalene is as pleasant to behold as her sinful counterpart. Jacobus, for instance, describes the saint as preaching with a "glad vysage" as well as a "dyscrete tongue," and her congregants as "admerueylled of" their speaker's beauty. Bokenham also notes that it is Mary's face, as well as her words, that captivated her audiences:

> Wyth a plesaunth chere up ded ryse,
> And with a feyr face in dysert wyse
> She hem reuokyd from hyr ydolatrye,
> And prechyd hem cryst most stedefastlye.

> All þat hir herdyn awundryd were,
>   What for hyr beute on þat o party,
> And for þe facundye whych she oysyd þere,
> And for þe swetnesse eek of hyr eloquency,

Whych from hyr mouth cam so plesauntly
Þat þei haddyn a uery delectacyoun
Stylle to stondyn & here hyr redycacyoun.[76]

However, references to the Magdalene's beauty, though ubiquitous, are not generous in their detail for, as Jansen shows, "preachers and moralists invented a woman called Mary Magdalene in order to preach on the evils of vanity, *luxuria*, prostitution, and the frailties of women." While the pre-Reformation treatments of the Magdalene's contrition, both visual and textual, do tend to articulate the penitent's corporeality, they do so modestly and in a manner that emphasizes bodily abjection rather than beauty. For instance, the penitent Magdalene's most celebrated attributes were her tears. While weeping features repeatedly in medieval accounts of Mary's life as a "multi-vocal symbol," to deploy Jansen's terminology, which simultaneously invokes the Magdalene's humility and her femininity, tears are not remarked upon as an aspect of her beauty.[77] The other component of the medieval Magdalene's penitential corporeality is her asceticism. She is featured, for example, in the thirteenth-century painting by the Magdalene Master (fig. 1) as an emaciated, naked hermit shrouded only in hair, and she appears in the Digby play as a figure of wild serenity partaking of Christ's "celestyall bred" rather than as a figure of mystical eroticism.[78] Late medieval representations of the Magdalene's postconversion life as preacher and as hermit do, as Theresa Coletti suggests, "capture the inescapable corporeality—of tears, hair, and touch—for which she was famous, consistently rendering her spiritual state in precise bodily terms."[79] And it is also the case that treatments of the saint's later life as preacher and contemplative "evoke the physicality of her renounced sexual past in hauntingly disparate ways." Yet it also seems safe to say that this investment in penitential/sacramental corporeality is never aestheticized to the degree that the Magdalene becomes obviously pleasing to the eye. That kind of pleasure is reserved, in the medieval tradition, for the sinful Mary. The sustained interest in the Magdalene's penitential beauty is an early modern— or baroque—phenomenon anticipated by Wager's Reformation interlude.

FIGURE 1.
Maestro della
Maddalena,
*Maddalena penitente
e otto storie della sua
vita* (1280–85).
Gallerie dell'
Accademia,
Florence.
Photograph:
Scala/Art Resource,
New York.

Hans Belting offers a possible explanation for this aesthetic turn. The medieval image, he argues, "rejected reduction into metaphor; rather, it laid claim to being immediate evidence of God's presence revealed to the eyes and the senses." The reception of the early modern image, however (and this is surely in part why it comes to be reviled), depended upon a new concept of art: "Form and content renounce unmediated meaning as art becomes the sphere of the artist who assumes control of the image as proof of his or her art."

> The [postmedieval] religious subject, in the end, could be invented only by the artist, since it could not actually be seen, like the objects in a still life or landscape. The new presence *of* the work succeeds the former presence of the sacred *in* the work. But what could this presence mean? It is the presence of an idea that is made visible in the work: the idea of art, as the artist had it in mind.[80]

There is a deep irony implicit in Belting's statement that plays itself out in Wager's Reformation interlude. As the figure of Mary Magdalene leaves behind the ornamental fictions and decorative embellishments that Wager binds to the "medieval imagination" (to invoke Simpson's term once again), it enters what Belting calls the "aesthetic sphere," where her job is to provide latter-day Christians, no longer able to experience or recall Christ's presence in eucharistic terms, with an artful, imaginative "idea" of how that presence might feel. We do not see much of this future in Wager's text—the narrative from Luke is too invested in the actor-Christ's real presence to sustain any kind of discussion of metaphor or of figure. But something like an idea of presence—the sweep of hair over the ghostly shadow of Christ's wet feet—can be found in Erasmus's blazon, which looks at Luke through Gregory but also provides supplemental detail that is far more sensual, far more aesthetic than any of its medieval precedents:

> She stood behind at his backe and (as well as she might dooe) begonne to washe his fete with teres of wepyng, marrying for her solle healthe the beautie of hir eyes, which of long tyme afore she was woontin the waie of abominacion to peyncte with Stibie:

and the fete of Iesus beying well washed with teres tryclyng down
from hir iyes lyke the droppes of rayne in a shower, she wyped
drie again, not with any towell of lynnen, but with ye heares of
hir own head, whiche she had vntill that daie, customablye vsed
for the delycate and sensuall pleasure of the fleashe, to enoynct
with swete perfume, to dye with colours, to kembe and to brede
with wrythes of golde enterlaced emong it. The woondrefull loue
also of this woman beeying a synner, was with all this not yet sat-
isfyed: but after that Iesus fete werso washed and wyped, she leaft
not kyssyng of them: But all the thinges which wer once ye instruments of her fylthye pleasures, she now turned to the obedient
seruice of hym, who onely, and none but he is to bee loued.[81]

Unlike the representations of John 20, which are the topic of the next
chapter, Christ is still physically present in this scene though the aesthetic turn is anticipated: Christ fades into the background, visible only
as a ghostly trace, while the Magdalene steps forward as the register or
site of his memory. The reader gets an idea of Christ from Mary Magdalene's feeling of him.

   After the Reformation the blazon becomes the most extensively
deployed conceit in the articulation of the Magdalene's penitential
affect. Robinson used it to great effect, and there are further examples
that suggest that the narrative had wider trans-Reformation ecumeni-
cal appeal. For instance, the blazon is central to *Saint Marie Magdalens
Conversion* (1603), a lengthy poem written by a Jesuit, known as J. C.,
who hoped, much like Wager, that his version of the penitent's contrition would be considered as "plaine and passionate" clothing "much
like a morning garment" for the devout mind to entertain.[82] The relevant passage appears at the end of an epic trial in the psychomachia
tradition. Mary Magdalene begins as Sin's disciple, a "many-headed
monster" who laments that "All seeme to wonder at me as I goe /
And Monster-like me to their children showe."[83] Midway, she is reduced
to blubbering incoherence, at which point she hears from Memory
(who tells her of others just like herself), Strong Opinion (who assures her of the possibility of success with God), Hope (who promises that her chances are good), and Free Will (who literally pushes

her to penance), though Distrust and Ever-Doubting Fear continue to torment her passage. She ends up, finally, as the emblazoned image of penance:

> Teares of true sorrowe for offences done,
> Her watrie eyes like prodigalles doe spend,
> Wherewith the feete of great *Iehouans Sonne*,
> For to imbalme, shee humblie doth intend,
> Those feete of his, these teares of hers, make faire,
> And being wett shee dries them with her haire.[84]

There is no historical allegory in place here; and yet, the aesthetic mobilized by Wager's treatment of Gregory is still the same. The past is not just the place where Mary's eyes were treacherous and her hair beguiling; it is also the place where Christ could transform the markers of sin into the signs of saintliness by virtue of his presence. Outside of history, however, that presence must be brought to mind, and one way to do this is to look at Mary Magdalene.

This is the point that Thomas Collins makes so evident in his treatment of the same moment in *The Penitent Pvblican*. This poem, written for Katherine Hastings, Countess of Huntington, a prominent figure in the court of Elizabeth, known for the godliness of her Protestant household, is a penitential testament offered by a "sinful publican."[85] The Magdalene enters the picture about halfway through as an example of a woeful sinner-turned-saint whose conversion provides a hopeful model for a desperate soul on the path to damnation. The publican's problem, however, is that he knows he can never touch Christ as Mary does. Because Christ will not be present to the publican as he was to Mary, the publican worries that his penitential gestures will not have the same effect.

> And humbly now (like Mary) Lord come I,
> As sad, and sorie, as e're she could bee:
> And for my sinnes repenting hartily,
> Yet though my teares I cannot powre on thee:
> As Christ to her (oh Lord) do thou to mee.

Remit my sinnes, and ere I leaue this place,
Expulse my euill, and fill me with thy grace.[86]

J. C.'s speaker and Collins's publican are, it would seem, reaching
into the past and drawing from it an abundance of relics: tears and
hair that seem to add a touch of beauty to the stark scriptural record
(in the first case) and to the bleak present reality (in the second)—
"Those feete of his," writes J. C., "these teares of hers, make faire."[87]

William Drummond, who was recognized variously as a Protestant and as a Royalist, also illustrates the same nostalgic process of recuperation in his revisiting of the Gregorian blazon in "For the Magdalene" (1630):

These eyes, dear Lord, once brandons of desire,
Frail scouts betraying what they had to keep,
Which their own heart, then others set on fire,
Their trait'rous black before thee here out-weep:
These locks, of blushing deeds the fair attire,
Smooth-frizzled waves, sad shelves which shadow deep,
Soul-stinging serpants in gilt curls which creep,
To touch thy sacred feet do now aspire.
In seas of care behold a sinking bark,
By winds of sharp remorse unto thee driven,
O! let me not expos'd be ruin's mark;
My faults confest, Lord, say they are forgiven.
　　Thus sigh'd to Jesus the Bethenian fair,
　　His tear-wet feet still drying with her hair.[88]

Before knowing what the Magdalene says (in the third quatrain), the
reader knows what she looks like, suggesting that the poised image
of the contrite Magdalene always precedes her speech and even her
actions. More importantly, both her body and her words stand before Christ, whose presence is not even acknowledged until the final
couplet, at which point the shadow of his feet come into view and he
is recognized as the recipient of the Magdalene's plea. The Magdalene emblazoned does not hide modestly behind a table as she does

in Luke or in Wager's *Life and Repentaunce*. She steps into full view, eclipsing the presence of the man who can no longer be known as such, and serves instead as a captivatingly beautiful register of the impression that he has made upon her. The subject of Christ's impression will be taken up more fully in the next chapter, which looks at representations of John 20, and which takes as its subject the problem of Christ's vanishing human presence. The point now, however, is to draw attention not to what has been lost but rather to what has been gained: the artful image of Mary Magdalene, as resplendent in penance as she was reviled in sin, as the aesthetic supplement to the scriptural truth. She is that which gives appreciable, material life to a story that risks being forgotten unless its importance is registered in moving, aesthetically appreciable ways.

I conclude with one last treatment of Luke's sinner, Joseph Sweetnam's *S. Mary Magdalens Pilgrimage to Paradise*. Here, the Magdalene's state of sin is, once again, a function of her misguided attachment to material things: "In my bed in the night I haue sought whome my soule loueth, I haue sought and haue not found."[89] But *Pilgrimage*'s distinctive feature is its rendering of Luke's narrative in self-consciously aesthetic terms. In the encounter at the home of Simon, Sweetnam introduces the subjects of courtesy and hospitality by suggesting that the presence of the Magdalene is akin to that of a painter who enters a home of a king and dines without invitation. Sweetnam explains that this painter, in order to make amends for his social gaffe, offers to paint the king's portrait, and the resulting work is "such a liuely image" of the king that the painter is henceforth honored at the palace. Likewise honored in the palace of our Lord is "our Blessed Magdalen" who has "in her hart and countenance expressed and imprinted the liuely image of Iesvs." Interestingly, while Sweetnam thinks of Mary as a painter whose subject is Christ, the portrait offered by his story is not of Christ but rather of Mary painting Christ—a creative act that makes an impression so vivid "that no age shall be able to blot it forth of memory, no iniury of tyme shall be able to blemish it, or any malice to defile it." The Christian artist cannot paint as Mary does; mortal artists, Sweetnam acknowledges, have not touched what Mary has touched and their painting will always be "but a shaddow of what indeed it representeth." But following in "the footesteps of her excellent Vertues," the artist can preserve Christ's memory secondhand by creating, as Sweetnam does, a register of the impression Christ made on those who felt his human form.[90] The Magdalen blazon thus becomes, for the next generation of painter-poets, a means to capture the art of Mary, which in turn captures a feeling lost to all latter-day Christians: the feeling of being close enough to Christ to reach out and touch him.

Touch Me Not

But Marie stoode without at the sepulchre weeping: and as she wept, she bowed her selfe into the sepulchre, And sawe two Angels in white, sitting, the one at the head, and the other at the feete, where the body of Iesus had laien. And they said vnto her, Woman, why weepest thou? She said vnto them, They haue taken away my Lord, and I know not where they haue laide him. When she had thus said, she turned her selfe backe, and sawe Iesus standing, and knewe not that it was Iesus. Iesus saith vnto her, Woman, why weepest thou? whom seekest thou? She supposing that he had bene the gardener, said vnto him, Sir, if thou hast borne him hence, tell me where thou hast laid him, and I will take him away. Iesus saith vnto her, Marie. She turned her selfe, and said vnto him, Rabboni, which is to say, Master. Iesus saith vnto her, Touch me not: for I am not yet ascended to my Father: but goe to my brethren, and say vnto them, I ascend vnto my Father, and to your Father, and to my God, and your God. Marie Magdalene came and told the disciples that she had seene the Lord, and that he had spoken

these things vnto her.

—John 20:11–18 (Geneva edition)

Thomas Walkington is probably best remembered as the author of *The Optik Glasse of Humours* (1607), a forerunner of Robert Burton's *Anatomy of Melancholy*.[1] Walkington's Magdalene sermon, *Rabboni; Mary Magdalens Teares, of Sorrow, Solace* (1620), shares with *The Optik Glasse* an extravagant and digressive prose style, and in both texts the author's interest in alchemy and humoral theory is probably more in evidence than his religious allegiances. Walkington was no defender of any particular church; *Rabboni* is replete with disparaging critiques of institutional hierarchy, and it is as hard on "Caluin's Presbytery" as it is on the papacy. "Downe with it," writes Walkington of all church authority, "downe with it, euen to the ground."[2] What is interesting about the text, however, and the reason it serves as a fit beginning to a chapter on the post-Reformation treatments of the Magdalene at the sepulcher, is its lugubrious reflection on the terms of Mary's intimacy with Christ—terms that shift, for Walkington, during the *hortulanus* scene in which Mary meets her Lord in the guise of a gardener.

The setting of *Rabboni* is derived from John 20. Mary Magdalene mourns Christ's death but also the apparent disappearance of his body. Her grief is exhausting in its lugubrious detail; Walkington's penitent, more than any before her, rages hysterically, "tearing her comely dangled haire." The prose is so wonderfully mawkish, it is impossible to resist citing at length:

Her heart is all sobby and swolne, like the lower vallies that drinke vp the drops of Heauen, her heart is thus surrounded with her retiring teares, that are run backe from their wonted sluces, her eyes,

the daily-dropping *conduit-pipes* of her greefe. Shee goes wringing her myrrh-dropping fingers, being robbed by the *Sabeans*,
the cursed *Iewes*, of her prizelesse pearle, the signet of her owne
right hand, *Iesus* her Sauiour, whom she tendred and loued as the
apple of her eye, she is grown *Extaticall*, intranced, in a *deliquium*,
a swound, ready to fall, ready to dye.[3]

Mary's grief over Christ's absence is, conventionally, a reflection
of her ardent, absolute love. Working in a deeply ingrained tradition,
Walkington makes extravagant use of the courtly resources of the
lyric as well as the erotic mingling of the sacred with the profane associated with the bride of the Song of Songs. Mary and Christ are a
"*Noble par*, a paire of sweet Turtle Doues, true Louers indeede, Louers in life, and Louers in death, their Loues as strong as death."[4] And
in Christ's absence, Mary is languid with longing: "O stay me with
flagons and comfort me with apples," she cries, "for I am sicke of loue."[5]

Despite her distraction, however, Mary sees something quite extraordinary. The vision is, of course, of Christ who has risen from the
grave but is unrecognizable in his gardener's guise. Only when Christ
addresses Mary by name do her senses recalibrate, allowing her to see
the obvious:

> *Rabboni?* what, *my* Lord and Master; and haue I now at length
> found my dearest Lord? my soule delight? And haue I now set
> happy eye on thee, *dimidium anime?* The halfe of my soule, nay,
> the whole life of my soule? The *Sepulcher* of my sorrowes, the
> *Paradise* of my blisse, the *Crowner* of all my miseries with eternall
> mercies, the *Balsame* of my hearts delight, the *Total Summe* of all
> my happines?[6]

As his title suggests, Walkington's interest is in this moment of recognition: the moment Mary turns to Christ and acknowledges him as
her master, the moment where vision becomes insight.

In most treatments of the *hortulanus* scene, Mary's single-word
address is followed (as it is in John 20) by an attempt to touch Christ's
body with the familiarity accorded to her in the past. Her hand is

rejected, and with Christ's words "touch me not" she ceases to be the woman whose privilege derives from an intimate, bodily connection with her Lord, and becomes the clairvoyant who sees things others can't. Walkington, intent on acknowledging Mary's new role as star pupil, makes the longing clear ("Oh let me graspe thee, ô Lord, and claspe and embrace thee, and cling to thee, and hold thee in the circles of my (in that happy) arms") but does not illustrate the *noli me tangere*. Nevertheless, *Rabboni* uses the garden sequence to intimate that there is a line to be drawn between the convert's knowledge of Christ before his death and her knowledge of him after his resurrection. Walkington's Mary no longer touches; instead, she comes to terms with the sensual experiences of her past, deriving from them the spiritual insight that makes her the "excellent Scholler of so worthy a tutor."[7]

And yet crucially, at this moment, all of Mary's past—all the "wantonesse vnto which she had been so long wedded"—comes flooding forward as Walkington revisits the site of conversion:

> She refuses to bee called the darling daughter of the world, chusing rather to suffer a short affliction, to endure a hard penance with the children of God, then to enioy the pleasures of sin for a season: she disrobes and strips her selfe of all her princely paludaments, her rich aray, her courtly acoutrements, her sumptuous weedes, and puts on the comeley attire of a true Penitentiary . . . shee comes trembling, and blushing, and crouching, and blubbring, to the table where *Iesus* was sit downe, she came quiuering behinde that Lord, that saw her well enough, she did her decent obeysance, she bowing downe her self, began to kisse the feet of her deare Sauiour [etc.].[8]

The life and repentance of Mary Magdalene are once again read as a narrative of divestment in which robes of luxury and decadence are stripped away, exposing the naked truth of penitence. But here, in the garden of the resurrection, the terms of Mary's relationship with Christ have been revised and so her exposure and physical vulnerability are less palpable (and less problematic) than they are in Wager's

Reformation interlude. In Walkington's text, repentance is recast as a memory rather than as a phenomenological event. The memory is significant because it is the foundation of the Magdalene's present knowledge and the basis of her current privilege; but the event is not material or tangible—at least not in the way that it once was. Nora has suggested that moments of rupture make us realize that "the past is a world from which we are fundamentally cut off." However, he also suggests that "we discover the truth about our memory when we discover how alienated from it we are."[9] Accordingly, just as Walkington's Mary realizes that her tangible, physical connection with a real presence has been severed, the memories of feeling and touch pour out and she is able to convey an idea of presence with extraordinary vivacity. Despite its histrionic propensities, Walkington's sermon is moving and articulate in this respect: the Magdalene's senses become the "Pen-men" of Christ's perfections, of his "exact pourtraiture, and liuely lineaments of face."[10]

Rabboni, along with other representations of the Magdalene at the sepulcher, is an obvious manifestation of "tears literature," an important subset of penitential writing.[11] And it has been argued by Patricia Phillippy, among others, that grief in tears poetry is always aestheticized in a process linked to the aesthetics of female lamentation informing cultural discourses of mourning.[12] Aesthetics are certainly at issue here, but I want to consider Walkington's investment in the *hortulanus* scene as an inquiry into the problems of portraiture facing the post-Reformation poet: Walkington essentially locates the Magdalene at the very moment in which religious poetics were being reformulated and revised. Mary's function, henceforth, is to supplement and mitigate the ghastly truth told in the Gospels with a memory that confirms Christ's enduring presence. By speaking one word, "Rabboni," Mary "awakes her glory" and acknowledges her master as well as her new vocation: she must figure forth a "liuely Idea" of Christ— an image of divine character and fair features that will comfort and revitalize all Christian hearts.

In the previous chapter I argued, in concert with Belting, that after the Reformation "the idea of art," as the artist had it in mind, eclipsed the presence of the sacred in works of art. Even Catholic artists needed, after the Council of Trent, to adopt the "Reformed kind of image, stripped of its offensive features—an image that stimulated theological reflection by a speculative content presented in artistic guise."[13] I argued that the postmedieval Magdalene enters what Belting calls the "aesthetic sphere," where she (or rather the visual poetics that constitute her) becomes a site of memory for the "idea" of bodily presence once captured in iconic art and in the sacramental ritual of transubstantiation. Here, I will use treatments of John 20 to show how Mary Magdalene's form registers the tremulous effects of a sublime encounter with an untouchable Christ. This moment is, for the writers that take up this subject, a moment of sensory disorientation, which, by necessity, brings the Magdalene's intimate memories of Christ rushing to the foreground. In the process, however, the texts also register a sense of monumental historical rupture by describing the bewildering effects that the Reformation had upon Catholic culture. Thus, by showing Mary's need to renegotiate her relationship with the resurrected Christ, these writers also highlight the effects of a larger cultural encounter with the Scriptures in which the memories of a much more material and iconic past come flooding forward as English Christians struggle to understand what it means to know and represent something that cannot be touched. Mary's form at the sepulcher is, therefore, doubly haunted—by Christ and by the Catholic past. Her narratives become ghost stories of disquieting intensity as they underscore the very pastness of the past. At the same time, this weeping figure is the herald of the baroque, anticipating a poetic tradition that registers the sublime effects of Christ's presence by making aesthetic sense of unruly and disquieted souls mournfully searching for something real to hold.

Walkington's sermon makes the point that devotional poetry, like the Magdalene, must bring forward an exact portrait of Christ. This chapter, however, will show that the literary images of Mary at the sepulcher, Walkington's included, do not (arguably, cannot) show us Christ. Mary Magdalene is very much the subject of these narratives. No longer a "profane pamplet," she becomes "the true *Enchiridion,* the *Manuell* of Gods mercies, in whom a Christian true Scholler may

reade with a blubbring eye, many lines of sorrow and hearty reformation."[14] Christ is a shadow in these texts, a filmy effect that brushes
across the exquisite body of the Magdalene—making his presence
felt in words that disturb and disorient the senses. Like ghost stories
which, according to Elaine Scarry, acquire extraordinary vivacity
by instructing readers to imagine, not a concrete object, but rather
the glide of something transparent across that object's surface, these
poems provide vivid images of the Magdalene by illustrating her encounter with a vision that can be seen but not touched.[15]

This haunted Magdalene is most intensely illustrated by Robert
Southwell who, like Walkington, saw Mary's singularity as residing in
her extraordinary ability to see Christ after his physical disappearance.
Southwell and his contemporaries who also write on the subject—
Henry Constable, Richard Verstegan (aka Richard Rowlands), William Alabaster, and Gervase Markham—are particularly concerned
with the Magdalene's ability to make sense of disturbing and disorienting sensory experience. Essentially, they argue that when Mary fixates on the absence of Jesus' body her physical senses overwhelm her
and she becomes distracted and confused. When she learns to look for
Christ within her soul, the deep and dark repository of her memory,
her senses align and Christ appears before her in ghostly form. I want
to suggest that early modern literary treatments of the Magdalene
at the sepulcher draw upon this "spiritual seeing" in order to articulate a sensual poetics of recollection that captures an *idea* of Christ's
haunting, ever lively presence.

The Sepulcher of the Heart

The story of Southwell's prose meditation, *Marie Magdalens
Funeral Teares* (1591), begins with the medieval source of Southwell's
narrative: the twelfth-century homily *De beata maria magdalena*. Tell-
ingly, the homily survives in at least 185 manuscripts in eight different
languages, including English.[16] There are 28 manuscript copies of the
homily in English libraries; there was at least one edition of the Latin

text printed in England in 1505, and English translations were printed in 1555 and 1565 under the title *An Homelie of Marye Magdalene, declaring her ferue[n]t loue and zele towards Christ.*[17] The scholarship on *De beata maria magdalena* has focused on the homily's debt to the Song of Songs in its refusal to privilege spiritual devotion and in the narrator's apparent reproach of the neglectful lover-Christ.[18] However, it is also the case that, for the medieval homilist, Mary's importance lies in part in her ability to weep for Christ's absence and to long for his presence ("Disce plorare dei absenciam at desiderare eius presenciam"). Because Christ is no longer part of the world of physical phenomena but rather to be understood as vital and vivid memory, the homilist argues that one can learn from Mary Magdalene to seek for Jesus in the sepulcher of one's heart ("Disce a Maria querere ihesum in monumento cordis tui").[19] The weeping penitent thus gives representational shape to a perennial theological problem no less troublesome to medieval writers than to those writing after the Reformation: the problem of invisible presence. The question of Christ's lasting place in the world, however, became particularly charged as liturgical reform challenged and reconceived the substance and function of the sacrament of the Eucharist. I would argue, therefore, that the homily's postmedieval popularity likely has much to do with its willingness to ask, can the Word be seen?

The homily's identification of Mary Magdalene's exceptional insight, as well as the role that her soul-searching serves in the representation of Christ's invisibility, have a long-standing history as part of the Easter liturgy in the form of the *Quem Quaeritis* topos. In this text, four members of the clergy enact the discovery of the empty sepulcher by the three Marys and the exchange between the women and the angel who announces the resurrection.[20] The importance of this brief scene, still widely understood as the first manifestation of liturgical drama, lies in the emphasis it places upon sight—that is, the ability to see absence—as evidence for the resurrection and, consequently, Christ's continuing presence in the world. For Michal Kobialka, who has written extensively on the subject, the answer to the question "Whom do you seek?" (which is "He is not here; he has risen just as was predicted. Go tell that he is risen from the sepulcher") becomes not only an imperative to preach the resurrection, but also a reflection of "the desire to give visibility to the body, which had disappeared," and to give "representational form to a complex theological thought." Kobialka concludes with the argument that the Fourth Lateran Council of 1215, which saw the consolidation of the principle of Real Presence within the doctrine of transubstantiation, was a turning point in the history of Christian representational practices because the constitutions of the council effectively located the production of images within the institution of the church. The fact that the Magdalene is one of the Marys participating in the exchange locates her at a moment in which discursive and mutable definitions of the nature and substance of representation itself were formulated and revised.[21]

In *De beata maria magdalena*, however, as well as in the sixteenth-century English translation of the homily to which I now turn, Christ's invisibility is considered initially to be the effect of Mary Magdalene's spiritual blindness—a blindness brought about by excessive grief.[22] Moreover, while Mary's wild lamentations are understood as a reaction to the death of her companion and leader, they are also, pointedly, the result of the disappearance of his corpse. This latter event is more disturbing than the former, for Jesus' body would have provided a material locus for the grief of the mourning woman. Because the body is missing, Mary's love is described as a tenuous thing—at least in her mind. She fears that if she cannot find Christ's body, "the loue of him her Mayster wold sone ware colde with in her breaste." Mary's soul is attached to a physical presence ("she could more easily seperate her liuing soule fro[m] her liuing body, the[n] her louing spirit from [his] dead body ... when she lost [his] body, she lost with it her own spirit"), and without her soul she is bereft, disoriented, and longs for her own death.[23] Her spirit can be content only when it lies with Christ, its lover, as it did in the past.[24]

> She had loste the life of her soule, & nowe she thought it better to dye than to liue, thinking perhappes in her death to haue founde, whome in her lyfe she could not fynde, withoute whom notwithstanding she was not able to lyue. Strong as the Deathe is loue: for what more could death do in Marye.[25]

A lost soul produces a loss of affect or rather an inability to master affect: "Hauing sence she used no sence: Seinge, she dyd not see: hearing, shee heard not, neither was she where she was."[26] And in this state of confusion, because she is "couered with a thicke cloude of wo and sorowe," Mary fails to recognize Christ when he approaches her in the garden. Her error (which proceeds not from sin but from love) is thus an error of the eye: she "didst seke Iesus, and didste not seke Iesus," and therefore in seeing Jesus, "she didst not knowe Iesus." Because she languishes in love she cannot see with her heart; "the eyes of her heart," concludes the homilist, have become "so dym."[27] The senses themselves, however, are not the problem; Mary's failure is that she cannot completely master her senses and, therefore, loses herself. Southwell later mobilizes this reading of Mary's wayward senses in *Funeral Teares.* "What maruaile then though sence faile, when the soule is lost, sith the lanterne must needs be dark when the light is out?" he writes, in concert with his medieval source, making it clear that he too thinks that Mary fails initially to make appropriate use of her passions and thus compromises her personhood.[28] Southwell also appropriates the homily's insistence that the tension between the soul and the senses comes into being only when the body is dispossessed of its soul—the interpreter and regulator of sense—without which the experience of the world becomes incomprehensible.[29]

Some precision is lent to the bond between sense and soul in two Southwell poems on the subject of the Magdalene. In the first, entitled "Mary Magdalens blush," Mary becomes a figure torn between the world of the senses and the world of the soul:

> O sence, O soule, O had [*sic*], O hoped blisse,
> You wooe, you weane, you draw, you driue me back.
> Your crosse-encountring, like their combate is,
> That neuer end but with some deadly wrack.
> When sense doth winne, the soule doth loose the field,
> And present happes, make future hopes to yeeld.

And yet Southwell is reluctant to cast away the potency of sensory experience, for in its absence sacred love lacks the ecstasy that confirms it to be genuine. Sensory experience may lead to sin, but a world deprived of the senses simply has no soul.

> O heauen, lament: sense robbeth thee of Saints:
> Lament O soules, sense spoyleth you of grace.
> Yet sense doth scarse deserue these hard complaints,
> Loue is the thiefe, sense but the entring place.
> Yet graunt I must, sense is not free from sinne,
> For theefe he is that theefe admitteth in.

In the second Magdalene poem, "Mary Magdalens complaint at Christs death," the death of Jesus and the disappearance of his body provide the unfortunate opportunity for the escape of the soul. The courtly understanding of imprisonment is put to work here as Christ's confining embrace is understood as pleasurable; captivity, a delight; and freedom, another word for nothing left to lose:

> O my soule, what did vnloose thee
>   From thy sweete captiuitie?
> God, not I, did still possesse thee:
>   His, not mine, thy libertie.
> O, two happie thrall thou wart,
> When thy prison, was his hart.[30]

With this understanding of the soul's role as the arbitrator of sense at hand, the meditative space of *Funeral Teares* allows Southwell to consider further the critical contents of Mary's soul—her memories of Christ's body.

Southwell's appreciation of the significance of memory in the interplay between soul and sense is, not surprisingly, largely derived from *De beata maria magdalena*. Both the Latin original and the English translation observe that Mary's disorientation is a product of her failing memory. "Jesus had forespoken that thus he should dye," writes the homilist, but Mary "had quite blotted out the remembraunce of these words."[31] Essentially, the more she weeps, the more she becomes obsessed with the corporeal and the more she forgets the promise that Christ will rise from the dead and live again. Moreover, memory can only be revived and the soul returned to its senses by means of sacramental nourishment. The narrator urges Christ on, fearing that Mary will faint of spiritual hunger:

> Refresshe and comforte the bowels of her soule with the plesau[n]tes of thy taste. For thou art the liuing bread whiche haste in the al maner delectablenes and all sauour of swetenes: for the life of her body will not long endure, onles y^u quickly shewest thy self, which art the life of her soul.[32]

Christ's single-word address, "Mary," thus restores her senses, revives her spirit, and allows her memories to live again. For the homilist, then, the *hortulanus* sequence explores the cognitive implications of Christ's absence, with explicit reference to the doctrine of transubstantiation, assuring the "transition between Christ as a living contemporary to a Christ who henceforth exists in memory—in the sacrament and in the church founded on and by those who witnessed his resurrection."[33] Mary shows how it feels to have Jesus present in one's soul, in one's heart:

> Learne sinfull man of a sinfull woman, whose sinnes notwithstandinge be forgeuen her: Learn to wepe for Gods absence, and to desire his presence. Learne of Marye to loue Iesus, and to trust in Iesus, and by seekinge Iesus in this search, to feare no aduersitie, and besides Iesus to receiue no comfort, and for Iesus to co[n]teinne all thinges. Learn of Mary to seeke for Iesus in the Sepulcher of thy Heart.[34]

For Southwell, however, the garden sequence does more than describe the sacramental urgency of Mary's encounter with Christ; it also delineates a new role for the Magdalene in the battle to preserve Christian memory in the face of Protestant tyranny. This shift in focus from Christ's potentially nourishing body to Mary's memories of that body is first registered in the English translation of the medieval homily, which opens with an invocation to the reader in which

Mary Magdalene is "recoursed" to the speaker's "remembrau[n]ce" upon the present occasion.[35] This setup, in which the reader observes the speaker remembering the Magdalene remembering, is preserved by Southwell and becomes an important topos in the development of the postmedieval Magdalen. As English Catholics are deprived of the doctrine of transubstantiation, the Magdalene is figured as the empty sepulcher/altar still illuminated or embellished by the body/host it no longer contains. "Though I haue beene robbed of the Saint," writes Southwell in his introduction, "I wil at the least haue care of the shrine, which though it be spoiled of the most soueraigne hoast, yet shall it be the Altar where I will daily sacrifi[c]e my heart, and offer vp my teares." And this altar, Southwell concludes, bears upon (or within) it a likeness of Christ's person: "Likenesse loue had limed [in the sense of illuminated or colored] in her heart, and treasured vp in her sweetest memories."[36] Now obliged to reconcile themselves to a greatly diminished sacrament, the weeper, with her memories painted upon her, is all that Catholics have left.

Southwell is doing his best to make the Magdalene figure topical and useful. Gary Kuchar has expertly broached this endeavor by showing how Southwell's work generally provided recusant subjects with "a devotional framework" through which they could "symbolically mitigate the lived experience of social and religious exile." Southwell's Magdalene meditation, in particular, "serves as a commentary on the recusant experience of social isolation and religious abandonment while providing a model example of how one should cope with such marginalization." Kuchar's reading ultimately argues that *Funeral Teares* makes the best of bad times by pointing to the distinctions between "subjection to the divine spirit and submission to national law" and between "genuinely devout grief over the absence of the true Church and unnecessarily hyperbolic grief that is the child of self-love." In this respect, Southwell's work is a socially symbolic act engaged in the production of ideal subjects in Reformation England.[37]

Southwell overcomes the anguish of present circumstances partly by tapping into the medieval notion of Mary Magdalene as physical vessel for a numinous idea of presence that puts the Reformation question of missing bodies at some remove. In the N-Town play, for instance, Mary Magdalene is metaphorically figured as a "chawmere" or chamber for her Lord's "swete sowle."[38] Jacobus, in the *Legenda aurea*, describes Mary as containing or enclosing a brilliant and yet indiscernible presence:

> . . . she is a lightar / ffor there she toke so largely / that she spradde it habundantly She toke the lyght there / wyth whiche afterward she enlumyned other[s] / And in that she chaas the best parte of the heuenly glorye: she is sayde the lyght for thenne she was enlumyned of parfyght knowlege in thought & with the lyght in clernes in body / magdalene is as moche to saye as abydyng culpable / Or magdalene is interpreted closed or shette / or not to be ouercomen Or ful of magnyficence[. . .][39]

And, in the resurrection pageant in the Towneley plays, Mary's heart becomes the fragile vessel, or sepulcher, for a body upon which no others can place their hands:

> My catyf hart wyll breke in thre
> when that I thynk on that ilk bodye
> how it was spylt;
> Thrugh feete and handys nalyd was he
> Withoutten gylt.[40]

In these texts, Mary is a figure who provides imaginative and even aesthetic supplement to an idea that can be difficult to fathom on its own. It is of this idea of Christ that Julian of Norwich speaks when she alludes to Mary Magdalene's mourning. Julian longs for that which she cannot have—immediate and intimate access to the suffering body of Christ—she wants to see, as Mary did, the "bodily sight" of his anguish so that she might have more "knowledge of the bodily peynes of our saviour." But Julian knows she cannot emulate Mary's experience of Christ's body—living or dead. Forever at a distance from the real thing, she turns to meditating upon Mary Magdalene in order to "have the more trew minde in the passion of Christe."[41]

And so when Southwell comes down hard on Mary's inability to recognize Christ when he appears before her, he is engaging the figure in a discussion that extends well beyond doctrine on transubstantiation. He is appealing to what medieval writers knew well: Mary is special because she has useful memories that others do not. When Mary dismisses Christ "for a ghost," Southwell writes, "shee deemeth [him] but a fansie, being yet better acquainted with [his] bodily shape, then with [his] spirituall power." Her eyes have become too familiar with the literal "trueth"—that is, the physical form of Christ's body—to "accept a supplie of shadowes" (a ghostly impression)—that is, his resurrected condition.[42] Only when she comes to terms with the circumstances that now face her, with the pastness of her own past, is her memory restored so that she can see and indeed recognize the ghost. Southwell may well bemoan the moment of violent historical rupture that "spoiled" the host and relegated memories of Christ to shadows. But he also wants to make it known that, given these horrible conditions, it would be best to make full use of a figure who can, because of her past, know a ghost when she sees one.[43] Southwell's meditation is not, therefore, just an elegy on the loss of the substance of the Holy Eucharist to the powerful agents of reform; it is also an appeal for an alternative—a purely figurative way of seeing, recorded in a language of affect, in a poetics of the senses.

Central to Southwell's formulation of this poetics is the *noli me tangere* sequence. In John a man appears to Mary as she weeps. She doesn't recognize him because he appears as a gardener. He asks her why she weeps; she explains and wonders if he knows of the body's whereabouts. He speaks her name, and instantly she knows him. She reaches to touch him—as she has done in the past—and he forbids the gesture; evidently something has changed, though it is difficult to discern what. Glenn Most, in his recent work on Doubting Thomas, shows that the synoptic Gospels do not include like prohibitions and, in fact, prove to be contradictory: in Matthew, the two Marys take hold of Christ's feet and worship them (28:9); in Luke, Jesus invites the disciples to "handle me, and see" (24:39). The contradiction is so flagrant, Most argues, that translators occasionally attempt to camouflage it with mistranslation.[44] Coletti, also recognizing the passage's strangeness, reminds us how harsh and jarring the prohibition seemed to Margery Kempe, who saw the Magdalene as "pursuing an utterly tactile religious epistemology, forever at odds with the deeper spiritual implications of the *noli me tangere*."[45] One might suppose that the difficulty posed by Christ's rejection of Mary's touch was at least partly resolved by the somatic phenomenology of medieval religious culture. Sarah Beckwith argues, for instance, that the discussion of absence and presence, as posited by the Magdalene's encounter with the empty sepulcher and then with the untouchable Christ, becomes sacramental in the York play because the enactment of the scene gives a scriptural idea tangible substance by introducing living form. The winedrawers' pageant (the dramatization of the *hortulanus* scene) provides "the regained sight that shows that we too can see that Christ is the sign of God." Beckwith expands as follows:

> It is the actuality of encounter in theatre that helps us to see and experience this drama as one of acknowledgment rather than knowledge. For what we have before our very eyes is all that has been missed. Like Mary, Christ is in front of us, but his presence is insignificant until woven into our memory. The continuity of Jesus with Christ will be part of a community of ourselves to ourselves; without that self-knowledge, belief in a risen Christ is pointless and empty dogma, the visible witness of which is Mary Magdalene's love for a corpse. Her recognition becomes to us, too, a communal achievement, one that has to be reexperienced, not merely repeated, for this version of presence to be real.[46]

For Southwell's Magdalene, however, as for all English recusants, the unsteadiness provoked by the loss of the body of Christ could not be resolved by the materiality of theater. Perhaps with his eyes cast back nostalgically upon a period of representational innocence, Southwell makes much more of the physical distance between Mary and her Lord than does the medieval homilist. Mary finds herself bereft once again, "like a hungry infant puld from a full teat, or a hart chased from a sweet fountaine."[47] Christ's ghostly touch tickles, leaving an itch that Mary cannot scratch. And yet because this is the case the *noli me tangere* moment becomes more useful than it is vexing because it commands a different kind of recognition. Mary's problem, according to Southwell, is that she presumes too much, too soon. Eager to recapture the intimacy they once shared, Mary charges at Christ's body without considering the implications of the resurrection. She cannot touch because she does not understand. Southwell concludes his meditation with the following advice to readers:

> if hee vouchsafe thee with his glorious sight, offering himselfe to thy inward eies, presume not of thy selfe to be able to knowe him, but as his unworthy suppliant prostrate thy petitions vnto him, that thou maiest truly discerne him, and faithfully serue him. . . . If with Marie thou crauest no other solace of Iesus but Iesus himselfe, he will answere thy teares with his presence, and assure thee of his presence with his owne words.[48]

Only when prepared to accept the idea of Christ, rather than the body, will his presence be made manifest. In this respect, Southwell becomes aligned with Erasmus, whose gloss of the *noli me tangere* likewise records the need for a new way of thinking about Christ's presence. Erasmus has Mary lingering at the sepulcher because she longs to tend the body of him "whome she had loued being aliue," and when she sees Christ again she does fall to the ground to touch his feet, doing so in "remembraunce thyr olde familiaritie." But, Christ's wrenching prohibition is then glossed as follows:

> Jesus knowying that as yet she thought no great excellent thyng of hym, although she loued him sincerely and arde[n]tly, did prohibite her to touche his bodye. For Marie saw well that he was aliue agayne, but she thought y^t he was reuiued for none other cause, but as he dyd before, to liue familiarlye with his frendes, beyng now a man aliue where as before he was deade, & ignoraunte she was y^t he now caryed about with hym an immortall bodye whiche

was to be handeled with muche greater reuerence, whiche bodye
the Lord did neuer exhibite or present to the wicked, nor suffered
it to be handled of euery man, to thentente he might litle by litle,
altogether withdrawe them from the loue of y^s bodye. Touche me
not (sayeth he) it is the same bodye whiche hong vpon the crosse,
but it is nowe beautified and adourned with the glory of immortalitie.[49]

For Erasmus, John 20 points to a significant epistemic shift from
a time when one could know God by touching him, to a time when
knowledge can come only to the blessed and only to those who have
altogether withdrawn from physical attachment.[50] The gloss suggests
that the prohibition on touch enables a form of "spiritual seeing," or
what Herbert Kessler identifies as an intermediate level of perception
between the corporeal and the intellectual which relies upon the "eyes
of the mind" (the term is Augustinian) to "think of bodies previously
known but now absent."[51] Mary's past is a world from which she is fundamentally cut off, and she can see the Truth only when she recognizes the extent to which she is alienated from it.[52]

Southwell's Magdalene is, however, a less willing student of Erasmus's ideal recollection than her Origenist antecedent. In fact, Southwell's most significant departure from his medieval source is found in
the sequence that follows the *hortulanus* scene. Mary's encounter with
the disciples and her announcement of the resurrection is a solemn
occasion in which she advises Christ's followers to "goe seeke to better thy selfe in some more happy breast." "I am nothing different from
that I was," she laments, for "in hauing taken a taste of the highest
delite, that the knowledge & want of it might drowne me in the deep-
est misery." Mary's fervent love then leads her back to the tomb where
she again "forgetteth her self, and loue carrieth her in a golden distraction, making her to imagin that her Lord is present." She dreams
of Christ's body, imagining that his "feete are in her folded armes, and
that hee giueth her soule a full repast of his comfortes." The Magdalene desperately wants to revel in real presence here but the point is
that it is just not possible. Southwell must acknowledge the imaginary

or figurative quality of his subject's experience, calling her dream a figment of her "imagination, being so delightfull."[53] Interestingly, Mary is not condemned for her fantasy; instead, her false rapture moves the passions of the reader. In the figure of Mary, the reader sees that spiritual vision is not fully accessible to the fallen, and presence can only be known as an uncanny memory so vivid it makes one's hair stand on end and yet so remote that the experience is profoundly saddening.

Southwell's contemplation of the Magdalene's fantasy also resonates against Erasmus's description of what Mary eventually comes to see—something "nowe beautified and adourned with the glory of immortalitie." Her vision is not a tangible presence; it is a spirit or phantasm whose beauty is figured by the sensual effect it has upon its beholder. Louis Martz has argued that, with the words of Southwell's "Epistle," "the aesthetic of the Counter Reformation establishes itself on English soil."[54] Martz's claim is that early modern articulations of the place of sensory experience in divine meditation originate in the Ignatian method, which teaches that the contemplation of the life of Christ involves seeing the scenes of the Gospels "with the eyes of the imagination" along with hearing what they say, smelling and tasting "the infinite sweetness and delight of the Divinity, of the soul, and of its virtues," and finally feeling "with the touch; as for example, to kiss and embrace the spots where such persons tread and sit."[55] As in the Magdalene poetry, the Jesuit experiences of the physical senses become the platform for a spiritual encounter with Christ. But I am arguing that, for Southwell, the object of Mary's love is not that which comes into focus at the moment of revelation—that is, one does not necessarily see what Mary sees. Magdalene literature tends to dwell on how it is that Christ becomes present to Mary: how his ghostly form opens the gates of her soul, allowing memory to return, and restoring the sensual experience of love. The object ultimately beautified here is Mary as her body registers the sublime effect the strange encounter at the sepulcher has had upon her.

Perhaps more useful than Martz's sense of the Jesuitical origins of the baroque aesthetic emergent in Southwell's meditation is Elizabeth Harvey's invocation of the centrality of tactile contact within religious representation where it attempts to signify the "dialectic between materiality and resurrection, between physical and spiritual contamination or cure." More than any other sense, touch is "a mediator—between the body and what transcends it." In broader terms, Harvey argues, touch becomes, within early modern culture, "a metaphor for conveyance into the interior of the subject, particularly the capacity to arouse emotion . . . Touch evokes at once agency and receptivity, authority and reciprocity, pleasure and pain, sensual indulgence and epistemological certainty."[56] For Maurice Merleau-Ponty touch is fundamental to any subject's orientation in the world. "My hand, while it is felt from within, is also accessible from without . . . a veritable touching of the touch," he writes, in order to illustrate that she who touches "passes over to the rank of the touched." Moreover,

> . . . since the same body sees and touches, visible and tangible belong to the same world . . . There is double and crossed situating of the visible in the tangible and of the tangible in the visible; the two maps are complete, and yet they do not merge into one.[57]

If touch comes to define the contours of self and world in such vital terms, to be deprived of it cannot be without consequence. Susan Stewart argues that Christ's interdiction to the Magdalene seems harsh and even cruel because touch, of all the senses, "is most linked to emotion or feeling. To be 'touched' or 'moved' by words or things implies the process of identification and separation by which we apprehend the world aesthetically." Any prohibition placed upon the anchoring capabilities of touch, then, "results in the effects of sublimity, magnitude, and ungraspability." This powerfully intense experience of vertigo enhances aesthetic perception even as it disallows the organizing functions of the imagination and the understanding. The disoriented figure of the Magdalene is thrust forward into the world, as is the disoriented English Catholic. Unable to make sense of immaterial experience, both must repeat to others in lyric utterances marked by the inarticulate passion of one who has seen (but not touched) a ghost of sublime proportions. "What propels us outward," concludes

Stewart, "will also transform us, and it is only by finding means of making sense impressions intelligible to others that we are able to situate ourselves and our experiences within what is universal."[58] The last words of Southwell's meditation are, in fact, Mary's: "I haue seene our lord, and these thinges he sayd vnto me."[59] For Southwell, then, the devotional lyric, and the society created around it, become the only available means to commemorate Christ's presence in a world where memory is no longer embodied in the living practices of a communal culture.[60]

An Ineffable Form

Ironically, the epistle that prefaces *Funeral Teares* denounces overtly sensual poetry, "especially this of loue." However, as I hope to have made clear, the expression of the passions is not what Southwell objects to, for while these may be "the chiefe commaunder of moste mens actions, & the Idol to which both tongues and pennes doe sacrifice their ill bestowed labours," Southwell thinks if poets could only "alter their obiect and better their intent," the experience of the senses could be used to improve literature on religious subjects. In fact, Southwell asks the wits of his day, "now giuen to write passionat discourses," to learn from his endeavors and "to make choise of such passions, as it neither should be shame to vtter, nor sinne to feele."[61] The plea did not fall upon deaf ears. My next two chapters will show just how important Southwell's maudlin poetics became to the devotional writers of the later seventeenth century. However, before I move on, I want also to suggest that Southwell was not thinking in isolation; rather, he was one of a number of English writers, early heralds of the baroque, intrigued by the Magdalene's potential to reshape Christian memory for the age after the icon.

In 1601 Richard Verstegan published "A Complaint of S. Mary Magdalene" in a collection of odes and sundry poems "tending to deuotion and pietie." The poem is perhaps not what Southwell had hoped for when he called for those "skilfuller pennes" to make up for his own "want of ability." And yet Verstegan does try to render a

Magdalene whose grief is more than just exemplary. This poem, like Southwell's, shows us how Christ becomes present to Mary Magdalene. "O let me know but where hee is," she says to the uncanny gardener whom she does not yet recognize, for "my harte shall be his toombe." Despite her distress, despite the eyes that "serue mee not to see," Mary knows already to make something of her mourning—something she can communicate to others. For Verstegan, Mary knows that she is the monument upon which Christ's memory shall be engraved:

> And thow thereon maist wryte,
> This epitaph in verse,
> Heer lyf that lately lay for dead.
> Liues and reuyues his hearse.[62]

And by calling the Magdalene to mind Verstegan instigates her as a site of memory that mitigates the horror of the Gospels (or of history) by showing others how it feels to encounter the presence of something thought to be irretrievably lost.

In William Alabaster's twenty-first sonnet, on the subject of the Magdalene, Mary's soul is again divided from her body in pursuit of her loved one. As in Southwell and his sources, the division is understood as profoundly disturbing and disorienting, producing tears that serve as lenses to reveal the sad truth of physical absence.

> I weep two deaths with one tear to lament:
> Christ, my soul's life, out of my heart is fled,
> My soul, my heart's life, from me vanished,
> With Christ my soul, and with my soul, life went.
> I weep, yet weeping brings mere discontent,
> For as Christ's presence my tears seasoned,
> When through my tears his love I clearer read,
> So now his loss through them doth more augment.[63]

The tears that once made vital contact with holiness, a reference to Mary's lachrymose tending of Christ's feet in Luke 7, now make the world, deprived of that holy presence, dreary and cold. Without the sight of Christ there can be no words to describe him.

However, the moment is part of a larger narrative in which Mary comes to see quite differently. Tears eventually become prismatic glasses through which a remarkably vivid image is made manifest. Another maudlin Alabaster sonnet makes this point:

> And let these thousand thoughts pour on mine eyes
> A thousand tears as glasses to behold him,
> And thousand tears, thousand sweet words devise
> Upon my lips as pictures to unfold him.[64]

Tears provide the perspective glasses that make spiritual vision clear, and the passage becomes a prescient synthesis of a specifically visual poetics: emotional affect (tears) takes verbal form (words) which in turn becomes utterance (lips) visible to others' eyes (pictures). The experience of the body sharpens the register of the senses, making the figurative or literary expression of the sublime a vivid but also, crucially, a shared experience. Like Mary, then, readers do not see Christ because a picture is held before their eyes; they see him because the figuration of Mary's new self-knowledge touches them, assuring them that they are not alone.

Southwell's sense of the poetic potency of the Magdalene image is also demonstrated by Henry Constable in a suite of Magdalene poems in the *Spiritual Sonnets* (1594). All four of Constable's sonnets conventionally turn around the relationship between matters of body and soul. The first describes unmeasured sensual experience, a "fewe nyghtes solace in delitious bedd," as paid for dearly in penitential tears. Mary's example is summoned to remind the speaker "how deare I should for triflyng pleasures paye" and "what hyghe Rewarde, by little payne ys wonne." The second poem places the Magdalene at the sepulcher where she serves as a penitential model for the speaker's soul, which must also bear "a breast with oyle of grace," making his heart "lyke to a lampe appere." The third sonnet dwells upon the location of the soul, initially trapped in a hellish body but ultimately settling peacefully into a contrite heart:

In such a place my sowle doth seeme to be
   when in my body she laments her synne:
   and none but brutall passions fyndes therin,
   except they be sent down from heaven to mee.
Yett if those graces, God to me impart,
   which he inspyr'd thy blessed brest withall:
   I may fynde heaven in my retyred hart:
And if thou change the obiect of my love,
   Thy wyng'd affection which men Cupid call
   may gett his syght, & lyke an Angell prove.

In the final poem, the speaker asks the Magdalene to declare to him "what pleasure ys obtayn'd by heavenly love." Mary's knowledge is more perfect than his; for only in death can he abandon the experience of the physical world and partake in a more perfect union with Christ:

My body ys the garment of my spryght
   whyle as the day tyme of my lyfe doth last:
   when death shall brynge the nyght of my delyght
My sowle vncloth'd, shall rest from labors past:
   and clasped in the armes of God, inioye
   by sweete coniunction, everlasting ioye.[65]

All four poems stress the impossibility of seeing Christ, whose form is too resplendent for mortal vision steeped in sin. But the contemplation of Mary's encounter with Christ does, nevertheless, provide an alternative form of Christian selfhood based not upon immediate access to Christ's suffering body, but on the dark and haunting impressions of presence that the Magdalene topos allows one to share.[66]

"Reflecting on *lieux de mémoire*," writes Nora, "brings history back to life, giving it a second level of existence." Ultimately, a writer's engagement with the Magdalene's account of Christ's presence relies, like all sites of memory, "on its ability to avail itself of a tenuous, intangible, almost ineffable bond" to something that has been intensely loved and lost. Nora says this kind of history-making calls to mind the mourning for lost love described by Marcel Proust: "that moment when the obsessive grip of passion finally loosens, in which the real sadness is that one can no longer suffer from that for which one has already suffered so much. The head takes over from the heart, and one is left with only reason where there was once sublime unreason."[67] This is a powerful suggestion with respect to the Magdalene for it hints that poetry in her name is less about the loved one himself but instead marks a somewhat bitter endpoint in the process of losing the loved one, the point where utterance replaces inarticulate grief. Each of these Catholic-identified sepulcher poems follows Southwell's *Funeral Teares* in its attempt to fill emptiness with words not only through the figure of the Magdalene (who finally finds her voice), but also by means of an authorial gesture that draws the subject matter out of its medieval sources and rearticulates it for a distinctly postmedieval audience.

Alison Shell has observed that Southwell's *Funeral Teares* enjoyed runaway popularity, as subsequent editions were published in 1594, 1596, 1602, and 1609.[68] And perhaps more significant than Southwell's impact in English Catholic literary circles is the perceived legitimacy of his Magdalene writing. The poet's work was not confined to publication by clandestine or Continental presses: *Funeral Teares*, printed by Master Gabriel Cawood of London, appears to have had the sanction of the archbishop of Canterbury, and its popularity suggests that it was read by Protestants as well as by Catholics.[69] Southwell's influence upon, and possibly even association with, Protestant writers is further suggested by the fact that Adam Islip and James Roberts, the printers of the 1594, 1596, and 1602 editions, were also the printers of a poem entitled *Marie Magdalens Lamentations for the Losse of her Master Iesus*, published in 1601 and again in 1604.

Though published anonymously, this text is now attributed to Gervase Markham, a figure whose religious convictions remain uncertain and who is now remembered primarily for his publication of practical manuals and guidebooks.[70] Nowhere is the awareness of the Magdalene's centrality to literary treatments of the Passion more evident than in *Lamentations*, which unapologetically borrows from *Funeral Teares* and yet removes the explicitly eucharistic material so evident in the Catholic work. For Markham's Mary, the loss of Christ's body is never associated with the loss of Catholic ritual. Instead, Markham adds to Southwell's *Funeral Teares* what probably amounts to a more conformist emphasis on the Word. At the end of the Fifth Lamentation, as Mary ponders her vision of the gardener, partial revelation comes to her before Christ speaks. Mary seems to recognize the figure, but her first instinct is to express her sense of the insufficiency of the site and form of the resurrection:

> Alas, and is a silly garden plot
> The best free-hold that my love can afford,
> Is this the highest office he that got,
> To be a Gardiner now that was my Lord:
>> He better might have liv'd and owned me,
>> Than with his death to have bought so small a fee.[71]

However, by the beginning of the next Lamentation everything has changed. Christ has addressed Mary by name, and the momentousness of her experience suddenly becomes clear. Christ's word is "proofe most sweet" of his living presence, and he stands before her not as a gardener but as a king ("in glorious robes I find thee"). For Markham, Christ's single word chases away despair, bringing about a calmness that awakens the senses and sets in motion the perception of inexplicable beauty.

> Yet now the clearnenesse of his lovely face,
> His words authoritie which all obay,
> This foggie darknesse cleane away doth chace,
> And brings a calme and bright well tempered day:
>> And doth disperse clouds of melancholie,
>> Awakes my sence, and cures my lethargie.[72]

The woman who stands before Markham's Christ is as much a figure of Protestant grace, alert and attuned to the sparkling vitality of the Word, as she is a figure of Catholic grief, mourning over the irretrievable loss of the Eucharist.

A further development in Markham's poem, which also suggests a growing interest in the sensory and aesthetic properties of the Magdalene's spiritual being, is the self-articulation of the conflict between body and soul. This poetics of introspection is most apparent in the Fifth Lamentation, where readers become spectators of a maudlin player's self-scrutiny:

And doe I in such zeale thus seeke for one,
Whom when I have found out, I do not know,
Or if I know him that of late was gone,
Now having him, why doe I seeke him so?
   Behold my Christ is come, he whom I sought,
   Doth talke with me, and I my selfe know nought.

Why doe I not then wipe my dazled eies?
Ah hath my Lord in this world liv'd so long,
Di'de with such paine, shed shours of tears with cries,
Laboured so much, and suffered so much wrong,
   And hath thereby no more preferment cought,
   But for to be a silly Gardiner thought?[73]

This sequence represents Markham's most radical departure from Southwell, whose manipulation of monologue never aspires to this kind of interiority. And yet the result of the self-scrutiny is familiar: Mary's struggle to remember does not produce Christ's presence. Though she is charged with keeping Christ's image alive "in sweetest memory" for others to witness, and though she continues to hope that she will "with teares his presence buy," emphasis falls even less on the absent Christ than it does in *Funeral Teares*. While sight, or the loss thereof, is still an issue ("In true loves hearts," Mary claims, "each part is made an eie, / And every thought prefixed for a looke"), Markham is more interested in what the reader sees than in what the subject does not. The Magdalene's articulation of her distraction, of the incomprehensible experience of her senses, is precisely that which inscribes both her person and her memory upon the scene of devotion.[74]

It would be tempting to explain Markham's appropriation of Southwell's weeping Mary by appealing to the former's reputation as a prodigious plagiarist with a flair for recognizing new literary markets. His *Lamentations* may be no more than an opportunistic attempt to exploit vestigial nostalgia for hagiographic romance or, even more unscrupulously, to profit from the unwarranted reproduction of the writing of a controversial Catholic. Recent scholarship, however, has argued for a reconsideration of Markham's translations and adaptations in the light of his interest in creating particularly English editions of important texts.[75] It is therefore possible that the Magdalene poetry deliberately separates the popular saint from pre-Tridentine and Counter-Reformation Catholicism in order to give the figure, and the devotional poetics that it inspires, a meaning that would be more productive in a Protestant environment. Bearing in mind that Mary Magdalene was the only female saint to figure in the 1549 Book of Common Prayer, Markham may have seen himself as repossessing an important biblical figure central to an increasingly English effort: the literary representation of the passionate affect of the resurrected Christ.[76]

Markham's own reluctance to put his name forward as the author of the versification suggests a desire to dissociate himself from its Catholic sources, but it need not follow that he was heedlessly seeking to profit from controversy. The unnamed W. F., in his preface to the 1604 edition, asks the author to reveal himself, pointing to both the magnificence of the Magdalene's vision and the worthiness of those authors who dare to transcribe it:

> Cherish thy Muse in hope of better dayes,
> Wrong not thy worth in keeping close thy name,
> No cunning workman that his skill displaies
> But seekes to let men know who did the same
>
> . . . .
>
> And though presumptuous *Zoilists* would taint
> The true deuotion of these contemplations,
> T'is not their fierie zeale, in zeale too faint,

Can burne the merit of thy commendations:
For after death, when they forgotten be,
Thy verse shall bring thee immortalitie.[77]

The Catholic associations of the Magdalene story are dismissed as the concerns of zealots. For W. F., the singularity of this Magdalene poem rests in its ability to act as a memorial to Christ, to "that which she hath done," and, most importantly, to Markham. The preface suggests that the Magdalene "idea," and the cognitive orientation that it inspires, lends a public coherence to the figure of the sinner-saint, to the tangible presence of Christ in the world, *and* to the lyric "I," here conflated with the anonymous poet. This is so because the *hortulanus* scene enables the reader to share the possibilities of sense impression, of memory, and of imagination and abstraction articulated by the writer, and thereby to encounter along with other readers a Christ who resides beyond the range of immediate experience. The "idea" is thus an articulation of religious community.[78]

Shell has argued that Southwellian writers, such as Markham, both reinforce and challenge the common equation of Protestantism with experiential inwardness: "reinforce because of their popularity in Protestant England, challenge because their inspiration is Catholic."[79] The affective quality of *Lamentations* certainly does anticipate the Counter-Reformation aesthetics that will be broached in detail later in this book. I would like to suggest, however, that Markham's debt to Southwell is formal rather than theological in that both are working out a poetics that uses the sensual figure of the Magdalene to permit the emergence of a narrative voice (or narrating self) that recounts to others, equally disoriented by religious upheaval, the eerie and yet somehow comforting experience of recognizing Christ again—albeit in a radically different form. Stewart writes that when darkness is understood as the "place of error and shattered being where humans are halted from movement and knowledge in a state of ignorance . . . the mind must attempt to forge connections of intelligibility and recognition that will be no less than the grounds for the creation of one's own consciousness." Poems like Markham's, which are based on John 20, are ghost stories or what Stewart calls "narratives of light in the darkness" that record "the emergence of the figures and forms of human making from conditions of unintelligibility."[80] Markham begins *Lamentations* with a preface in which he thanks his muse, Mary, for providing him with a subject that "graver pens" have refused. The poet's intent is described as bent on turning perverted hearts, stifled by a diet of "fond fancie," toward a rediscovery of the passions or senses which Southwell also anxiously advances:

> Ah could they see what sinne from sence hath shut,
> How sweet it were to summon deeds misdone,
> To have their lives in equall ballance put,
> To waigh each worke ere that the judge doe come:
>   Ah then their teares would trickle like the raine,
>   And their eye-flouds would helpe to fill the maine
>
> They would with *Marie* send forth bitter cries,
> To get the ioies of their soule-saving love,
> They would gush forth fresh fountaines from their eies,
> To win his favour, and his mercie prove:
>   Eyes, hart, and tongue, should poure, breath out, & send,
>   Teares, sighs, and plaints, untill their love they find.[81]

By positioning the Magdalene as an agent who reinvigorates the senses of bodies and minds debilitated by darkness, Markham creates a space for the emergence of his own narrative voice.

The final stanza of the preface asks the reader to favor "Maries memorial of her sad lament." As part of this appeal, the figure of Colin is summoned from the pastoral tradition as an alternative example of a lover also stricken by the loss of his loved one.[82] The reference is likely an allusion to *The Shepherd's Calendar* and to "Colin Clout's Come Home Again," in which Edmund Spenser appropriates Catholic, and specifically Marian, imagery, in the service of singing Cynthia's, or Queen Elizabeth's, praises.[83] The presence of Spenser's Colin in Markham's versified garden of the resurrection suggests that the icon of the Magdalene has in some vital sense become the subject of poetic art. She is no longer a vehicle for simply access-ing knowledge of Christ's image or even just for understanding the ghostly impression that he left behind. She is, rather, a haunting fig-ure of meditation in her own right, acknowledged not only for her exceptional insight, but also for her ability to provide to the religious poet the sensory and aesthetic resources needed to invoke in himself, and in others, the form and feeling of the divine. If, as Stewart sug-gests, lyric expression is propelled by the desire to make mystifying sense impressions intelligible to others so that the individual can un-derstand her experience as, in some way, shared, Southwell and his contemporaries—Catholic and Protestant alike—used the Magdalene as a force against effacement—she is a lonely soul who can recognize another like soul and draw it "out of the darkness."[84]

CHAPTER

THREE

The Task of Beauty

Nowe it came to passe, as they went, that he entred into a certaine

towne, and a certaine woman named Martha, receiued him into her

house. And she had a sister called Marie, which also sate at Iesus feete,

and heard his preaching. But Martha was combred about much seru-

ing, and came to him, and saide, Master, doest thou not care that my

sister hath left me to serue alone? bid her therefore, that she helpe me.

And Iesus answered, and said vnto her, Martha, Martha, thou carest,

and art troubled about many things: But one thing is needefull, Marie

hath chosen the good part, which shall not be taken away from her.

—Luke 10:38–42 (Geneva edition)

In "To the Lady *Magdalen Herbert*, of St *Mary Magdalen*" (1607), John Donne addresses a dear friend whose spirituality commanded his respect and admiration:

Her of your name, whose fair inheritance
    Bethina was, and jointure *Magdalo*:
An active faith so highly did advance,
    That she once knew, more than the Church did know,
The *Resurrection*; so much good there is
    Deliver'd of her, that some Fathers be
Loth to believe one Woman could do this;
    But, think these *Magdalens* were two or three.
Increase their number, *Lady*, and their fame:
    To their *Devotion*, add your *Innocence*;
Take so much of th' example, as of the name;
    The latter half; and in some recompense
That they did harbour *Christ* himselfe, a Guest,
    Harbour these *Hymns*, to his dear name addrest.[1]

Manuscript versions of what have come to be known as the "Divine Poems" suggest that this tribute was a dedicatory verse that prefaced either *La Corona* or perhaps a more random collection of holy sonnets.[2] The poem begins with a playful allusion to the controversy over the Magdalene's biography, and with the gentle mocking of post-Tridentine attempts to distinguish the various Gospel Magdalenes by suggesting that Magdalen Herbert add her name to the lot. Despite its wry humor, however, the dedication is a marvelously synthetic manifestation of the topos, popularized by Southwell and his imitators, in which the subject of the poem is charged with the task of gathering, forever, memories of Christ's life. It is also a superior example of the habit of posing pious women in the posture of the Magdalene. To the saint's collective attributes, Donne wants to add Magdalen Herbert's pious composure in a gesture that seems to erase all trace of the Magdalene's prurient past. Donne's Magdalene is a distinguished Protestant contemplative, recognized for her mind as well as her beauty, poised to receive and to read Donne's lines of true devotion.

The affinity Donne finds between Magdalen Herbert and the Gospels' sinner-saint is not as jarring as it might initially seem to be, for, as Jansen has shown, the Magdalene's legendary aristocratic parentage had made her a worthy patron for the nobility of the Middle

Ages.[3] The latter-day Magdalenes to whom I now turn—first to Mary Herbert (née Sidney), Countess of Pembroke, and then, very briefly, to Margaret Clifford (née Russell), Countess of Cumberland—are, much like their medieval antecedents, models of pensive serenity. They are, crucially, figures of moderation rather than excess, who lead their servants, Nicholas Breton and Aemilia Lanyer, to a poetic practice most evocative (and most eerie) in its restraint—in what it leaves out—rather than in what it provides in full detail.[4] This chapter returns to the sepulcher scene in order to consider it a site of reading and contemplation in the light of Luke 10 in which Mary of Bethany's quiet attention to Christ's words, in contrast to Martha's bustling housewifery, is the "good part." Mary makes the better choice, according to the Gospel, because Christ's words can never be taken away from her. They remain a part of her, even much later at the sepulcher, where they reverberate again, helping her to contemplate Christ's still-living presence. Like Mary of Bethany (and in contrast to Southwell's protobaroque weeper), Breton's and Lanyer's mourning Magdalenes are calm, placid, and alert to the Word; they are listeners (or readers) lost in thought. There is something special, even clairvoyant, about them for they seem to know something the rest of us cannot. I will show that spiritual insight, in these instances, is related not only to the Gospel account of Mary of Bethany, but also to the medieval legends in which Mary journeys to France and then retreats into the desert to live as a hermit. The medieval saint's mystical insight, born of isolation and tranquil study, is impressed upon the dedicatees of Breton's and Lanyer's poems—poems that also seem to describe the vertigo experienced by a poetic persona in the face of a devout patron who, by virtue of her ability to see beyond the range of normal human vision, is, like Christ, out of reach. The Magdalene's encounter with Christ, in all its emotional depth, is thus reconfigured in analogous encounters between tormented speakers and their shadowlike muses. As with the Magdalene, the poet experiences sensory disorientation at the thought of his hauntingly beautiful patron, and his vision becomes subject to doubt.[5] The result of the exchange is the realization that the description of the experience, lyric poetry, need not convey Christ's likeness with the precision of a looking glass; instead, the restrained obscurity of figurative language provides the most vivid way to see.

The Beauty That Comes of Stillness

The work at the center of this chapter is Breton's sustained and intricate treatment of the Magdalene, the poem "The blessed Weeper" (1601). However, before I turn to this particular example, I want to consider Breton's other literary Magdalenes, dedicated for the most part to his patron, the Countess of Pembroke.[6] These works are remarkable portraits of piety that find beauty in the quiet stillness associated with Mary of Bethany and in the contemplative aspect of the Magdalene's medieval legend.

In a number of his prefaces Breton explicitly addresses his female readers, asking them to turn their "good mindes" to the memory of "some women in his especiall fauour," including Mary Magdalene.[7] This appeal to the female reader may be a reiteration of the common-place assumption that women were, like Mary Magdalene, prone to visionary lapses of the imagination induced by an excess of passionate feeling. Breton's prose work, *Marie Magdalens Loue* (1595), certainly reflects this concern:

> how vncomely a thing it is in a maiden, to be giggling and laugh-ing, and how vngratious a thing it is for a woman, to be tighing [*sic*] and babbling, in the Temple of God, at the time of the reading, or preaching, of his holie Gospell: Alas what will they bee thought on among the wise? The one but an idle gossip, and the other a fool-ish girle, but here you see *Mary* did not of these, and as I said be-fore. . . . Learne then of Mary to loue Christ, to bee Constant in louing Christ, and to vse Modesty in your loue to Christ: so shall you surelye please Christ, and I am fully perswaded, bee most commended of Christians.[8]

However, Breton's invocations of the Magdalene are not exclusively directed at women; the figure is more frequently offered to both sexes as a "sweet example of care."[9] As is the case with Donne's dedication to Magdalen Herbert, Breton's work sets aside the more effusive feminine aspects of the saint's biography in order to dwell extensively on her pensive, and less gendered, goodness.

This Magdalene is much calmer and more attentive than the Southwellian figures of the same period. While the influence of the Origenist tradition is apparent in Breton's prose—the reader is advised, for instance, to "learne [of Mary's] sorrowe to bee without [Christ]"—Breton's interest lies more squarely in a milder Magdalene whose attributes are spiritual and intellectual rather than corporeal. In *Marie Magdalens Loue*, emphasis ultimately falls on Mary's efficiency and timeliness—it is because she was not idle, because she rose early to attend the sepulcher, that she is privileged with the knowledge of the resurrection. Breton, furthermore, refuses to linger on the Magdalene's inarticulate lugubriousness: "Now it is not said, shee cryed or sighed, or sobbed, and coulde not speake a worde," he writes. Instead, the Magdalene is commended for her modest use of speech and her model calm in the face of adversity:

> I woulde wish that all men and women woulde learne to imitate Mary in this manner of hir speaking, to talke as shee did of Christ and to his Ministers, to learne their instruction for their knowledge of him. Then would there not bee so many wicked men and women, Witches, and Sorcerers, Gluttons, Drunkards, Adulterers, Thieues, Traytours, and Murtherers, besides other vayne and idel headed people.

The Magdalene's tears, if they must be acknowledged at all, are signs of genuine grief—remarkable because they are seen by no one: "the earth had no eyes to behold her teares."[10] The text shows its readers a solitary, contemplative figure poised in her thoughtfulness, her constancy, and her humility.

The same figure is found in the Magdalene prayers included in Breton's *Auspicante Iehova. Maries Exercise* (1597). Here again, the subject is Mary's decision to listen rather than to act:

giue me leaue not with Martha, to complaine of a sister, but to accuse my selfe of to much euill in so long combring my hart with the wretched cares of this wicked world, that I haue had almost no care to humble my soule to the happie hearing of thy holie word: let mee therefore beeseech . . . that casting of all the combersome cares of this vncomfortable worlde, I maie not onelie serue thee in bodie, on the knees of my heart, worshipping thy diuine will, but in the humilitie of my soule, sit with Mary on the ground, with the tears of true repentaunce to wash the feete of thy mercie: that being both vnable and vnworthy to behold the glory of thy presence, I maie yet ioye in my soule to heare the sweetnes of thy preaching.[11]

The pious Mary that Breton invokes here, and in *Marie Magdalens Loue*, is Mary of Bethany, whose decision to listen to the Word rather than to act in the ministry of Christ's person bolsters Breton's preference for a spiritual life rooted in the Scriptures rather than in holy deeds.

To suggest, however, that Breton finds in Mary of Bethany a rational, intellectual model of a stalwart, masculine Protestantism stripped of all the feminine elements of her Catholic past would be to overstate the case precisely because the figure is also linked to recognizably female forms of mystical spirituality. In medieval accounts, Luke's listener merges seamlessly with the legendary accounts of Mary of Egypt, transforming "Jesus' attentive student," as Jansen describes her, "into a veritable medieval mystic."[12] The most accessible account of this composite Magdalene is found in the *Legenda aurea*, which describes the contemplative's retreat, after the resurrection, to a place "deyned by thangele of god." This "ryght sharp desserte" had "no comfort of reynnynge watter / ne solace of trees ne of herbes," making it clear that God had "ordeyned for her refection celestial / and no bodily metes." Every day, for thirty years, at the seven canonical hours, Mary was "lift up in thayer of thangellis / and herd the glorious songs of the heuenly companies with her bodily eeres / Of whiche she was fedde and fylled with right swete metes."[13] Very little of this eremitical tradition survives in English; however, of what remains the Digby play provides the most memorable representation of Mary's retreat to the desert and her daily transportation to the "clowddys" by angels.[14] The scene is a magical iteration of the Magdalene's weightless mystical serenity—a quality echoed again in the *The Southern Passion* in which the saint's attributes, "myldhede and goednesse," surpass those of any other creature on earth.[15] This characteristic mildness is most strikingly depicted in the visual art commemorating the desert retreat. In Giuliano da Rimini's *Virgin and Child Enthroned with Saints* (1307; fig. 2), for example, the Magdalene's calm, innocent receptivity (featured in the top right-hand corner) not only mirrors the quietude of St. Francis (top left-hand corner), it also reflects the maternal serenity of the painting's subject, the Virgin Mary.[16]

The subject of the Magdalene's mystical withdrawal resurfaces in the sermons of Breton's contemporary, Henry Smith, an evangelical clergyman referred to as "Silver-Tongued Smith" by Thomas Nashe, who also likened him to Ovid.[17] In "Mary's Choice" (1598), Smith does not specifically link the Mary of Luke 10 with the "sinner" of Luke 7, and yet he clearly retains vestiges of the ancient legend. In this case, domestic labor (exemplified by the figure of Martha) is less favored than contemplative exercises that permit Mary to receive, from God alone, all necessary sustenance:

> As for all other things, whether they be honours, promotions, pleasures, and what not, they serve only for the maintenance of this present life, which is so short and subject to mutability; but the Word of God is the food of the soul, the bread of life, that immortal seed which bringeth forth fruit unto eternal life.[18]

And yet Smith's sermon is unquestionably conformist. Drawing on the Protestant habit of seeing the Magdalene's attentiveness to Christ's words as support for a piety based in the mind rather than in the world, Smith argues that "although the care of Martha in entertaining of Christ be not to be misliked, yet, Mary's diligence in hearing His doctrine is purpose preferred, to teach us, that it is much better with Mary to study in the Word, and first to seek the kingdom of God, (Mat. vi. 33) than with Martha to labour in the world, and to

FIGURE 2. Giuliano da Rimini, *Virgin and Child Enthroned with Saints* (1307). Isabella Stewart Gardner Museum, Boston.

neglect that heavenly kingdom." Mary is the "pattern of a good hearer," and she conveys both beauty and wisdom in her stillness:

> Mary sitteth to hear the Word, as Christ used to sit when He preached the Word, (Mat. v. 1.) to shew that the Word is to be preached and heard with a quiet mind. In a still night every voice is heard, and when the body is quiet, the mind most commonly is quiet also. . . . As often therefore as we come to hear the Word of God, we must not come with distracted minds, we must not trouble ourselves with the cares of this life, which (as our Saviour said) are thorns to choke the Word, and to make it unfruitful: (Luke vii. 14). . . . When our minds are quiet, we are fit to deal with heavenly matters.[19]

The dominant features of this portrait are once again serenity and beauty, born of wise decisions.

And yet, because of her association with the fictional (or imagined) mystical experiences of female saints, Mary of Bethany could not be uniformly accepted as a model of Protestant piety. Calvin, for instance, argues that Christ does not disparage Martha's domestic energy but only suggests, as Breton does, that it is poorly timed. "Luke saieth that Mary was at Iesus feete," writes Calvin with typical indignation, but "doth he meane that she did nothing else al her lyfe time?" Mary chooses the good part because she takes full advantage of the circumstances and occupies herself in "a holy and profitable exercise, fro[m] which she ought not to be drawn" because "such opportunitie is not had alwayse." Calvin's unease likely reflects a recognition of Mary's relationship to the legendary Magdalene and is an attempt to discredit readings of Luke 10 that see Christ's praise for Mary's choice as an argument for choosing a profligate life of the imagination (*vita contemplativa*) associated with the Catholic trappings of the past over a wholesome life of godly productivity (*vita activa*) more in line with the principles of Protestant reform. Calvin wants to be sure that goodly housewifery remains a viable means of demonstrating one's predestined election.[20]

The very same concern is evident in the 1549 Book of Common Prayer, which, as I have observed already, preserves the provisions for the feast of Mary Magdalene. The first readings are predictable: Luke 7, Psalm 146 (on the mercy and omnipotence of the Lord who "helpeth them that are fallen" and who "careth for the righteous"), and a collect that asks that "we may truly repente, and lamente the same, after the example of Marye Magdalene." However, the orthodox emphasis on sin and salvation shifts in the final prayer as the holy penitent is domesticated by the reading of Proverb 31 on the household virtues of a good woman:

> Whosoeuer fyndeth an honest faythful woman, she is muche more worth then perles. The hart of her husband may safely truste in her, so y^t he shall fall in no pouertie. Shee wyll do hym good and not euyll, all the daies of her lyfe. . . . Strength and honour is her clothynge, and in the latter day, she shall reioyce. She openeth her mouth with wisedome, and in her tongue is ye law of grace. She loketh well to the waies of her housholde, and eateth not her bread with idlenes. Her children shal aryse, and call her blessed: & her husband shall make much of her.[21]

The proverb initially seems an odd choice for the celebration of a saint whose virtue is typified by her fervent love for Christ (both before and after his death) or, as in Luke 10, by her studious disregard of home and family. However, if the text is read in the light of Calvin's gloss of Luke 10, the emphasis on domesticity is less peculiar. The ideal Protestant woman is both Mary and Martha.

Even more interesting than this claim, however, is the possibility that reformist attempts to work around the inevitable link between Mary's choice and female mysticism necessitated the invocation of yet another aspect of the Magdalene's medieval past—an aspect that validated the centrality of marriage and motherhood within the spiritual lives of Protestant women. In this case the relevant narrative is the Magdalene's alleged journey to France after the resurrection. In this story, also a significant component of the *Legenda aurea*, Mary encounters the pagan ruler of Provence and his wife. Mary first convinces the couple to convert to Christianity, at which point she brings about a fertility miracle allowing the royal couple to conceive a child. She then safely delivers the baby amidst a storm while the couple is traveling to Rome to undertake a pilgrimage. The queen dies in childbirth, and the king abandons both mother and child on a rock in the middle of the sea. Mary effects a second miracle by allowing the child to nurse, for two years, at her dead mother's breast. The king, meanwhile, studies with St. Peter in Rome and learns the ways of a Christian leader. On his return to France, he finds his child miraculously still alive. He prays to the Magdalene, and she resurrects his wife, who claims to have been on a holy pilgrimage also guided by the Magdalene, and the integrity of the family is restored. As Jansen notes, the essential elements of this narrative point to the saint's "maternal qualities and her patronage of concerns relating to motherhood." Moreover, these qualities, in conjunction with Mary's great penance, were channeled by uncloistered, married, and widowed women who wanted to indicate that their vigilant attention to spiritual matters made them a *hortus conclusus* on the model of the Virgin Mary.[22] Thus, the Magdalene's association with wifely and motherly virtue found in both the Book of Common Prayer and Calvin's gloss of Luke 10 is, at least in part, facilitated by the cultural memory of a legend which assured that the iconic beauty that comes of Mary's good choices was not beyond the reach of Protestant wives and mothers.[23]

By 1552 the Magdalene's feast had been jettisoned from the Book of Common Prayer. But, as Christine Peters argues, "the 'liberation' of Mary Magdalen from the ranks of the saints allowed her to emerge as a more useful and powerful model" for English women.[24] While it is the case that the characteristics of Mary of Bethany, her wisdom, her grace, and her stillness, could be appropriately bestowed upon married Protestant women like Magdalen Herbert or the Countess of Pembroke, it is the legendary aspects of the Magdalene's life that allow these goodly characteristics to come into greater relief. The saint's mystical life in the desert, as well as the domestic miracles associated with her mendicant vocation, confirm Mary's piety to be singularly blessed, making it clear that her person effects wonder beyond ordinary understanding. It is to these luminous qualities, particularly as retained in Breton's "The blessed Weeper," to which I now turn.

In the poem's preface, Breton draws attention to his dedicatee's grace in terms of the imaginative talents of her remarkable intellect. He explicitly addresses the countess's inward self, trusting that his poetry will "lay before [her] eyes a diuine humour of a rauisht soule"— a vision Breton hopes will be pleasing to Pembroke's "good fauour":

> Right Honorable, matter of most worth to most worthy mindes, is most worthily presented. What matter, in worth may compare with diuine meditation? What minde more worthy honour, then the heauenly enclined? and whose minde more truly worthy of that blessed Title, then your Ladiships.[25]

The matter of Magdalene is offered to a woman whose eyes and mind are turned toward the matter of God. Pembroke is, Breton argues, already Mary Magdalene, and the portrait that follows is presented as a tribute to the inspirational beauty radiating from her pious person.

The blessed weeper appears to Breton's speaker as the first witness of the resurrection. As in Southwell's *Funeral Teares*, the Magdalene's grief is intensified by the fact that Christ's body has apparently been removed from the tomb. Referring to Jesus as "the heavenly substance of my life and loue," Mary asks, "Why should I liue and looke vpon the light? / Now I haue lost the ioy of such a sight?" Because Mary's soul was attached to the physical body of Christ, the disappearance of that body means that her soul is jettisoned into the world, leaving the body bereft of sense:[26]

> But, what speake I of either sinne or grace?
> My sinnes too greeuous, and my g[r]ace is gone;
> My life is dead, the earth is all too base,
> For my loues Lord, to deigne to looke vpon,
> Where liues not one good creature, no not one,
> And what should I but weepe to liue to see
> I cannot see where my sweete Lord may be.[27]

Once again, not only has Mary become blind, but in Christ's absence seeing becomes a base and even loathsome experience.

However, despite her distraction, or more likely as a consequence of it, Mary's tears provide a lens for a spiritual insight that refocuses her senses and allows her to see differently. Mary says, "Let me see thee, and I desire no more." Unlike the heroine of *Funeral Teares*, this weeper would be as satisfied with an ethereal vision as with a corporeal presence:

> Oh, sight more pretious then tongue can expresse,
> Wherein the eye doth comfort so the heart,
> The heart, the soule, and all in their distresse,
> Doe find an ease, and end of euerie smart.
> When eie and heart, and soule and euerie part
>   Concluded in ioy, that comfort did beginne;
>   Better to weepe in grace, then laugh in sinne.

Breton's Mary, of course, does see "the substance of her bliss" and experiences the return of her senses. More importantly, the *noli me tangere* is glossed as reflecting Mary's understanding that she needs "but a looke / Of that sweete heauenly holy eye of thine" to feel satisfied.[28] The reader observes Breton's noble patron and the Magdalene becoming one as both turn inward to that still and silent place where they see the likeness and feel the presence of Christ.

The Substance of Her Bliss

Breton repeatedly creates this scene of introspection in his work dedicated to Pembroke. In *The Countesse of Penbrookes loue*, the countess is represented as lamenting her sins in the fashion of the Magdalene ("looke on thy Mary with her bitter teares, / That washt thy feete and wipte the[m] with her heares").[29] And in *The Passions of the Spirit*, the dedicatee is found sitting with the Magdalene "at the graue / As full of griefe / as euer loue maye liue."[30] There is, admittedly, an oddness to the optics that Breton generates in these portraits:

the sensuality of an image premised so vividly on sight means that the Pembroke/Magdalene figure is not just the subject of Christ's scrutiny; Breton, and any reader who happens upon the intimate scene of contemplation, also look upon her. Such an observation could, I suppose, bolster an argument on the politics of male voyeurism or even be seen as evidence of the alleged romance between Pembroke and Breton. But I would suggest that Breton puts the speaker/writer, subject/patron problem at some remove by appealing, once again, to the contemplative tradition. Like his erudite patron, Breton's blessed weeper is a reader and Christ is her book:

> I will not presse one foote beyond the line
> Of thy loue's leaue, vouschafe me but a looke
> Of that sweete heauenly holy eye of thine,
> Of my deere Loue the euer-liuing Booke.[31]

The conceit is intricately fashioned: the weeper's "feet" lend meter to Christ's lines as she looks upon the leaves of Scripture only by his leave. In this posture, contrite and tearful eyes become contemplative or reading eyes, invoking what Beckwith has described as the long-standing association between tears and words, weeping and reading or writing.[32]

There are many examples in painting of the reading Magdalene, all of which draw upon medieval iconography in which Christ (the Word) is figured as a book, and the Magdalene (in a bizarre moment of reflexivity) is figured as the exemplary reader of both his and her history.[33] Correggio's Magdalene, for example, looks away from her book to meet her viewer's eye with calm regard, as if to say, "I understand now" (fig. 3). Tintoretto's Magdalene also looks up from her book and toward the light emanating from heaven as if listening attentively, registering the full implications of her text.[34] An English example of this same posture is Isaac Oliver's ink drawing in the British Museum collection (fig. 4). Titian as well depicts the saint with eyes looking upward and away from a book that rests upon a skull. Here again, understanding is registered on the woman's face (fig. 5). Rogier van der Weyden paints the Magdalene more modestly: this figure is

FIGURE 3. Correggio, *The Magdalen* (c. 1518–19). The National Gallery, London.

FIGURE 4. Isaac Oliver, *The Penitent Magdalene* (1556–1617). © The Trustees of the British Museum, London.

FIGURE 5. Tiziano Vecellio, *Repentant Mary Magdalene* (1560s). © The State Hermitage Museum, St. Petersburg.

FIGURE 6. Rogier van der Weyden, *The Magdalen Reading* (before 1438). The National Gallery, London.

indoors, possibly reading in a library (fig. 6). As in the other images, the reader's pale, nearly translucent features suggest a serenity born of study and of knowledge. Another Magdalene—an English sculpture on an outside wall of the Church of St. Mary Magdalene in Launceston, Cornwall (fig. 7)—is depicted *allongée* as if to convey the restful

FIGURE 7. *Reclining Magdalene*, Church of St. Mary Magdalene, Launceston, Cornwall. Photograph: Ryan Smith.

solace that comes of her reading.[35] In many of these images the subject's eyes look down or look away from the pages open before her. These eyes could be interpreted as "come hither" bedroom eyes and, as such, reminders of the penitent's prurient past. And yet, while it is certainly the case that all of these images, even the van der Weyden, invoke a certain coy sensuality, I would argue that Mary's diversion registers satisfaction—a principal affect of reading—rather than sexuality. These figures, like Mary of Bethany and the desert hermit of medieval legend, are filled with Christ's words, and this fact makes them serene and even Christ-like. What is most remarkable about these images, and what Breton appears to channel in his poem, is the peaceful beauty of the sitters. Their faces are characterized not by ecstasy but by mildness. Even in a state of *déshabillé*, as is the case in the Tintoretto, the Oliver, and the Titian, the emotions conveyed are less of rapture than of contentment and quiet goodness.

One of the loveliest literary renditions of the reading topos is found in the pseudo-Chaucerian *The complaynt of Mary Magdaleyne* (1520). In *The complaynt*, a text also heavily indebted to the pseudo-Origenist homily that inspired Southwell and Markham, Mary's lingering memories of ablution and crucifixion lead her into a distraction that seems impossible to contain.

> Which rufull sight when that I gan beholde
> Out of my wytte I almost distraught,
> Tare my heer, my ha[n]des wrange & folde
> And of y^t sight my hert dra[n]ke such a draght
> That many a fall sownyng there I caught;
> I brused my body fallyng on the grounde
> Whereof I fele many a greuous wounde.

However, when Christ appears before Mary, everything slows down as the Magdalene discovers the haunting truth of Christ's presence in her own stillness. Crucially, at this moment Mary's vision of ungraspable divinity takes the form of a printed page as she says, "Thy blessed visage" is the place "wherin is printed my parfyte solace." The act of reading Christ transforms the Magdalene into a figure of contemplation and tranquility.[36]

There is also an important case to be made for the recognizability of the reading Magdalene topos within late medieval devotional culture. Catherine Sanok, in her rich discussion of exemplarity and female saints' lives, reflects significantly on the reception of Margery Kempe, pointing to the fact that Kempe's conspicuous public display of weeping often confounded her audiences and went unrecognized as a form of *imitatio Magdalenae*. On the other hand, Sanok finds evidence for the familiarity of the figure of the reading Magdalene. Bokenham, for instance, in his narrative of the *Legendys*' commission, redirects his patron's (Lady Bourchier) interest in the Magdalene away from the saint's public display of spirituality toward her private meditative reading:

> To hyr [Lady Bourchier] goostly confourth is especyal,
> And of them generally wych it redyn shal;
> By wych redyng þat þae may wynne
> Fyrst remyssyoun here of al here synne,
> Lych as Mary Mawdelyn dede purchace,
> And þat aftyr þis lyf þey may [þorgh grace]
> To þat blys comyn wher-yn is she.

As Sanok observes, "Bokenham suggests that Lady Bourchier, and future readers, seek the grace that Mary Magdalene enjoys, not by imitating her extravagant weeping or her itinerant preaching nor even by embracing a life of chastity, but through the far more socially acceptable practice of private devotional reading."[37]

The most familiar early modern appropriation of the reading topos is found in Richard Hooker's *Of the Lawes of Ecclesiastical Politie*. Seventeenth-century editions of the book feature a frontispiece that includes, in the top left-hand corner, a reading Magdalene (recognizable because of the familiar iconography of the skull and belt; fig. 8).[38] Shuger has argued that the picture "offers an extraordinarily accurate visualization of Hooker's treatise" in its illustration of "the disencorporation of the subject from the mediating hierarchies of both state and church" (the beams that issue from the divine light at the top of the page fall separately upon the king, the church, and the third figure, Mary Magdalene). The presence of the Magdalene in this formulation thus shows how "the exemplary figure of the Middle Ages's highly materialist erotic mysticism is also the decorous symbol for the Protestant (although not Calvinist) *individual* subject, the *suppositum* existing apart from the mystical conjunctions of both church and state, with room (and book) of her own." In the case of the Hooker frontispiece then, Mary's "sacred eroticism," although proscribed as cultural praxis, "inhabits a traditional construct of religious subjectivity, one that passes from the cloistral devotions of the Middle

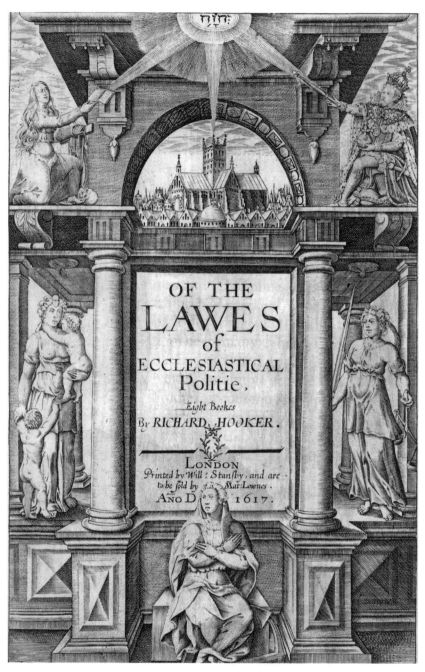

OF THE
LAWES
of
ECCLESIASTICAL
Politie,

Eight Bookes

By RICHARD HOOKER.

LONDON
Printed by Will: Stansby, and are
to be sold by Mat:Lownes.
Ano D 1617.

FIGURE 8. Richard Hooker's *Of the Lawes of Ecclesiastical Politie* (1617). Bancroft Library, University of California, Berkeley.

Ages into early modern representations of a privatized, autonomous inwardness."[39]

Shuger's recognition of the service Mary Magdalene performs for Hooker is exactly right, though I am less convinced by her emphasis on the figure's eroticism. The significance of the image resides, as it does in both pre- and post-Reformation literature and art, in the interplay between the sign of absent presence—the book—and the experience of that presence as depicted upon the face of a placid reader absorbed in thought. The frontispiece thus claims a slightly different iconic continuity with the Catholic past: the Magdalene is the avatar of the Word; she represents the literary possibilities of the future and not the plastic trappings of the past. But to return once again to Breton's desolate speaker, how much satisfaction (or insight) is there to be gained from watching Mary read?

Crucially, the speaker of "The blessed Weeper" is never sure of what stands before him. The poem begins with a confession of altered states:

> My thoughts amaz'd, I knowe not how, of late,
> Halfe in a slumber and more halfe a sleepe;
> My troubled senses, at a strange debate,
> What kind of care shoud most my spirit keepe;
> Me thought, I sawe a silly woman weepe.[40]

The dreamlike disorientation described here is much like that experienced by the Magdalene herself when, as discussed in the previous chapter, she finds herself confronted with a vision she knows but cannot fully comprehend. Like the Magdalene, the speaker finds himself recalling an event both seen and heard but somehow inaccessible and incomprehensible:

> As to her words my vision witness beares,
> And my remembrance may for truth approoue;
> The whole discourse, her passions seem'd to moue;
>   In hearts deepe griefe, & soules high ioy conceiued,
>   Was as I write, were not my thoughts deceiued.[41]

These are the words of one who is certain of the affect of his experience but uncertain of its meaning. If the passage is taken literally, the speaker thinks he sees the Magdalene's words—or perhaps he even reads the reading Magdalene. If the latter is the case, the next passage reveals how reading makes him feel:

> If euer sorrow in a sinners hart,
> Liud', to distill those droppes of bitter teares,
> That to the world in passions can impart,
> Part of that paine, the troubled spirit beares;
> Smoothring the woes, wherein all pleasure weares;
>   Oh let her shewe the deepest of her skill,
>   In drawing out the essence of mine ill.[42]

The tears that form as the weeper reads are distilled into words that tell her readers of remorse over lost opportunities. These words in turn draw out the speaker's own experience of loss and regret, producing ultimately the poem we read.

The stanzas that follow this one are even more disorienting as one figure slides over the other and the contours of the Magdalene and those of the speaker become indistinguishable. At times, it seems as though the abject speaker is male, stumbling in misery before someone (God, Christ, Mary Magdalene, or Mary Herbert) too great to entertain his wretched presence.[43] In other places, the speaker is clearly the Magdalene recalling her desperate ministrations at the Pharisee's house, Christ's boundless mercy, and her own insufficient gratitude. The haunting presence of the Magdalene makes the speaker feel Magdalene-like, provoking him to reach out and recount his experiences, as his vision does. Breton's dedication of the poem to Pembroke, a formidable reader and writer in her own right, also suggests that the countess served not only as Breton's personal Magdalene but also as a model of the self-reflection and stillness necessary for the production of his own godly words.[44] Furthermore, the Magdalene provides a sense of the form these words must take—a poetry in which narrative vivacity resides not in the full explication of sensory experience, but in figurative language that invokes something of the obscurity and incomprehensibleness of spiritual experience.

The Specter of the Magdalene

I have already suggested that the *hortulanus* scene is a site of haunting. Appealing to Scarry's work on the narrative vivacity of ghost stories, I have argued that Magdalene narratives in the tradition of the Origenist homily describe the glide of Christ's untouchable form across the surface of the Magdalene's body, and moreover that the vivid portrait that emerges from these poetic encounters is not of Christ but of Mary, whose affective response to a vision that can be seen but not touched provides an "idea" of Christ's presence.[45] Breton's poem also describes an intimate encounter between his speaker (presumably a man) and his speaker's vision—a dream, a spirit—but the ghost in this instance is not Christ, it is Mary Magdalene. The speaker's wobbly, tentative, almost incoherent attempt to describe the terms of his encounter does not amount to a portrait of the Magdalene as it does in *Funeral Teares*; rather, it records the impression that this exquisite ghost has upon her distracted witness. At this moment, a new person comes into view—a person whose sense of himself comes into being in the memory of a Magdalene (Pembroke) itself constituted in recollections of ancient but not forgotten Magdalenes (Mary of Bethany, Mary of France, Mary of Egypt). This newly present person, Breton's speaker (and likely Breton himself), is both a reader and a writer, and as such he is the very epitome of the early modern Christian subject.

At the end of "The blessed Weeper," the Magdalene suddenly disappears, leaving the speaker alone to puzzle over what he may or may not have witnessed:

> And with that word, she vanisht so away,
> As if that no such woman there had beene,
> But yet me thought, her weeping seem'd to say,
> The Spirit was of Marie Magdalen;

Whose bodie now, although not to be seene,
  Yet by her speech, it seemed it was she,
  That wisht all women might such Weepers be.[46]

This speaker has seen a ghost, who bears a startling resemblance to his own exceedingly devout patron. Breton is summoning all the resources of the Magdalene tradition here—the saint's contemplative mysticism and spiritual acuity, her ability to inspire conversion and to effect miracles, and finally her sense of peace and satisfaction as discovered in Christ's words—in order to show that encounters with the divine can, and indeed must, be made known through a glass darkly. Perhaps then it does not matter that the speaker cannot trust either the clarity of his vision or the accuracy of his memory. The possibility of deception or misperception that troubles the somnambulist speaker (he was "halfe in a slumber, and more halfe a sleepe") arises from the prescient inkling that one of the truths the Magdalene reveals is that figurative language succeeds only when it constitutes presence ambiguously, haunting the mind and obliquely challenging it to question the substance of the forms it makes manifest.[47] The stillness, or even rest, that comes to the exhausted speaker at the end of the poem thus suggests an acceptance of the incompleteness of spiritual seeing and a weary willingness to try to write it all down.

And Breton is not alone in this project. Lanyer's *Salve Deus Rex Judaeorum* (1611), a poetic meditation on the Passion dedicated to a congregation of illustrious Protestant ladies including the countesses of Pembroke and Cumberland, understands the conditions of spiritual receptivity in terms similar to those Breton invokes. At the very end of her work, Lanyer addresses "the doubtfull Reader" in order to explain the origin of the title of her book. "It was delivered unto me in sleepe," explains the author, "many yeares before I had any intent to write in this maner." Lanyer also writes that the title was "quite out of my memory" until such time as the work was completed, "when immediately it came into my remembrance, what I had dreamed long before." Lanyer reads the dream as a prescient herald ("a significant token") of her authorial vocation and thus finds "the very same words

I received in sleepe as the fittest Title I could devise for this Booke."[48] For Lanyer, the importance of her writing becomes apparent when the resources of her strangest and most dimly lit memories are called upon.

Some of the authority that Lanyer assigns, at the end of her poem, to memory is infused into her account of the Passion, particularly the moment that finds Mary Magdalene at the site of the crucifixion. It has been noted that the corporeality of Lanyer's verse seems at odds with what has been described by biographers as the poet's concerted attempt to make a place for herself as a devotional writer within court culture. For example, following the description of the crucifixion, Lanyer's speaker provides for the reader—the Countess of Cumberland, at this moment—a "brief description of [Christ's] beautie":

> This is that Bridegroome that appeares so faire,
> So sweet, so lovely in his Spouses sight,
> That unto Snowe we may his face compare,
> His cheekes like skarlet, and his eyes so bright
> As purest Doves that in the rivers are,
> Washed with milke, to give thee more delight;
>   His head is likened to the finest gold,
>   His curled lockes so beauteous to behold.[49]

The passage is a palpably corporeal blazon in the Petrarchan tradition, here applied to Christ. And yet in a subsequent stanza the speaking persona withdraws from visceral description, requesting permission to lay aside "this taske of Beauty" as she fears she may "wade so deepe" and in so doing deceive herself before she has completed the image ("before I can attaine the land"). In the same way that fleeting memories can seem to be more vivid than photographs that record with precision every detail of a person or event, poetic perfection lies in the incompleteness or partial obscurity of the image. While the addition of more visual material may make the scene appear more magnificent, it would also, she claims, diminish the reader's affective experience. While it is important that the countess see Christ as "a God in glory, / And as a man in miserable case," it is also crucial that she, like the

Magdalene, "reade his true and perfect storie," for in words "his bleeding body there you may embrace."[50] Lanyer wants to deliver unto her reading patron something of the experience of the reading Magdalene who finds in the Word a memory that has no material substance and yet has the power to move her. To accomplish this task, Lanyer portrays Christ, as he appears elsewhere to the Magdalene, as in a recollection or in a dream:

> Sometime h'appeares to thee in Shepheards weed,
> And so presents himselfe before thine eyes,
> A good old man; that goes his flocke to feed;
> Thy colour changes, and thy heart doth rise;
> Thou call'st, he comes, thou find'st tis he indeed,
> Thy Soule conceaves that he is truely wise:
> 　　Nay more, desires that he may be the Booke,
> 　　Whereon thine eyes continually may looke.[51]

Rather than fully describe anything, Lanyer withdraws and provides her principal reader with the memory only a Magdalene can have. In so doing, she shows the rest of her readers an image of Cumberland as the Magdalene: the blush of her cheek and the flutter of her heart as Christ's words echo in her ears and as his ghostly person appears just beyond the full perception of her eyes.[52]

By dedicating their poems to noble Protestant women, Donne, Breton, and Lanyer move the medieval contemplative into conformist court culture where she becomes identifiable as the image of Christian subjectivity—the reading Magdalene. I will argue, in chapter 5, that the convention of representing aristocratic ladies *à la Madeleine* becomes decadent, as the erotic features of the penitent reader prove, in a later political context, impossible to contain. But these three writers not only succeed in containing the erotic; they are also able to attribute to their patrons something of the Magdalene's stillness by dwelling not just upon their composure and their grace, but also upon their ability to haunt the poetic imagination. The Magdalene is thus not always the vestigial remnant of a more erotic eucharistic piety, nor is she an aestheticized emblem of a newly formed female devotion premised upon silent reading and meditation. Like these majestic women, she is, as was her medieval counterpart, a tranquil mystic and a serene clairvoyant who channels the Word, making its vitality apparent only mysteriously, as if in a dream. As such, the Magdalene's enduring presence suggests a new vocation for early modern devotional writers charged, in the wake of incontrovertible historical change, with the responsibility of articulating the Christian subject's relationship to Christ in terms of words that linger and visions that vanish.

Penance in a Sheet

And behold, a woman in the citie, which was a sinner.

—Luke 7:37 (King James Version)

In his first Easter sermon, preached before the king in 1620, Lancelot Andrewes considers the significance, for ordinary Christians, of Mary Magdalene's extraordinary mourning:

> Thus she, in her love, for her supposed loss or taking away. And what shall become of us in ours then? That lose Him. 1. Not once, but oft; 2. and not in suppose as she did, but in very deed; 3. and that by sin, the worst loss of all; 4. and that not by any other's taking away, but by our own act and wilful default; and are not grieved, nay not moved a whit, break none of our wonted sports for it, as if we reckoned Him as good lost as found. Yea, when Christ and the Holy Ghost, and the favour of God, and all is gone, how soon, how easily are we comforted again for all this! that none shall need to say, *quid ploras?* to us, rather, *quid non ploras?* ask us why we weep not, having so good cause to do it as we then have?[1]

The mourning Magdalene is summoned as an alarm for a constituency that has become insensitive to Christ's sacrifice. Andrewes renders Mary's desolation elegantly, moving his congregation from indifference to a like melancholy: "There was no taking away His taking away from her." Christ's departure is figured as cruel and absolute and Mary's grief as enduring and inconsolable. And yet, in a familiar segue that links the Magdalene of the sepulcher with Mary of Bethany, comfort can be found in listening to the words of Christ: "Such power is there in every word of His." Mary's choice, her decision to hear, is beautiful in its simplicity for it is the sound of just one word, "Mary," that makes Christ available again in some way. For Mary, "His taking away, is taken away quite" because listening is the way to understanding:

> *Voce quam visu,* more proper to the word. So *sicut audivimus* goes before, and then *sic vidimus* comes after. In matters of faith the ear goes first ever, and is more use, and to be trusted before the eye. For in many cases faith holdeth where sight faileth.[2]

There is more than a hint of Southwell in Andrewes's treatment of the Magdalene. He writes with an air of nostalgia, for instance, with reference to the supper at Emmaus, observing that it is folly to see, "as the fond fashion now-a-days is," word and sacrament at "odds" with each other. And yet, as in *Funeral Teares* or in Breton's "The blessed Weeper," Mary's attentiveness to matters spiritual transforms her from a wretched creature of lugubrious excess into the ideal congregant—silent and spiritually attentive. This redirection is even more explicit in Andrewes's second Easter sermon (1621), in which Christ's prohibition of Mary's touch reluctantly marks devotion premised upon touch (or taste, or smell, or sight) as receding into history:

> Mary Magdalene touch, and Mary Magdalene not touch! The difficulties grow still. For I ask, if at the second appearing, why not at the first? Why after and not now? Why there, touch and spare not; and here *noli Me tangere,* not come hither?[3]

That was then; this is now. Granted, there is nothing transparent about the state of "now," and Andrewes, like others before him, feels the need to rationalize the restriction placed upon physical contact by concluding that it contains both a forbidding and a bidding.[4] The forbidding is in two parts: a restraint ("Touch me not") and a reason ("I have not yet ascended to my Father"). The forbidding, cruel in its own right, is mediated by the bidding that creates an imperative: go and tell my brothers that I have risen from the dead. This bidding, according to Andrewes, is the very text of salvation:

> They call it Mary Magdalene's Gospel, for glad tidings it contains; and what is the Gospel else? The first Gospel of glad tidings after Christ's resurrection. The very Gospel of the Gospel itself, and a compendium of all the four.[5]

The sermon is returning to the preaching Magdalene of the Middle Ages, but she is no longer the mendicant of ancient legend converting the heathen of France. In his last Easter sermon, preached in 1622, Andrewes writes again:

> This day, with Christ's rising, begins the Gospel; not before. Crucified, dead and buried, no good news, no Gospel they in themselves. . . . The first Gospel of all is the Gospel of this day, and the Gospel of this day is this Mary Magdalene's Gospel.[6]

This is a most radical reading, which anticipates the discovery of the Nag Hammadi Gospel.[7] If Christ is the Word, then Mary is its first iteration.

This last observation is in keeping with Peter Lake's illustration of Andrewes's opinion that preachers ought to set aside the finer points of doctrine and instead present to their listeners "the figure of Christ as an object of faith, adoration and emulation." Preachers should act, Andrewes writes, as "the Lord's remembrancers," occupied by calling their congregants' minds to "the things they know and have forgot, as in teaching them the things they know not, or never learnt."[8] Andrewes's ideal preacher, then, is a lot like the postmedieval

Mary Magdalene. However, Andrewes's own Magdalene, like the others, is pretty much silent. One can listen all one wants, but there is nothing to hear. Instead, as Luke instructs, one is asked to "behold, a woman in the citie, which was a sinner" (7:37). If Andrewes's sermon teaches that Mary will not see Christ until she hears him, it also suggests that the rest of us, less privileged auditors, will not hear Christ until we, in some sense, see Mary Magdalene. While Andrewes may well have expected his audience to model the saint's exemplary silent attention, the success of his plea rests upon his sermons' ability to leave their readers haunted, like Breton's speaker, by the spectral sight of the blessed weeper.

The petition to the visual in Andrewes's sermons needs, I would argue, some contextualizing. Graham Parry has recently characterized Andrewes as "a noncontroversial figure"—a preacher and counselor to King James—whose engagement with the tenets and principles of the English Church was central to the consolidation and dissemination of mainstream Protestantism. And yet, as Lake has argued, Andrewes's conformity can also be interpreted as "avant-garde" in its espousal of an emotionally compelling style of piety—one centered more on the sacrament and on public worship than on preaching—which begins with Richard Hooker and culminates in the High Church ideals that, by the beginning of the 1630s, were endorsed by Archbishop Laud.[9] The Laudians, as they have come to be called, generally adhered to the patterns of worship identified in the Book of Common Prayer; however, they were also more inclined to find a place for visual culture within the church, the library, and the gallery. And thus, for a brief period of time—a period Parry identifies as the Anglican Counter-Reformation—the English Church, along with its more illustrious congregants, became a great patron of the arts.[10] As Lake makes clear, Andrewes was not Laudian *avant la lettre*; and yet his sensitivity to the Psalmist's imperative—"O worship the Lord in the beauty of holiness" (Ps. 96:9)—an imperative that would be fully appreciated by the aesthetic movement associated with Laud and his circle, is evident in the Magdalene sermons that beg the eye to behold the modest comeliness of the Magdalene image in order to contemplate that which lies beyond it.[11]

What, then, are the visual analogues to Andrewes's sermons; or to which images does he refer his readers? Sometime between 1628 and 1632, Anthony van Dyck sketched a picture of Mary Magdalene in chalk (fig. 9). There is no evidence to suggest that the image is an illustration of Andrewes's sermons—and I do not think that it is— though the picture is roughly contemporary and van Dyck was in London in 1620 at the request of King James, making it possible to conceive of a relationship between the two.[12] What I find intriguing about the image, and what links it to the Easter sermon, are the Magdalene's hands, which grasp at something that appears, at first, to have some substance. A quick glance at the image might lead the viewer to assume she clings to a body part, a leg perhaps or even an arm, belonging to a figure just outside the frame. But closer examination reveals the object of Mary's grasp as less tangible; she holds fabric that appears to be draped over some kind of architectural feature. The scene might be a study for a fuller realization of Luke 7 and the draped fabric a substitute for a Christ figure that has yet to be realized. Or the sketch meditates upon John 20 and serves to illustrate what Mary wants at the moment of the *noli me tangere* rather than what she has. If the latter is the case, the image becomes a striking rendering of the lyric interplay between the desired and the inaccessible found in Andrewes's sermons as well as in other treatments of the sepulcher scene. The Magdalene's hands capture the hallucinatory longing for substance where there isn't any. Also remarkable is the look on the Magdalene's face: she is neither enraptured nor particularly penitent. She simply looks sad. Her face invokes precisely the same loss as the Easter sermons, which, when read alongside the image, become less persuasive: there really is no taking away his taking away from her.

And yet the exquisiteness of the Magdalene sketch lies in its capture not of the lost object but of the experience of loss itself and the attendant realization of the irretrievability of the past. The picture is a *lieu de mémoire* that serves, citing Nora once again, to reveal that the "whole dynamic of our relation to the past is shaped by the subtle interplay between the inaccessible and the non-existent." The picture, then, insists that "if the old ideal was to resurrect the past, the new

FIGURE 9. Anthony van Dyck, *Saint Mary Magdalene* (1628–32). The Samuel Courtauld Trust, Courtauld Institute of Art Gallery, London.

ideal is to create a representation of it" in some way. The van Dyck Magdalene *shows* that while Christ can no longer be touched, he can be recalled and represented in art that captures the lingering effect of his presence. Likewise, the rhetorical persuasiveness of the sermon lies in its ability to confront indifference to the past with an idea of presence that effectively saddens the listener because it lingers somewhere just out of reach, beyond the narrative frame.

I am invoking both words and pictures here because, when it comes to sites of memory, Nora reminds us, "everything is in the execution."[13] On the one hand, the Magdalene serves to commemorate things (the fabric of Christ's body, the fabric of the church) that cannot be touched (or smelled or tasted) because they are long gone. On the other hand, her commemoration of those things will be executed in ways that appeal to what is left, not just to the ear but also, always, to the eye. The circumstances of this mode of execution are historical, but they are also formally engaging: in the same way that a man, deprived of sight, reports a new intensity to his experience of smell, the Magdalene, no longer able to touch or smell or taste, lends new intensity to the acts of listening and looking. Until this point, I have been discussing the Magdalene's vision in terms of spiritual insight — that is, her ability to see Christ when no one else can. Furthermore, I have argued that the vision of the Magdalene — that is, the depiction of her shame, her contrition, her mourning, and her revelation — was understood, in the period in question, as a viable means of accessing some idea of Christ's affective presence. I now want to turn to actual pictures — early modern paintings and prints — in order to make explicit, and historically specific, a claim that has been only implicit to this point: literature written in the seventeenth century which takes the Magdalene as its subject does not ask us simply to imagine a blessed weeper; it asks us to look at one.

As historians of postmedieval religion, we tend to think of the epistemological experiences of sight, scent, taste, and touch as oriented differently from the experience of sound: Catholics actively look, smell, taste, and feel, while Protestants simply listen. Even reading, the devotional mode most frequently attributed to Protestant observance, is not really considered an act of looking: words ought not to unfold as images before the eye, and only when read aloud do they appeal to the senses at all. Therefore, despite a number of significant interventions to the contrary, we still tend to think of visual art—and paintings on religious themes in particular—as aligned primarily with Catholic aesthetics and with pre-Reformation, recusant, or Counter-Reformation culture.[14] I have already argued that the figure of the Magdalene proposes a different set of oppositions between the sensual activities of the body (touching, smelling, and tasting) and those of the mind (seeing and hearing). The first are understood as inarticulate registers of loss, reminders not of what one has but, like the van Dyck image, of what one does not have; while the second are the makers of memories, aesthetic tools, which lend the inexpressible sadness some kind of hearable, seeable form. I want to push these assumptions further now by suggesting that in the two decades preceding the Civil War, literary representations of the Magdalene appealed to pictorial representation. This appeal was facilitated by two related phenomena: the return, through the 1620s and 1630s, of the visual arts to devotional culture under the direction of Laud; and the development of a connoisseur market for Continental religious paintings and their print spin-offs. While the treatment of religious themes in English art was more or less prohibited, the purchase of art, and of print reproductions, produced elsewhere, was difficult to regulate—so much so that images of Mary Magdalene were, in certain circles, ubiquitous. If Andrewes's congregants did not know van Dyck's picture, I would conjecture that they knew a print very much like it.

The next two sections of this chapter trace a growing affinity between text and image in the Magdalene material of the 1620s and 1630s. I first turn to the epigrammatic economy of George Herbert's "Marie Magdalene" in the context of an evolving sympathy for emblematic treatments of religious subjects. I then argue that devotional writing, in this context, is brought into close proximity with a growing taste for luxury goods, including printed reproductions of Continental artwork. The chapter closes with readings of the Magdalene poems of Robert Herrick, Henry Vaughan, and Richard Crashaw that acknowledge the precariousness of this proximity and that, once again, retrace the boundaries between the verbal and the visual.

The Maudlin Epigram

When blessed Marie wip'd her Saviours feet,
(Whose precepts she had trampled on before)
And wore them for a jewell on her head,
   Shewing his steps should be the street,
   Wherein she thenceforth evermore
With pensive humblenesse would live and tread:

She being stain'd her self, why did she strive
To make him clean, who could not be defil'd?
Why kept she not her tears for her own faults,
   And not his feet? Though we could dive
   In tears like seas, our sinnes are pil'd
Deeper than they, in words, and works, and thoughts.

Deare soul, she knew who did vouchsafe and deigne
To bear her filth; and that her sinnes did dash
Ev'n God himself: wherefore she was not loth,
   As she had brought wherewith to stain,
   So to bring in wherewith to wash:
And yet in washing one, she washed both.[15]

Unlike other Magdalene texts that seek to connect the reader to Christ by means of the feelings and experiences of the penitent saint, Herbert's poem consciously distances both the speaker and the reader from the scene in order to claim visual control of the subject matter. The poem is a dramatization of Luke 7, but it is a tidier, refined rendition reduced to its simplest elements: a question—how can one so sinful touch one so saintly—and an answer—her deed demonstrates her grace. Crucially, the poem depends upon prior knowledge of the Gospel stories, and the speaker addresses these in the past tense ("When blessed Marie wip'd her Saviours feet"), making it clear that this account of the scene is not original or unfolding in the same time and space as the reading. The poem works from Luke, but as if to answer the question that Herbert poses in "The Thanksgiving" ("how then shall I imitate thee, and / Copie thy fair though bloudie hand?"), it also acknowledges its distance from its source and its status as a reading whose value resides in its capture of the distilled essence of the original.[16] "Marie Magdalene," I would argue, becomes most poignant when considered within a representational tradition in which the challenge lay in the masterful execution of a ubiquitous conceit. Herbert's Magdalene is not new, but she is more concise. In this orderly structure, the paradoxical details of the medieval Magdalene— her corporeality and her holiness—are resolved and set aside as the poem becomes a refined, emblematic engraving that tells us precisely what we need to see and how we need to see it.

Much ink has been spilled over the question of where Herbert stood with respect to the aesthetic practices of the English Church, and not surprisingly his Magdalene lies at the center of the debate.[17] Martz has argued for Herbert's poem's "participation in a time-honored line of hyperbole" that begins with Southwell and carries on through Andrew Marvell and Vaughan to Crashaw, while Ann Pasternak Slater finds Herbert's Magdalene to be "well washed" of her past. Richard Strier concurs with Slater, arguing that "Herbert does not present Mary erotically in his poem; the single allusion which he makes to her past is studiedly abstract."[18] The poem also corroborates Barbara Lewalski's contention that the religious lyric does not try to relate its work to "ineffable and intuited divine revelation" after the Magdalenes of Southwell. Herbert's effort here is mediated by and modeled upon the biblical text. But, as Michael Schoenfeldt senses, the attitude the speaker expresses is not properly "Protestant," precisely because of the relationship it has to sensual experience. Elaborating upon Helen Vendler's sense that the subject of the poem is social courtesy, Schoenfeldt detects a discomfort that he ascribes to unease "with regard to the relationship between feminine sexuality and religious devotion." He argues that the poem "negotiates unsuccessfully between body and soul, between action and significance, between filth and ablution," and ultimately that it "represents an abortive attempt to locate religious devotion in relation to human sexuality."[19]

Schoenfeldt's articulation of Herbert's unease is important; however, beneath it lies the same fundamental assumption that underpins the Protestant readings of Herbert's poetry—the assumption implicit in the very definition of the religious lyric—that the poetic process always involves "the painstaking analysis of the personal religious life."[20] And yet if there is any common ground in Magdalene poetry of the Counter-Reformation period (the poems of Herbert, Marvell, Herrick, Vaughan, and Crashaw), it is the distance between the poetic subject and the persona of the poet. Attention turns outward rather than inward. The speakers are no longer present at the scene, as they are in Breton's and Lanyer's poems. Instead, they stand back, one more step removed as if, to quote Herbert, all is veiled "while he that reads, divines, / Catching the sense at two removes."[21] Taking a cue from Martz's recognition of the "neatness" of Herbert's poetry, I want to argue that the affect Schoenfeldt reads as personal uneasiness is better understood as the mannered "self-consciousness of the artist who knows that he has mastered every form and technique that the earlier masters of the Renaissance have taught."[22]

The affinity Martz detects between Herbert's poetics and visual art is most dynamic with respect to the Magdalene, although her English history is not a simple one to trace. Only the rare pre-Reformation artifact survives: the Launceston statue discussed in chapter 3 is a particularly evocative example; the Anglo-Saxon Ruthwell Cross, so tender in its simplicity, is another (fig. 10).[23] More common than the three-dimensional images that once adorned churches and chapels are the images found in illuminations and in the odd pre-Reformation printed text. Woodcut examples include the image found in Richard Pynson's 1526 edition of *The complaynt of Mary Magdaleyne* (fig. 11).[24] Another example is found on a sixteenth-century broadside, "A Newe Ballade of a Louer. Extollinge his Ladye," signed by M. Osborne (fig. 12). While the text suggests the speaker's love is secular, the song is clearly a reconfiguration of a ballad in the tradition of the Song of Songs, and the images, including a picture of the Virgin and two of Mary Magdalene (fig. 13), are vestiges of the ballad's previous life.[25] These late medieval images, despite their beauty and longevity, are testament to an aesthetic environment different from that under consideration here. They work as thumbnails that point directly at familiar stories. They index narrative without claiming any

FIGURE 10. The Ruthwell
Cross, Ruthwell Church,
Dumfriesshire, Scotland.
Crown Copyright: RCAHMS
(Royal Commission on the
Ancient and Historical
Monuments of Scotland).

FIGURE II. The image accompanying *The complaynt of Mary Magdaleyne* in *Here begynneth the boke of fame* (London: Richard Pynson, 1526?). Harry Elkins Widener Collection, Harvard University, HEW 15.11.8 F.

mastery over the subject, and for this reason they seem out of step with seventeenth-century texts more self-consciously preoccupied with the aesthetics of narrative than with narrative itself.

There is not, however, a lot of English material to look at between the relics of medieval visual culture and Peter Lely's sumptuous Restoration Magdalenes to be discussed in the next chapter. A very rare example is Isaac Oliver's drawing of the reading Magdalene discussed in the previous chapter (fig. 4). Oliver was Nicholas Hilliard's student and was appointed limner to Queen Anne in 1605.[26] The drawing's Renaissance provenance is unknown, though it was in the possession of John Spencer (the first Earl of Spencer, 1734–83), and its connection to the court of James I is likely.[27]

Parry has noted that in the period under Laud's influence, "the conditions were propitious for a modest revival of religious painting,"

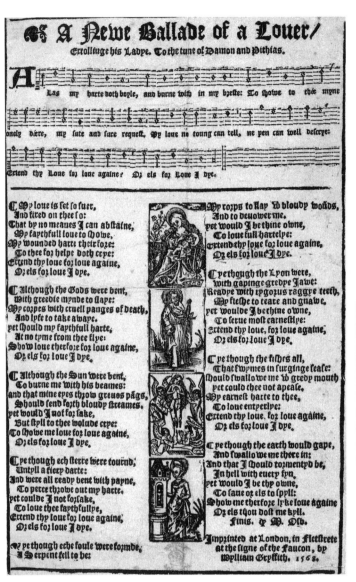

FIGURE 12. "A Newe Ballade of a Louer. Extollinge his Ladye. To the tune of Damon and Pithias" (Wyllam Gryffith, 1568). © The British Library Board. All Rights Reserved. Huth.50.(27).

FIGURE 13.
Detail from figure 12.

but, likely as a result of the iconoclastic surge of the 1640s, little of this indigenous work survives.[28] It is well known, for instance, that King Charles had an impressive collection of Continental masterpieces, some of them given to him as gifts and others commissioned of visiting artists. Orazio Gentileschi, for example, was invited to court in 1626, and the biblical scenes he painted at the king's request were likely the first paintings commissioned by an English monarch since the onset of the Reformation. Among the work commissioned was a penitent Magdalene, presented to George Villiers, Duke of Buckingham, in 1626 (fig. 14).[29] The queen's chapel at Somerset House, according to the inventory compiled in 1649, contained twenty-three paintings, thirteen of them depicting the Virgin and five depicting Mary Magdalene.[30] There is a window in Lincoln Chapel, Oxford, featuring the Magdalene with Christ, the latter sporting the beard and mustache made fashionable by Charles I (fig. 15).[31] There are also records of religious works in the private collections of elite courtiers. Buckingham and his wife, Katherine Manners, were renowned collectors, and the Earl of Arundel, the Earl of Pembroke, the Marquess of Hamilton, and the Earl of Somerset were likewise great purchasers of foreign art. Laud also had an enviable collection of religious paintings in his gallery at Lambeth Palace.[32]

A more modest example of private collecting is alluded to in John Donne's will, which lists a number of religious paintings apparently in his home—including, rather tantalizingly, a painting of Mary Magdalene in his "chamber."[33] But this kind of information is hard to come by, and it is difficult to know how widespread private collecting would have been. There is, however, considerable evidence that religious prints, copied from painted masterpieces both locally and abroad, did circulate in Stuart England. Tessa Watt writes that while "there is no evidence of a large-scale attempt to replace medieval 'images of pity' with cheap and acceptable pictures which might disseminate Protestant ideas to a wide audience," the period of Laud's influence did "see a resurgence of sacred images" in print and on glass.[34] The immediate attraction of these prints may have something to do with their acceptability within moderate conformist culture. As Parry has observed, by the 1620s a less defensive attitude toward the illustration

FIGURE 14. Orazio Lomi Gentileschi, *Büßende Maria Magdalena*.
Kunsthistorisches Museum, Wien oder KHM, Wien.

of the Scriptures was in the air: "The possession of religious engravings by European artists was a modest and discreet way of helping
the imagination to conceive of divine events in history."[35]

An example of English investment in religious prints is provided
by a series of images that was originally produced as an accompani-
ment to a volume of meditations entitled *Vitae, passionis et mortis Jesu
Christi*, by the Jesuit Johannes Bourghesius. Included in the volume are
seventy-six plates engraved by the Antwerpian Boethius Bolswert.[36]
The collection begins with the annunciation and concludes with the

Quem Deus | fuscitauit, So | lutis dolori-
bus inferni, | iuxta quod | impoſſibile
erat teneri | illum ab eo : | Actor: Cap 2:24

FIGURE 15.
Abraham van Linge,
"Resurrection Window"
(1629–32). Lincoln College
Chapel, Oxford. Reproduced
by kind permission of the
Rector and Fellows of
Lincoln College Oxford.

assumption of the Virgin, including four images that feature Mary Magdalene: in the home of Simon the Pharisee (fig. 16); together with Christ and her sister Martha; at the sepulcher with the other Marys; and in the garden with Christ just after the resurrection (fig. 17).

In 1640, after Laud's arrest and imprisonment in the Tower of London, his study at Lambeth Palace was searched by William Prynne (author of *Histriomastix*, and Laud's longtime enemy). In his shamelessly biased account of Laud's trial, *Canterburies Doome*, published in London in 1646, Prynne describes finding a bound volume "containing in all 74 Idolatrous Superstitious Pictures"—the volume in question was a bound collection of the Bolswert plates, gathered this time without the Jesuit meditations.[37] Prynne alleged that the controversial pictures found in Laud's study were all licensed by the archbishop's chaplain, Doctor Bray, and were also included in an edition of the authorized Bible produced by the archbishop's printer (and kinsman), Badger, in 1638 for Robert Peake—a stationer/bookseller of Holburn Conduit who was "in armes" against the Parliament. The Bible in question, a New Testament, has come to be known as "The Bishop of Canterbury's Bible," and indeed the Bolswert images feature prominently within it, though new plates, with English subtext, were evidently commissioned for the printing.[38] These plates are the only set of Bible illustrations produced in England before the Civil War, and prints from the plates can be found bound in a number of authorized Bibles of the 1630s (figs. 18 and 19).[39]

George Henderson has observed that Peake's engraver made very few attempts to modify potentially controversial aspects of the images, making his reformation "only very partial."[40] One of the quirks of the Peake editions is that they deploy the Geneva Bible translations and thus do not correspond with the Authorized Version of the Gospels that they purport to illustrate. It is tempting to consider the choice of text as an attempt to pre-empt the ire of iconoclasts: an identifiably Protestant epigram makes the print reminiscent of textually informed Reformation art in which the image is an execution, or reading, of the Scripture inscribed below it.[41] However, Henderson observes that it is unlikely that Laud would have ever encouraged Peake

De Conversione Magdalenæ. *Lu. 7.*

1. Magdalena pænitens medio in conuiuio et domi alienæ prosternit
se ad Christi pedes, quos lacrymis lauat, osculatur, vnguento pretioso
vngit, ac capillis suis detergit.
2. Murmurantem Pharisæum Dominus compescit proposita parabola de
duobus debitorib⁹ cuiusdam fæneratoris.
3. Dimittit Magdalenam cum indulgentia et pace. Remittuntur ei
peccata multa quia dilexit multum.

25

FIGURE 16. Engraving by Boethius Bolswert in Johannes Bourghesius, *Vitae,
passionis et mortis Jesu Christi Mysteria, piis meditationibus, exposita. Figuris aeneis
expressa per Boetium a Bolswert* (Antwerp, 1622). Bancroft Library, University of
California, Berkeley.

FIGURE 17. Engraving by Boethius Bolswert in Johannes Bourghesius, *Vitae, passionis et mortis Jesu Christi Mysteria, piis meditationibus, exposita. Figuris aeneis expressa per Boetium a Bolswert* (Antwerp, 1622). Bancroft Library, University of California, Berkeley.

The Conuersion of Magdalen. *Luc: 7*

37. *And beholde a woman in ȳ cittie, which was a sinner, when shee knewe that Jesus sate att table in the Pharises house, shee brought a boxe of oyntment.*

38. *And shee stoode att his feete behind him weeping, and be: ganne to wash his feete with teares, and did wipe them with the heares of her head, and kissed his feete, and anoynted them with the oyntment.*

FIGURE 18. "The Conversion of Magdalen," engraving by Robert Peake, *The New Testament of our Lord and Saviour Jesus Christ* (London: Robert Barker, 1638). Reproduced by permission of The Huntington Library, San Marino, California. RB 82003.

Christ appeareth to Mary Magdalene *Matt: 28.*
Mar: 16. Ioau: 20

*11. *But Mary stood without att ẏ Sepulchre weeping etc:*
12. *And saw two Angels in white, sitting, etc:*
13. *And they sayd unto her, woman, why weepest thou?*
     Shee sayd unto them, they haue taken away my Lord, and
     J know not where they haue lay'd him.
14. *When shee had thus say'd, Shee turned her selfe backe, and*
     Saw Jesus standing, etc

FIGURE 19. "Christ appeareth to Mary Magdalen," engraving by Robert
Peake, *The New Testament of our Lord and Saviour Jesus Christ* (London: Robert
Barker, 1638). Reproduced by permission of The Huntington Library, San
Marino, California. RB 82003.

to engrave the Calvinist text that the Authorized Version was intended to supplant, and it may be that the translation in question is less relevant than the act of "Englishing" that the new engravings perform.[42] This latter possibility, one anticipated by Markham's mainstream versification of a Jesuit meditation, speaks to a growing market for appropriately English copies of Catholic art—a market interested in recovering something of the visuality of the past, "the beauty of holiness," without fully abandoning the spirit of reform.

In the first Peake image ("The Conversion of Mary Magdalen"), for instance, Christ's spoken teachings are witnessed in the same time and space as Mary's bodily ministrations. As if to make it clear that goodly precepts are inseparable from tender deeds, Christ's narrative—the parable of the two debtors—is illustrated in the bubble floating above the central image. In the second image ("Christ appeareth to Mary Magdalen"), the overt sensuality of the weeper is controlled within a framed narrative that moves from left to right, like words on a page. Mary weeps, rather modestly, with her back to the viewer in the middle ground of the picture; she kneels before Christ as he speaks her name in the foreground; and, in the background, her touch is rebuked. The image is, in both cases, held at some distance. These Magdalenes lack passion. They are stylized and invested in the intellectual tension between word and image rather than in affective immediacy.

Herbert's Magdalene epigram, to return to the poem that initiated this digression on images, approaches the visual picture in a similarly restrained, intellectual manner. In the first instance, text precedes image: before tears and hair can be visually conceived, Herbert redirects the reader's attention to text. Christ's holy feet become "precepts" or words, possibly even poetry (metered feet), blindly trampled by ignorant souls' soles. Words then work to materialize a model of Lutheran assurance or Calvinist predestination, a figure that knows "who did vouchsafe and deigne / To bear her filth" and yet still is not loath to show her sin. This Mary's faith is absolute and comforting, as her salvation, residing in only the Christian text, is emblematized in the feet (words) she holds. When the picture finally emerges before the reader's eyes, the kneeling image of grace is bound by the motto "in washing one, she washed both."[43] If the first stanza forces the reader to step with the Magdalene into a world of precepts, the second stanza reveals just how hopeless that journey would feel for the average human, steeped in sin. At this moment of greatest doubt, the Magdalene is brought forth ("As she had brought wherewith to stain, / So to bring in wherewith to wash") and only then is the answer provided: "in washing one, she washed both." Here, the image deftly steps out from under heaps of thoughtless words, idle works, and sinful thoughts to provide the gloss (or glass) that makes the Gospel story sensible. The work does not privilege the Magdalene's image, nor does it suggest that the image is the source or inspiration for work. Rather, the image nimbly illustrates the grace that lies at the center of reformed piety.

The link I am establishing between Herbert's Magdalene epigram and the Bolswert images is admittedly more intuitive than sustained. It is, however, possible to provide a more immediate connection between the two by considering how Herbert's poems may have crossed paths with religious images in Laudian circles of the 1620s and 1630s. It was once commonplace to think of Herbert's poetry as lying in relative obscurity during his lifetime; however, recent scholarship has challenged this assumption by pointing to dedications that draw attention to Herbert's influence both before and shortly after his death. Greg Miller has noted, for example, that while Herbert had political reasons for limiting the circulation of his poems during his life, he certainly shared his work with a small coterie of sympathetic readers gathered around Nicholas Ferrar and his religious community at Little Gidding.[44]

The Little Gidding community was a religious sanctuary, established by Ferrar and his mother, Mary, in 1625.[45] This "Protestant Monastery," as it came to be known, was equipped to encourage a life of prayer and study. Because the community drew artists, including Donne, Herbert, and Crashaw, into its midst, and because it was renowned for its commitment to the beautification of its church and to the celebration of an ordered liturgy, it became notorious for its High Church sensibilities in an increasingly Puritan age. The community's reluctant entanglement in religious turmoil became indisputable when Charles I sought refuge there in May 1646 just days before his arrest.

The most astonishing products of the community are its Bible harmonies. These are handmade collage "concordances" of the Scriptures, produced in the Little Gidding workshops by Ferrar's nieces, the Collet sisters, who meticulously cut out, collated, and reassembled texts using multiple print editions of the Bible. The purpose of the volumes was to reduce individual books of the Bible into one complete narrative that related to the reader in a variety of different formats.[46] Of greatest interest to me is the production of the New Testament volumes collated, according to Ferrar's brother and biographer, John, as a devotional exercise that sought to achieve, through respect for scriptural integrity, a coherent life of Christ. The page shown here (fig. 20), from the "King's Concordance," prepared for Charles I, renders the story of Mary's visit to the home of Simon the Pharisee.[47] The page includes a "Comparison" of Matthew, Mark, and Luke achieved by cutting and pasting together the three accounts. Next, there is a "Collection" or assembly of all possible accounts of the same narrative. There follows an extraction of the Gospels into one complete text, or "Composition." And, finally, the narratives are illustrated with an array of "sundry pictures" added to express "either the Facts themselves or their Types and Figures or other things appertaining thereto." One of the illustrations on the page is a Bolswert.

The connection between the harmonies and Herbert's poetry has been thoroughly discussed by Herbert scholars. Ferrar was Herbert's first editor, and it was to Ferrar that Herbert sent *The Temple*, requesting that he judge the poems' value and then either publish or burn them.[48] Herbert was also a privileged recipient of his own harmony, remarking upon the occasion that he "most humbly blessed God that he had lived now to see women's scissors brought to so rare a use as to serve at God's altar."[49] Stanley Stewart has argued that the harmonies acknowledge, in a manner consistent with Herbert's poetry, that "the meaning of the written Word was not immediately accessible but somewhat mysterious" and that the act of reading the Gospels involved complex processes of compilation and collation in

De Conuersione Magdalenæ *Luc.7.*

S. Matthew.   COMPARISON.   S. LUKE.

De cæcæ manu sanatâ, sermone muto, & laude SS Matth. 12.

1. Magdalena gemitus medio in conuiuio se domi aberat prostrata ad Christi pedes, eos lacrymis lauat, siccatque, vnguentis perfusis vngit, &c capillis suis detergit.
2. Murmurantem Pharisæum Dominus exeuso proposita parabola de duobus debitoribus quaestione soluit.
3. Dimittit Magdalenam cum indulgentia ei pax. Remittuntur ei peccata multa quia dilexit multum.   25

1. Dum Dominus æcilem cæcudem brachum sanaret, aegrum illum manu apertæ quatra senata est, sc quo sanatu.
2. Egit Dæmona humoratam mutum cum admiratione populi, sed circumstantibus Pharisei multa obtrectant.
3. Quædam mulier vocem attollens laceram praedicat restore, qui Christum peperit, &c vbera quibus lactatus est.   26

C

hath washed my feete with teares, and wiped them with the haires of her head

45 Thou gauest me no kisse: but this woman, since the time I came in, hath not ceased to kisse my feete.

46 Mine head with oyle thou didst not anoint: but this woman hath anointed my feete with oyntment.

47 Wherefore, I say vnto thee, her sinnes, which are many, are forgiuen, for she loued much; but to whom little is forgiuen, the same loueth little

48 And he said vnto her, Thy sinnes are forgiuen.

49 And they that sate at meate with him, began to say within themselues, who is this that forgiueth sinnes also?

50 And he said to the woman, Thy faith hath saued thee, goe in peace.

IT CAME TO PASS AFTERWARDS &. Ch. 8.5 first.

COMPOSITION:

A Nd they went into an house. And the multitude cometh together again, so that they could not so much as eat bread. *Then was brought vnto him one possessed with a devil blinde and dumbe:

A Nd he was casting out a devil, and it was dumbe. And it came to passe when the devil was gone out, the dumbe spake: And he healed him, insomuch that the blinde and dumbe both spake and saw. And the people wondred. And all the people were amazed, and said, Is this the sonne of David?

M And when his friends heard of it, they went out to lay hold on him: for they said, He is beside himself. But when the Pharisees And the Scribes which came down from Ierusalem heard it, they said, He hath Beelzebub, and I through Beelzebub the prince of the devils casteth he out devils This fellow doth not cast out devils, but by Beelzebub the prince of the devils. And Iesus knew their thoughts, and he called them vnto him, and said vnto them in parables, How can Satan cast out Satan? Euery kingdome diuided against it self, is brought to desolation, and euery citie or house diuided against it self, shall not stand. A house diuided against a house, falleth. And if Satan rise vp against himself And if Satan cast out Satan, he is diuided against himselfe. If Satan also be diuided against himself, how shall his kingdome stand? because ye say that cast out devils through Beelzebub he cannot stand, but hath an end. And if I by Beelzebub cast out devils, by whom do your sonnes cast them out? therefore shall they be your iudges. But if I cast out deuils by the spirit of God with the finger of God then I no doubt the kingdome of God is come vpon you. Or els how can one enter into a strong mans house, and spoil his goods, except he first binde the strong man? and then he will spoil his house. When a strong man armed keepeth his palace, his goods are in peace. But when a stronger then he shall come vpon him, and ouercome him, he taketh from him all his armour wherein he trusted, and diuideth his spoils. He that is not with me, is against me, and he that gathereth not with me scattereth abroad. Wherefore verily I say vnto you, All sinnes shall be forgiuen vnto the sonnes of men, and blasphemies wherewithsoeuer they shall blaspheme but the blasphemie against the holy Ghost shall not be forgiuen vnto men And whosoeuer speaketh a word against the Sonne of man it shall be forgiuen him: but whosoeuer speaketh against the holy Ghost, it shall not be forgiuen him. But he that shall blaspheme against the holy Ghost hath neuer forgiuenesse neither in this world, neither in the world to come, but is in danger of eternall damnation. Because they said He hath an vnclean spirit. Either make the tree good, and his fruit good Or else make the tree corrupt, and his fruit corrupt

COLLECTION:

CHAP XLIX.

and they went into an houses 20 And the multitude cometh together againe, so that they could not so much as eate bread.

A2   22 Then was brought vnto him one possessed with a deuill, blinde and dumbe:

C   14 And hee was casting out a deuill, and it was dumbe. And it came to passe when the deuil was gone out, the dumbe spake: and the people wondered.

and he healed him, insomuch that the blinde and dumbe both spake & saw 23 And all the people were amazed, and sayd, Is this the sonne of Dauid?

21 And when his friends heard of it, they went out to lay hold on him, for they said, Hee is beside himselfe. 22 And the Scribes which came downe from Hierusalem, said, He hath Beelzebub, and by the prince of the deuils, casteth he out deuils.

A   24 But when the Pharisees heard it, they sayd, This fellow doeth not cast out deuils, but by Beelzebub the prince of the deuils.

B   15 But some of them said, Hee casteth out deuils through Beelzebub the chiefe of the deuils. 16 And other tempting him, sought of him a signe from heauen. 17 But hee knowing their thoughts, said vnto them, Euery kingdome diuided against it selfe is brought to desolation: and a house diuided against a house, falleth.

B   23 And he called them vnto him, and in parables, How can Satan cast out Satan?

order to articulate the complete story of the Passion.[50] Paul Dyck has suggested that the exegetical practices put on display in the harmonies shed light on Herbert's own interest in the Bible as the "ultimate source and locus of life-giving texts, a 'storehouse' to which readers and writers can go to find the most important knowledge." Drawing from Herbert's *The Country Parson*, Dyck shows how the ideal reader of Scripture is one who, in a manner not unlike that deployed by the assemblers of the harmonies, "digests" the mother text, settling and arranging it methodically in the mind.[51]

To these observations, I would add that Herbert's aesthetic sympathy with the Little Gidding enterprise is afforded greater specificity if one considers the odd experience of print that the harmonies provide. Many have noted the images as striking and have remarked upon their controversial (at least from the Protestant perspective) inclusion, as well as upon the "medieval" or "monastic" aura the Bibles acquire by virtue of their print illuminations. However, it is also the case that the volumes sit right at the point where the rarefied exegetical practices of monastic artistry meet with the democratic culture of the printing press. John Ferrar observes the following of the harmonies' making:

> The concordance was a year in making at first. . . . There was a fair large room near the great chamber wherein he [Nicholas Ferrar] spent one hour of the day in the contriving of it and gave direction to his nieces that then attended him how and in what manner with their scissors they should cut out [of] each evangelist such and such verses and thus and thus lay them together to make and perfect such and such a head or chapter. What they had first roughly done, then with their knives and scissors they neatly fitted each verse so cut out to be pasted down on sheets of paper. And so artificially they performed this new-found-out way, as it were a new kind of printing, for all that saw the books when they were done took them to be printed in the ordinary way, so finely were the verses joined together and with great presses for that purpose pressed down upon the white sheets of paper.[52]

While each book is one of a kind, it is in keeping with the "prayer book Protestantism" of Little Gidding to observe that there is nothing original about the books' content: every word and, crucially, every picture is a printed copy.[53] Pictures could trouble reformers, because they are signs that pretend to not be signs, "masquerading as (or for the believer, actually achieving) natural immediacy and presence."[54] But prints make no such claims. They are evidently copies to be read as one might read a book. Thus, the books' achievements lie in their display or execution of Scripture and not in the inimitability of their content; they are, essentially, skillfully rendered Bible studies.

Returning to Herbert's "Marie Magdalene" with columns 141 and 142 of the Royal Harmony alongside makes it possible to read the epigrammatic poem as a "new-found-out way" of printing or copying that excises "such and such verses" and illustrates them with images "to make and perfect such and such a head or chapter." The status of the imagined image is the same as that of the text: both are forms of imitation, and both are recognizable reiterations or reproductions of Scripture, lovingly and laboriously reassembled to make the original more memorable. The appeal to the visual in Herbert's poem, then, does not work in quite the same way as Reformation art, wherein images are said to emanate from words; instead, Herbert's epigrammatic style arranges words and images in the manner of the Little Gidding volumes. The spiritual significance of the text comes not from content—that is, predetermined by Scripture—but from the reunion of images, skillfully rendered, with precepts, cleverly composed.[55]

A Mannered Gallery of Contrition

There is a modesty (something Cristina Malcolmson calls "the sincerity effect") to Herbert's reconciliation of words and pictures which also characterizes the Peake plates and the work of the Ferrar family at Little Gidding.[56] This modesty was not always sustainable, however, particularly as religious works entered into public circulation where their value as works of art surpassed their value as instruments of faith. John Ferrar's account of Charles I's reception of the Royal Harmony makes the point:

> The king said that it was a most rich present for the greatest king upon earth in many respects: the matter it contained the richest treasure in the world, then the rare and singular composition of it in that excellent form, the rare contrivement in the method of it; the exquisite workmanship in the so neatly putting on and cutting off as few men but must take it really to be so printed as it showed to be; the finest curious laying on those costly pictures and the no less art showed in the binding of it as not to be paralleled he thought by any man; he concluded that he must needs say that for the whole and each part of it there wanted no skill, no care, no cost.[57]

The book impresses not because it is an extraordinary devotional labor, nor because it illuminates Scripture in an unprecedented manner. The king cherishes his gift because it is fine, rich, and rare. Its workmanship is exquisite and unparalleled, and its contents are, above all, costly. Laud was, apparently, in agreement, finding the King's Concordance to be a treasure "not in the world to be seen . . . a precious gem and worthy of [the king's] cabinet."[58] Above and beyond their value as devotional tools, these books were quenching a developing thirst, in elite circles, for rarefied objects of art.

Further evidence for the growing culture of art appreciation is the description of Laud's collection of Bolswert prints brought forth at his trial. Prosecutors were initially unimpressed with the volume and dismissed it as a vestige of Catholic populism: "a meer ignorant Laymans [book], not a learned Archbishops Book, consisting meerly of unlawful Pictures." Laud essentially concurred, arguing that "it is lawful for every learned man to have those Books to peruse and refute them, as there is occasion, there being no great Schollers but have them in their studies for this end." However, this defense was undermined when prosecutors further observed that the book was colored, gilded, and luxuriously bound, and it was concluded that the volume was intended to be looked at and not studied, its owner evidently prizing it "more than ordinary to help him in his Devotions." To support this claim, further evidence, allegedly found inside the Bolswert volume, was offered: "12 severall loos Pictures in fine Vellom, about the bignesse of playing cards of the largest size, gloriously and curiously guilded, and set forth with most exquisite colours, some having one, others, two or three Pictures a peece in them." This find, likely including Magdalenes, offered "a pregnant proof" that Laud "very much doted on these Puppets in his declining age," and the volume emerges from the record as akin to the Little Gidding harmonies: a rare and highly personalized presentation copy of the sort one might display in a cabinet of treasures.[59] Despite their genesis in print, a purely mechanical form of production, these collected pictures, like those in the King's Concordance, acquired the aura of art.

The value of Continental prints was, by the 1620s and 1630s, well established in stylish court circles. Anthony Wells-Cole's study of the Elizabethan and early Jacobean aristocratic taste for Continental elegance argues that, while few English examples of European prints survive, a case for their importance can be built by gauging their influence upon English decorative arts. And Antony Griffiths, in an important survey of prints in Stuart England, attributes the growth of the English market to the sophisticated Europhilia of the royal court, to the arrival of talented engravers from the Netherlands, and to the entrepreneurship of newly established publishers. While both Wells-Cole and Griffiths are cautious in their endorsement of Watt's assertion of the availability of religious prints, and both make claims for the English preference for Flemish and Dutch works, recent work by Parry and by Linda Levy Peck makes confident claims for the presence of a wider range of such material within refined circles in which iconophilia was indistinguishable from art appreciation.[60] In her study of the circulation of luxury goods through European society, Peck points to the practice of copying pictures, both in painting and in print, in order to meet the increasing demand for European masterpieces. Charles I, for instance, did a lot to disseminate his collection by allowing favorite courtiers to copy his pictures. Thomas Howard, Earl of Arundel, also had many of his sculptures, paintings, and drawings copied by Wenceslaus Hollar, who was recruited from Germany. Arundel's London house eventually became a famous repository of art open to "all gentlemen . . . or artists which are honest men." Two leading Flemish engravers, Lucas Vorsterman and Robert van Voerst, also worked in England, primarily in court circles. Painted copies of pictures, such as the Gentileschi described earlier or Rubens's *Feast in the House of Simon the Pharisee* (1618–20), circulated among kings and courtiers, while print editions, such as Claude Mellan's *La Madeleine allongée*, probably after Gentileschi (fig. 21)[61] or those collected by Ferrar (figs. 22 and 23),[62] may have been for sale at the New Exchange. "Collecting was not only a private passion," writes Peck, "but also a public performance, which created new wants and new wares . . . increasingly available for view and for sale in seventeenth-century London even before the Civil War."[63]

Many of the Magdalene poems of the mid- to late seventeenth century, like their visual analogues, seem to be responses to an increasingly discriminating taste, from all moneyed walks of life, for mannered, refined observations upon familiar subjects. John Stradling, for instance, dedicated his Magdalene to Charles I.[64] Edward Sherburne, a courtier himself, had an aristocratic audience in mind for his Magdalene, which is found in a collection of poems and translations divided into four parts: *erotica, ludicra, ethica,* and *sacra.*[65] Thomas Bancroft dedicated his Magdalene poem to "two top branches of the gentry," and Thomas Pecke directed his translations of John Owen's Magdalene epigram to "the ingenious, and deserving Persons of all sorts."[66] All of these poems set aside the complexities of the saint's history, altering her status as a site of memory. Her controversial affiliations to the past (the Catholic past, Christ's past presence) are resolved as she invokes an aesthetic of sheer elegance and *sprezzatura* rather than of haunting likeness and presence. Like Herbert's Magdalene, these poems are emblematic and epigrammatic in quality; that is, they are short, concise expressions that appeal simultaneously to the mind and to the eye, and that aspire to a stylish ingenuity. But unlike Herbert's more earnest achievement, these works are characterized by a sly awareness of the ubiquity of the images they employ—almost as if they were written in competition with each other, for collection

FIGURE 21. Claude Mellan, *La Madeleine allongée* (1627). Bibliothèque nationale de France.

Magdala.
BEATI QVI LVGENT,
QVONIAM IPSI
CONSOLABVNTVR
BEATI QVI ESVRIVNT ET SITIVNT IVS
TITIA QVONIA IPSI SATVRABVNTVR
Primus es hic Simeon,
A
4 Blessed are they that mourne: for they shall bee comforted.
5 * Blessed are the meeke: for they shall inherite the earth.
6 Blessed are they which doe hunger and thirst af-

FIGURE 22. Page from *The Actions & Doctrine & other Passages touching our Lord & Sauior Iesus Christ, as they are related by the foure Euangelists* (1635).

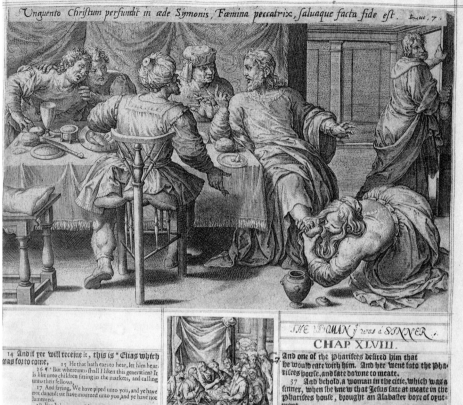

Unguento Christum perfundit in æde Symonis, Fæmina peccatrix, saluaque facta fide est. *Luc. 7.*

14 And if yee will receiue it, this is * Elias which was for to come,   15 He that hath ears to hear, let him hear.
16 ¶ But whereunto shall I liken this generation? It is like unto children sitting in the markets, and calling unto their fellows,
17 And saying, We have piped vnto you, and ye haue not danced: we haue mourned vnto you, and ye haue not lamented.
18 For John came neither eating nor drinking, and they say, He hath a devil.
19 The Son of man came eating and drinking, and they say, Behold, a man gluttonous, and a wine-bibber, a friend of Publicanes and sinners: but wisedome is iustified of her children. THEN BEGAN IHE TO VE-RAVDE &c. chap. 79 p. 274.
29 And all the people that heard him, and the Publicanes, iustified God, being baptized with the baptisme of John.
30 But the Pharises and Lawyers ‖ reiected the ounsell of God ‖ against themselues, being not baptized of him.
31 ¶ And the Lord said, * whereunto then shall I ken the men of this generation? and to what are hey like?
32 ¶ They are like vnto children sitting in the market place, and calling one to another, and saying, Wee haue piped vnto you, and ye haue not danced: we haue mourned to you, and ye haue not wept.
33 For John þ Baptist came, neither eating bread, or drinking wine, and ye say, He hath a deuil.
34 The Sonne of man is come, eating, and drinking, and ye say, Behold a gluttonous man, and a winebibber, a friend of Publicanes and sinners.
35 But wisedome is iustified of all her children.

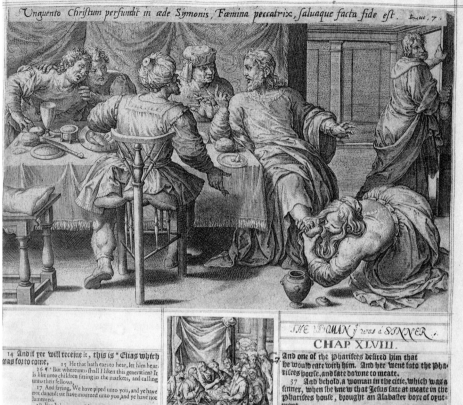

24.
Iesu pedes rigat, tergit, osculatur, vngit Magdalena. Luc 7

THE VOMAN y was a SINNER.
CHAP XLVIII.

And one of the Pharisees desired him that he would eate with him. And hee went into the Pharisees house, and sate downe to meate.

37 And behold, a woman in the citie, which was a sinner, when she knew that Iesus sate at meate in the Pharisees house, brought an Alabaster boxe of oyntment,

38 And stood at his feete behind him, weeping, and began to wash his feete with teares, and did wipe them with the haires of her head, and kissed his feete, and anoynted them with the oyntment.

39 Now when the Pharisee which had bidden him, saw it, he spake within himselfe, saying, This man, if hee were a Prophet, would haue knowen who, and what maner of woman this is that toucheth him: for she is a sinner.

40 And Iesus answering, said vnto him, Simon, I haue somewhat to say vnto thee. And he saith, Master, say on.

41 There was a certaine creditor, which had two debtors: the one ought fiue hundred ‖ pence, and the other fiftie.

42 And when they had nothing to pay, hee frankely forgaue them both. Tell mee therefore, which of them will loue him most?

43 Simon answered, and said, I suppose that hee to whom he forgaue most. And he said vnto him, Thou hast rightly iudged.

44 And he turned to the woman, and said vnto Simon. Seest thou this woman? I entred into thine house, thou gauest mee no water for my feete: but shee

FIGURE 23. Page from *The Actions & Doctrine & other Passages touching our Lord & Sauior Iesus Christ, as they are related by the foure Euangelists* (1635).

and for comparison. Marjorie Swann has demonstrated that "texts—both as physical objects and as vehicles of representation—were vitally important to the negotiation of the meanings of collections and collectors in early modern England, and . . . that modes of textuality and authorship were shaped by sixteenth- and seventeenth-century collecting practices." I would like to suggest that the ubiquity of the Magdalene epigram is an illustration of what Swann describes as the "interrelationships of material and literary culture," and that the texts form collectively a gallery of stylishly dressed figures for readers (and collectors) more invested in fashion and technique than in devotion.[67] In order to give a sense of how this literature accumulated, like fine gowns in a closet, I list the examples here one after the other:

> Those feet, for which a Bath as salt as bryne,
> Blest *Magdalen* prepared at a dinner,
> With tears distilling from her blubbred eyne:
> (Now holy woman, Once noted sinner)
>   Kissing them with her lips incessantly,
> Wip't them with her haire, till they were dry.
> (John Stradling [1625])

> "Upon Mary Magdalen"
> What faults her eyes were guilty of, in years
> Of wantonness; she blots out with her tears.
> A faculty to weep, resides in eyes:
> For by their Treachery; most sins surprize.
> (John Owen [1659])

> "On Mary Magdalene, weeping etc."
> How fast doth Mary let her floud-gates goe,
> As if the bottome of her loue to shew!
> Catching with folden nets (o rich device!)
> That presious prey, true bird of Paradise.
> (Thomas Bancroft [1639])

"To penitent Magdalen"
Mary, but late the cage of Hell,
Thy heavenly change what Muse can tell?
Those twinkling eyes that did allure
To sordid lust, now droppe the pure
Pearl of Contrition; and that haire
That wandering *Cupids* did ensnare,
And wav'd its pride in every streete,
Now humbly licks her Saviours feete,
And from those blessed roots derives
Vertue, more worth than thousand lives.
To cleanse thy stain'd affections then,
Still weepe and wipe, kind *Magdalen*.
                    (Thomas Bancroft [1639])

"And she washed his Feet with Her Teares,
    and Wiped them with the Hairs of her Head"
The proud *Aegyptian* Queen, her *Roman* Guest,
(T'express her Love in Hight of State, and Pleasure)
With Pearl dissolv'd in Gold, did feast,
    Both Food, and Treasure.
And now (dear Lord!) thy Lover, on the fair
And silver Tables of thy Feet, behold!
Pearl in her Tears, and in her Hair,
Offers thee Gold.
                    (Edward Sherburne [1651])

"Draw me, and I will Follow Thee"
Through devious Paths without Thee, Lord! I run,
And soon, without Thee, will my Race be done.
Happy was Magdalene, who like a Bride,
Her self to Thee by her fair Tresses ty'd.
So she thy Presence never did decline,
Thou her dear Captive wert, and she was Thine.
Behold another *Magdalene* in Me!
Then stay with Me, or draw me after Thee.
                    (Edward Sherburne [1651])

These are poems that attempt to assert a mastery over their subject by bringing it forth in new and visually appealing ways. The epigrams push aside the expression of feeling and of sensuality to make room for the meticulous, stylish exploration of the subject's aesthetic components. The poems are compact. The concise language of Stradling's text, for instance, reduces the image to its most essential elements as Mary's tears "distill" or purify her soul. Feet, eyes, lips, and hair are isolated, enlarged, and then combined in a mannered portrait of contrition. In Owen's epigram, the biblical scene actually disappears, leaving a near-grotesque study of the Magdalene's bulbous eyes. The first Bancroft poem morphs eyes into other things, assuring that symbolic abstraction, rather than narrative illustration, dictates the final form of the image. Bancroft's second poem moves on from glistening eyes to winding hair as the blatant corporeality characteristic of earlier manifestations of the Magdalene blazon is disembodied, abstracted, and emblematized. Sherburne begins with Luke, but then departs from Scripture to gloss the passage with reference to the rich, intensely visual, value-laden tradition of Cleopatra. But here the allusion is less affective than it is clever. When asked to "behold" the Magdalene, the image of the weeper is adroitly superimposed, producing an image that is decorous and learned, rather than sensual or sexually evocative. Sherburne's second epigram creates a space for a third player, a penitent figure reminiscent of Breton's speaker. The emblem made manifest is one of a Magdalene-like lover, by "fair Tresses ty'd" to his beloved Christ. But the act of submission seems less an acknowledgment of the feminine posture assumed by all Christians in the face of God than a witty, stylized play on the bondage topoi associated with amorous lyrics as the speaker self-consciously assumes an artful transvestite stance that alludes to, and possibly even mocks, the aristocratic habit (to be discussed in the next chapter) of posing for a painter *à la Madeleine*. These are more than formulaic expressions of a subject; they are stunningly synthetic interrogations of the Magdalene's iconography in which the subject of prayer becomes the object of art, and in which Gregory's blazon is recalled in strikingly ornamental terms.[68]

An even greater rapprochement between word and image is apparent in the dexterous epigram embedded within Marvell's "Eyes and Tears":

> *So Magdalen, in tears more wise
> Dissolved those captivating eyes,
> Whose liquid chains could flowing meet
> To fetter her Redeemer's feet.[69]

Nigel Smith has argued that this stanza alone "may be regarded as part of the English tradition inaugurated by Robert Southwell." The rest of the poem, he insists, is secular.[70] However, Gary Kuchar has recently contested this view, suggesting instead that Marvell's entire poem needs to be read as a critical reassessment of Southwell's postmedieval poetics. Kuchar's argument rests upon the anamorphic quality of Marvell's tears, "the varying perspectives" that "slow down and momentarily fix the flux of time." These perspectives do not work, Kuchar shows, as "analogies of transcendence but as emblems of the liminal nature of the present itself, its suspension between all and nothing, eternity and oblivion."[71] By heeding this gap—a gap between Nature and God—Kuchar concludes that Marvell, like Southwell, fashions a poetics that arrives "at a less deluded because less narcissistic, relation to Deity." Kuchar's reading of the poem's emblematic perceptiveness is a sophisticated complication of Joan Hartwig's sense of its possible links to Henry Peacham's "Hei mihi quod vidi" from *Minerva Britanna* (1612), which depicts an image of a tearful eye above an epigram that voices the traditional Petrarchan complaint. Hartwig suggests that the Magdalene passage activates the poem's efficiency by showing that the saint wisely dissolved her eyes with tears, assuring they can no longer enchant in the "gallant" or "Cavalier" sense.[72] However, to these articulations of the poem's clearsighted economy I would add that there is something particularly mannered, and almost hideous, about the image of "wise" tears (tears are not usually wise; quite the opposite) acting as a solvent to melt the eyes that have captivated lovers, turning them into the chains of liquid that capture feet.

The footnote tagged to the passage in the 1681 edition is further illustration of the author's participation in what was becoming a rather bizarre game of learned referentiality. The note reads as follows:

Magdala, *lascivos sic quum dimisit Amantes,*
Fervidaque in castas lumina solvit aquas;
Haesit in irriguo lachrymarum compede Christus,
Et tenuit sacros uda catena pedes.[73]

It is assumed that Marvell wrote the Latin epigram first, but why it lingers as subscript to the larger poem has never been convincingly explained. Perhaps, like the emblems in Peacham's or George Wither's collections, the Latin text forms by way of synecdoche a picture: burning lights ("fervidaque lumina") dissolving in chaste waters ("castas aquas") metamorphosing into wet chains ("uda catena") to bind sacred feet ("sacros pedes"). The English text then becomes the epigrammatic gloss. Or, because the Latin came first, the subscript becomes a nimble reminder of the historical and cultural depth of the Magdalene legacy as well as of its "pastness" and obscurity. Here, only the more learned reader can entertain Mary's "lascivos amantes," which are, like Sherburne's erudite translations of ancient erotica, refined and abstracted by Marvell's expert English précis. The Latin epigram may recall the Magdalene's representational history and her link to the affective religious culture of the past, but it does not do so to invoke past associations. Marvell, like the mannerist painter, considers his subject "through the glass of the prior achievement" in order to take his work further in the direction of aesthetic abstraction.[74]

The discussion of the Maudlin epigram is nicely concluded with Robert Whitehall's book *Exastichon hieron* (1677), a text that physically brings together epigram and emblem on the same page. The volume includes 258 images on biblical subjects which Whitehall imported from Holland. The images are pasted onto pages printed with accompanying verses. This, once again, is a rare book. Twelve versions were made, and the recipients included the king and the young son of John Wilmot, second Earl of Rochester, for whom it may have been "chiefly composed."[75] One of the plates is a copy of a Marcantonio Raimondi print rendered after a painting by Raphael (fig. 24). Here, epigrammatic poetry and illustration come together in a practice, born of the image controversy of the previous generation, of essentially reading art. To look at a picture in this printed format makes one a reader rather than a naïve consumer of images, and to bind these pages and collect them in a volume makes one a connoisseur not just of literature but also of art.

Ekphrastic Poetry: Herrick, Vaughan, and Crashaw

"Observation"
The Virgin-Mother stood at distance (there)
From her Sonnes Cross, not shedding once a teare:
Because the Law forbad to sit and crie
For those, who did as malefactors die.
So she, to keep her mighty woes in awe,
Tortur'd her love, not to transgresse the Law.
Observe we may, how *Mary Joses* then,
And th'other *Mary* (*Mary Magdalen*)
Sate by the Grave; and sadly sitting there,
Shed for their Master many a bitter teare:
But 'twas not till their *dearest Lord* was dead;
And then to weep they both were licensed.[76]

In Robert Herrick's "Observation," the Virgin stands in the background — a pictorial representation of time indicating she was there before the others, before the death of Christ, and, by law, too early to display outward signs of grief. The other two Marys inhabit the foreground of the picture as they have arrived later and their weeping is therefore sanctioned. The reader is, as the title commands, implored to observe first here, then there, as if guided by a master's pointer, across an image, much like those produced by Bolswert, in which a sequence of events unfolds across a two-dimensional canvas. The parenthetical

Cap. 7. Ταπεινὸν ὑψωθήσεται·

A *Pharisee* Christ at a Dinner treats,
Where *Mary Magdalen* staies while he eats,
Half drown'd in Tears; her penitent behaviour
Gains her offences pardon from our Saviour.
A broken Contrite Heart, with swolen Eyes,
The God of Mercy never will despise.

FIGURE 24. Plate from Robert Whitehall's *Exastichon hieron* (1677).
© The British Library Board. All Rights Reserved. C.51.d.2.

asides of the first and eighth lines offer extra guidance for those less informed—the third Mary, in case you are unsure, is Mary Magdalene.

The poem is not exactly an example of *ekphrasis;* that is, it doesn't purport to describe a specific picture or painting in poetic terms. And yet the poem owes some debt to the poetics set in motion by the verbal documentation of the visual thing. While the preceding discussion of emblems and epigrams gestures toward *ut pictura poesis*—an equalizing term describing the sisterhood of the visual and verbal arts—what follows is an attempt to consider the explicit desire to make poetry about art, and in so doing, draw attention to the friction between the two forms.[77] W. J. T. Mitchell's working definition of *ekphrasis* includes the expectation that the ekphrastic poem will do "something special and magical" with language, that it will (to use Murray Krieger's terms) "convert the transparency of its verbal medium into the physical solidity of the medium of the spatial art." And yet there is nothing "to distinguish grammatically a description of a painting from a description of a kumquat or a baseball game." The difference between ekphrasis and pictorial representation is therefore a "thematizing of 'the visual'" as somehow "other" to language. The ekphrastic poem simultaneously aspires to a kind of sameness between the visual and the verbal and fears that very sameness.[78] I want to argue that this tension between hope and fear enables, for Henry Vaughan and also for Richard Crashaw, a poetics that allows the Gospels to materialize in visual form while simultaneously acknowledging, in a manner that anticipates the final chapter of this book, that the illustration of the Word lends it an aura of decadence that puts the devotional project in jeopardy.

In the preface to *Silex Scintillans,* Vaughan presents himself as a "son of Herbert." This inheritance is evident to some degree in the poet's "St Mary Magdalen" (1655), which, after Herbert, takes up the representation of the Magdalene at Christ's feet. The poem first acknowledges medieval precedent, beginning with an invocation to the speaker's ladylove, reminiscent of lyric poetry to the Virgin. Like the other Mary, this figure is "more white than day" and "fresher then morning-flowers." Vaughan's poem also recalls the Magdalene Castle "where all was sumptuous" and recounts the conversion from sin to holiness in familiar terms. But there is nothing medieval about Vaughan's portrait:

> Why lies the *Hair* despised now
> Which once thy care and art did show?
> Who then did dress the much lov'd toy,
> In *Spires, Globes,* angry *Curls* and coy,
> Which with skill'd negligence seem'd shed
> About thy curious, wilde, yong head?
> Why is this rich, this *Pistic* Nard
> Spilt, and the box quite broke and marr'd?
> What pretty sullenness did hast
> Thy easie hands to do this waste?
> Why art thou humbled thus, and low
> As earth, thy lovely head dost bow?[79]

This is the Mary of John 20, but the introverted clairvoyance characteristic of Southwell's solitary weeper is replaced here with unapologetic display. Like Herrick's Julia, this woman's image is marked by a "skill'd negligence" as her hair falls, modestly covering that "much lov'd toy," her breasts. The broken pot and spilled precious oils have olfactory valence and become a focal point that enhances the Magdalene's disheveled contrition.

Vaughan tries to argue that there is nothing artful about this Magdalene. Artifice, he claims, belongs to the figure's profligate past. Freed from the snares of her own vanity, Mary is free to roam "native and pure" in the pretty pastures of Christian mercy:

> Dear, beauteous Saint! More white than day,
> When in his naked, pure array;
> Fresher then morning-flowers which shew
> As though in tears dost, best in dew.
> How art though chang'd! How lively fair,
> Pleasing and innocent an air
> Not tutor'd by thy glass, but free,
> Native and pure shines now in thee!

> But since thy beauty doth still keep
> Bloomy and fresh, why dost thou weep?

But there is more than a hint of artifice in the Magdalene's "pleasing and innocent air." Just as the phrase remarking on the saint's altered state cannot resist slipping "art" into the picture, so the rejected "glass" serves as a reminder of the tenacity of the *vanitas* trope.

There are a number of baroque visual treatments of the Magdalene that invite comparison to this poem. One possible example is Theodore Galle's engraving of the three Marys at the sepulcher (fig. 25). The image itself is conventional as is the text that glosses the subject. The inscription on the tomb (*tulerunt dominum meum*) and the subtext (*considerauit quod fecit, noluit moderari quid faceret*) point to the events at hand and to the Magdalene's appropriately woeful response. The most notable feature of this print is its border of flowers emanating from jars of holy oil. As Herrick describes Calvary, from an outside space as if looking in, the floral frame serves to remind the viewer of the artifice of the illustration it contains. It records something of the sensual experience of the image, how the oil might smell, how the dark, dank air of the tomb might feel, but it also declares, without apology, the unnatural aestheticized beauty of that experience. The frame also alludes to the pastoral motif that begins with the Song of Songs and later surfaces in Markham's references to Colin Clout at the end of *Marie Magdalens Lamentations*. In this chain of images, oil is linked to odors and odors to flowers, which transform the grim scene of the sepulcher into the garden of the resurrection.

Bound along with the Galle print into James II's personal Bible is another Magdalene print, by Martin de Vos, which situates the encounter between Mary and Christ in a meticulously cultivated knot garden (fig. 26). The print's presence in the royal Bible is a testament to the correspondence between Scripture and decorative art sustained by court enthusiasts after the Restoration, but it can also be found in the Little Gidding Royal Harmony where it evidently spoke to an earlier generation of connoisseurs. The image was first published in Gerard de Jode's *Thesaurus veteris et novi Testamenti*, a picture Bible published in Antwerp in 1579. Wells-Cole has shown that the Bible

S. MARIA MAGDALENA *consyderauit quod fecit, noluit moderari quid faceret.*
Theod. Galle excud.

FIGURE 25. Theodore Galle (1571–1633), plate bound into *The New Testament of our Lord and Savior Jesus Christ Newly Translated out of the Original Greek, and with the former Translations diligently Compared and Revised by his Majesties Special Command. Appointed to be read in Churches* (Cambridge, 1674). © The British Library Board. All Rights Reserved. C.7.d.18.

FIGURE 26. Martin de Vos, plate bound into *The New Testament of our Lord and Savior Jesus Christ Newly Translated out of the Original Greek, and with the former Translations diligently Compared and Revised by his Majesties Special Command. Appointed to be read in Churches* (Cambridge, 1674). © The British Library Board. All Rights Reserved. C.7d.18.

images were a popular source for decoration in England, and he provides examples of textile copies, wall paintings, and plasterwork indebted to de Vos's pictures.[80] One can see why the images were put to this use. They are exceedingly elegant works that present ample opportunities for viewers to luxuriate in the pleasures of sumptuous decorative detail. In the de Vos print, the garden—located just beyond and in relation to the city—is a purely aesthetic space artfully shaped to appeal to urbane tastes and stylish sensibilities. The significance of the fortunate encounter between Christ and Mary is registered in fine embellishments: the luxurious fall of the penitent's expensive clothing and the rippling muscles of Christ's well-appointed chest. If there is reference here to the Magdalene's privileged vision, it is registered in her aristocratic composure, a feature that recalls the figure's pre-conversion life of opulence. The human longing so poignant in van Dyck's freehand sketch (fig. 9) is lost beneath the refined complexity and infinite reproducibility of the printed engraving.

As Vaughan's poem progresses, the speaker is obliged to admit that there is, after all, art in the Magdalene's eyes. This "art of tears" or "art of love" is, however, good art that moves Mary's beholders to imitation and to a greater understanding of God:

> Learn *Marys* art of tears, and then
> Say, you have *got the day from men.*
> Cheap, might Art! her Art of love.
> Who lov'd much, and much more could move.

The next two stanzas, much more abrupt than the first, perform a common maneuver, shifting the ground from the subject of the Magdalene to the object of the poem by suggesting that this truly beautiful art works as a *lieu de mémoire* for the lost presence of Christ:

> Her Art! whose memory must last
> Till truth through all the world be past,
> Till his abus'd, despised flame
> Return to Heaven, from whence it came,
> And send a fire down, that shall bring
> Destruction on his ruddy wing.
>
> Her Art! whose pensive, weeping eyes,
> Were once sins loose and tempting spies
> But now are fixed stars, whose light
> Helps such dark straglers to their sight.

The topos is familiar: Mary is the image that recalls the idea. But the deliberate and repeated references to the penitent's "art" draw attention to the representational, aesthetic nature of the poem itself. As if in an attempt to regulate the degree of absorption in the image, the poem—like the floral borders of the Galle print—frames the artifice of the "bloomy and fresh" image it describes. If Vaughan's poem first displays the ekphrastic hope that the description of a lovely image will give permanent shape to an intangible experience that risks being forgotten, it also registers a concern that the reciprocity between the visual and the verbal can steer poetry away from "lively fair" art toward the manicured, stagy artifice, embodied by the de Vos print, that Mary is supposed to have left behind. Vaughan thus creates space between the Magdalene image and her beholders by confirming that the poem describes a picture but does not aspire to be one. The reader is indeed commanded, after Luke's *Ecce*, to behold the "beauteous Saint" as the speaker describes her artful contours. And yet a warning that pictures can also belie and beguile interrupts the reader's pleasure. It is as if the speaker is holding the reader back, or telling him to look away and to think for just a moment, in case the image becomes deceitful. The poem ends with the following stanza:

> Self-boasting *Pharisee!* How blinde
> A judge wert though, and how unkinde?
> It was impossible, that thou
> Who wert all false, should'st true grief know;
> Is't just to judge her faithful tears
> By that foul rheum thy false eye wears?
> *This Woman* (say'st thou) *is a sinner:*
> And sate there none such at thy dinner?
> Go Leper, Go; wash til thy flesh
> Comes like a childes, spotless and fresh,
> He is still leprous, that still paints:
> Who Saint themselves, they are no *Saints.*

As the perspective opens up and the garden scene expands, rather surprisingly, to include the Pharisee and his dinner guests, the pretext to the resurrection is abruptly reinstated, and attention is redirected from the elegance of the Magdalene's pastoral posture back to the book and to the moral of the story. The tenuous negotiation between the hope that the visual will capture that which words fail to constitute and the fear that imagistic embodiments will deceive is what makes this poem broach ekphrasis. Building on Herbert and others before him, Vaughan works out a formal interest in the Magdalene that negotiates controversy over visual representation of religious things by describing pictures in words. If submersion in the picture becomes altogether too real, then the words reassert the picture's artifice, reminding the readers that they are, in fact, reading an image that is far removed from the fragrant bouquets of the original scene.[81]

If Vaughan worries about the dangers of pictures, Crashaw does not—at least not in the same way. Much has been made of the poet's feminine imagery and of his Catholic sensibilities, and there is no poem that expresses these characteristics more than "The Weeper," first published in 1646 as the introductory poem to Crashaw's collection of sacred verse *Steps to the Temple*. If the Magdalene of the beginning of the century was read for her ability to trace an absent presence, then this one is read and re-read for her maudlin visuality.[82] Here infamous metaphors of feminine beauty are invoked to test the limits of the distinction between the sacred and the profane. Renowned and reviled for its obsession with liquid abjection, the poem invokes springs, snow, milk, dew, showers, fountains, baths, oceans, and other watery substances in praise of the Magdalene's tears. Crashaw's metaphoric extravagance is boundless, at one point notoriously describing the saint's tears as flowing upward where "Heavens bosome drinks the gentle stream." Despite its lavishness, however, the poem invigorates the Magdalene conceit as it resolves into a soothing portrait of alliterative contrition:

> Not in the Evenings Eyes
> When they red with weeping are,
>   For the Sun that dyes,
>   Sits sorrow with a face so faire.
> Nowhere but heere did ever meet
> Sweetnesse so sad, sadnes so sweet.

Crashaw's speaker's courtly pose—that of a lover before a half-naked, wholly desirable, and yet entirely unobtainable woman—recalls medieval Marian lyrics perplexed by the simultaneous veneration of the Virgin's youth and beauty and her maternal qualities. However, Crashaw's Magdalene does not materialize in the flesh, as does Southwell's weeper; nor does she appear as a phantasm as in Breton's poem. Crashaw does not recreate an absent presence or make something lost real again. Instead, his weeper represents, as Richard Rambuss elegantly argues, a culmination of the metaphysical style:

> In "The Weeper," Mary Magdalene's contrition is drained of its interior content—of the spiritual psychology of penance—and is stylized, as we have seen, in the form of a gushingly porous body. Indeed, the penitent herself is all but dissolved into a superflux of fluids, into an inconceivable hyperbole of liquefacient conceits, into oceans of penitential tears.[83]

Rambuss shows that the qualities for which Crashaw's verse is often assailed, "the opulence of his conceit-making; his indecorous commingling of disparate fields of reference or meaning; his extreme physical, often erotic renderings of spiritual states and events; the disconcerting mélange of affects that all this induces in even the most sympathetic reader," are all derived from a storehouse of tools and techniques available to the poets of the period. An incarnational Christianity that relies heavily upon embodied, physical moments like the one Luke asks his readers to "behold" demands, Rambuss concludes, "a metaphysical poetics for their rendering, for their entrance into representation, whether as text or image."[84]

Martz has suggested that while the metaphysical conceit "is based on the philosophical doctrine of correspondences" producing "the effect of truly exploring the nature of some metaphysical problem," the baroque conceit "views the same paradox or symbol from various angles, reviewing and revising and restating and expanding the issue until some truth of emotion gradually grows out from all that glittering elaboration." Another clear illustration of the process is found in Crashaw's other Magdalene poem, "The Teare," in which a single, gemlike drop is held, trembling, to the light, then softly placed in a jewel case ("A pillow for thee I will bring") so to be carried, like its maker, to heaven where it becomes a bright and shining star ("an eye of Heaven").[85] In the more intricate poem, "The Weeper," Crashaw moves in on Mary Magdalene herself and then withdraws, only to return from another angle or by means of a different metaphor or analogy. "It is not so much a poem," writes Martz, "as a series of experimental epigrams, testing how far a baroque conceit can be carried."[86] Peter Schwenger has similarly observed of "The Weeper" that the proliferation of metaphors for tears actually exposes the illusionism inherent in metaphoric expression. When metaphors multiply as they do in "The Weeper," "any claim of the individual metaphor to truth must be correspondingly weakened, and we are cast into a kind of relativistic view of the universe." This effect is compounded by the fact that the Magdalene story, much more present in "The Teare," fades into the background in "The Weeper" as the poem's formal poetic concerns overtake its narrative. The effect, Schwenger argues, is dazzling. While the metaphors themselves are unremarkable, "it is the multiplicity and movement" of the comparisons, "the reiterated sense of transition that creates a sense of the marvelous here."[87] These expressions of the dizzying effects of Crashaw's poetics are curiously evocative, from my perspective, of the overwhelming experience of sorting through baroque images of the saint: Mary comes dressed and meditative; undressed and rapturous; sitting in a library, posing before a mirror; or reclining in a grotto. The impact of these images is derived not so much from their individual artistry, or even from the stories the pictures tell, but from the profusion of possibilities, from the abundance of forms, from the sheer volume of postures.[88]

Crashaw's immediate counterpoints are the luxuriously penitent Magdalenes of Titian, Tintoretto, Correggio, and Rubens. By far the most flagrant example of the posture is Titian's painting (1531–35) in the Palazzo Pitti in Florence (fig. 27). The print progeny of this Magdalene was likely well known to English collectors. Cornelius Cort's copy is one commonly found example, and Martin Rota's later version also had many editions (fig. 28). Another contemporary example

FIGURE 27. Tiziano Vecellio, *Santa Maria Maddalenna* (c. 1530). Palazzo Pitti, Galleria Palatina, Florence. Photograph: Nimatallah/Art Resource, New York.

FIGURE 28. Martino Rota, *The Penitent Magdalene in the Desert* (16th century).
Fine Arts Museums of San Francisco, Achenbach Foundation for Graphic Arts.

is Hollar's 1646 engraving, possibly a copy of a work in an English collection (fig. 29).[89] The baroque features of "The Weeper" come then, at least in part, from its encounter with an image that had already been copied in both words and pictures many, many times. Indeed, Mario Praz, also remarking upon the epigrammatic quality of "The Weeper" denounces it as

> little more than a rosary of epigrams or madrigals clumsily linked together, without progression: the stanzas might be arranged in a different order (as indeed the poet arranged them in the various editions) and the poem be augmented indefinitely, or reduced (as it has been not improperly in many of the anthologies which have included it).[90]

I am reminded at this point of a passage in Southwell's preface to *Funeral Teares*, in which he explains that he has authorized the rather risky English publication of his work, because he feared that copies would fly "so fast, and so false abroad" that the text "was in danger to come corrupted to the print." It would be better, he writes, for his Magdalene to "flie to common viewe in the natiue plume . . . then disguised in a coate of a bastard feather, or a cast off from the fist of such a corrector, as might happily haue perished the sound, and imped in some sicke and sory fethers of his own phantasies."[91] Southwell makes the dangerous decision to pursue English publication because he is worried his work will be exploited wantonly; that it will move into markets beyond his control; and that it will be misread and abused. Is Crashaw, then, doing something similar? Is he taking up Luke's *Ecce* by attempting to gather the proliferation of "loos Pictures" in order to mediate and regulate their consumption?

In a move that James A. Heffernan describes as "Joseph Frank revisited or W. J. T. Mitchell anticipated," Krieger uses the term *ekphrasis* to describe poetic operations that capture "the frozen, stilled world of plastic relationships" and superimpose them upon literature's "turning world to 'still it.' "[92] Krieger's understanding of ekphrasis is suggestive, but his terms need to be reversed if they are

FIGURE 29. Wenceslaus Hollar, *The Penitent Magdalene* (1646). Fine Arts Museums of San Francisco, Achenbach Foundation for Graphic Arts.

to shed light on Crashaw's weeper. It is literature, this time super-imposed upon a dynamic proliferation of art, which, by the end of the poem, stills the eye and allows one to luxuriate in the beauty of holiness:

> Thus dost thou melt the yeare
> Into a weeping motion,
> Each minute waiteth heere;
> Takes his teare and gets him gone;
> By thine eyes tinct enobled thus
> Time layes him up: he's pretious.

Crashaw suspends the passage of time as the speaker hangs on the shape and movement of every tear. At this point the picture becomes as much an emblematic study of time and of memory as it is of shim-mering eyes and artful tears:

> Time as by thee he passes,
> Make thy ever-watry eyes
> His Hower-Glasses.
> By them his steps he rectifies.
> The sands he us'd no longer please,
> For his owne sands hee'l use thy seas.

The baroque images that clutter the content and the context of the poem recede from view as tears evaporate into the sands of an hour-glass. The well-established plasticity of the image dissipates and the Magdalene form becomes, more simply, a site of memory:

> Not, so long she liv'd,
> Will thy tombe report of thee
> But *so long she greiv'd*,
> Thus must we date thy memory.
> Others by Dayes, by Monthes, by Yeares
> Measure their Ages, Thou by Teares.

In these last stanzas, tears become nothing more than punctuation:

> Does thy song lull the Ayre?
> Thy teares just Cadence still keeps time.
> Does thy sweet breath'd *Prayer*
> Vp in the Clouds of Incense climbe?
> Stil at each sigh, that is each stop:
> A bead, that is a teare doth drop.

As drops turn into stops, even the picture disappears, leaving only the sound and cadence of poetry resonating in the ear. If "The Weeper" embodies an exchange between the tricky conventions of metaphysical poetry and the rich array of baroque images of Mary Magdalene, it may also reference the wanton proliferation of both, as the printing press assured that more and more Magdalenes, both visual and verbal, were put into circulation. In its attempt to slow everything down and to subject the image to the scrutiny of time and language, the poem acquires an element of the ekphrastic by asking the reader/viewer to stop looking and to listen. Crashaw uses the Magdalene, and the sound of her tears, to consider the borders between the verbal and the visual and to re-establish "firm distinctions between the senses, modes of representation, and the objects proper to each."[93]

However, an argument that speaks to the stillness of "The Weeper" works better for the first version of the poem than it does for the second (1652), which is decidedly different from the first. The revised poem is longer and the order of the final stanzas is different. Individual lines are altered, passages are removed, and new text is added, in most cases, to the middle of the poem.[94] The text of the second edition is also preceded by an image—a woman's face (eyes cast toward heaven) above a winged, flaming heart (fig. 30)—and an epigram:

> Loe where à WOVNDED HEART with Bleeding EYES conspire.
> Is she a FLAMING Fountain, or a Weeping fire!

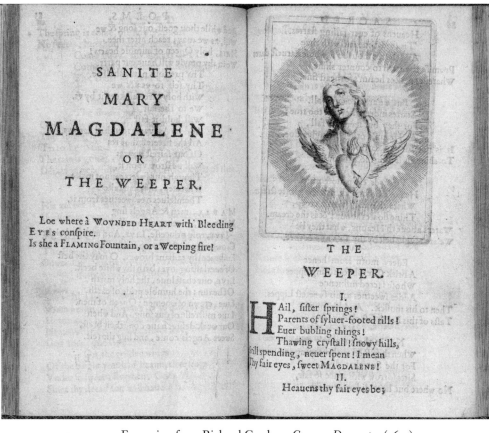

FIGURE 30.   Engraving from Richard Crashaw, *Carmen Deo nostro* (1652). By Permission of the Folger Shakespeare Library. C6830.

All of these revisions, as Paul Parrish has argued, serve to draw attention to the paradox of "weeping eyes and flaming heart, emanating as it does to both the sinner and the saviour."[95] However, while the alterations arguably lend the poem a new thematic coherence, they also shift aside the earlier edition's emblematic emphasis on time, dismantling in the process the stillness that characterizes the first ending. Particularly significant, in this respect, is the removal of stanza seventeen, the stanza that includes the hourglass that stills, at least to some degree, the poem's visual extravagance.[96] The inclusion of new thematic material, along with the addition of a picture, thus diminishes the tension, or self-conscious interplay, between the verbal and visual which characterizes the earlier version.

The second version of the poem appears in a collection of Crashaw's work, *Carmen Deo nostro*, posthumously published in Paris. The collection was compiled by Miles Pinkney (aka Thomas Carre), a Roman Catholic priest who frequented the exiled court of Queen Henrietta Maria and accompanied her back to England in 1660.[97] *Carmen Deo nostro* is a very different kind of book than *Steps to the Temple*.[98] It is dedicated to Susan Fielding (née Villiers, d. 1652), Countess of Denbigh, sister to George Villiers, Duke of Buckingham, Mistress of the Robes to the queen, a good friend of Crashaw, and a potential convert to Catholicism.[99] If Carre's prefatory "Epigramme" is credible, the printed volume was based upon a manuscript that Crashaw gave to the countess while in Paris, attending the court of the exiled queen. The manuscript included a number of engravings, also featuring flaming hearts, conceived and rendered by Crashaw himself. These images were preserved in Carre's printed edition:

Vpon the pictures in the following Poemes
Which the author first made with his owne hand, admirably
well, as may be seen in his Manuscript dedicated to the
right Honorable Lady the L. Denbigh.
Twixt pen and pensill rose a holy strife
Which might draw virtue better to the life.
Best witts gaue votes to that: but painters swore
They neuer saw peeces so sweete before
As thes: fruites of pur nature; where no art
Did lead the vntaught pensill, nor had part in th'worke.
The hand growne bold, with witt will needes contest.
Doth it preuayle? ah wo: say each is best.
This to the eare speakes wonders; that will trye
To speake the same, yet lowder, to the eye.
Both their aymes are holy, both conspire
To wound, to burne the hart with heaunly fire.
This then's the Doome, to doe both parties right:
This, to the eare speakes best; that to the sight.[100]

Carre's epigraph supports Parrish's argument that the revisions to "The Weeper" were intended to consolidate the poem's investment in the flaming heart image. Moreover, the suggestion that Crashaw's pencil effectively works in tandem with his pen to impress, by means of words and pictures, the image of Christ upon his reader's ears and eyes is remarkably in keeping with earlier English Catholic iterations of the Magdalene impression (Southwell and Markham after the pseudo-Origenist homily). However, if the second poem is something less, or at least something other, than a verbal representation of a graphic thing, it is because it strives to erase the tension between words and pictures established in the first version.

Ekphrasis, at its most basic, requires language that exceeds the pictorial or the imagistic by drawing attention to a form of representation, beyond the text, that is not linguistic. In Vaughan's poem, the ekphrastic qualities emerge from the fear that the reader will become too immersed in the visual field. The reader is asked to withdraw from the imaginary scene invoked by words and to look at the poem as one looks at a painting—from a distance and in two dimensions. In the 1646 version of "The Weeper," the reader is obliged to step back from a whirling mass of prints and pictures in order to listen to poetry. In *Carmen Deo nostro*, however, the verbal and the visual arts are equalized upon the surface of a manuscript that is invoked but is no longer present. Carre's publication captures the aura of Crashaw's manuscript gift to the Countess of Denbigh in a printed book, and in so doing he places a collectible rarity within the reach of more ordinary collectors and iconophiles. Less a consideration of art than a reproduction of art, the meaning of the second edition of "The Weeper" lies not in its contribution to the development of a visual poetics, but in the importance it holds for its readers as a printed text—an object of admiration and ultimately of desire.

"And Justly Take up an Ecce*"*

One last Magdalene text, William Hodson's meditation *The Holy Sinner,* published in London in 1639, neatly summarizes the productive tension between word and image that has been the subject of this chapter. Hodson makes what are by now familiar statements on the unreliability of human vision as it is made possible by the eyes. He writes that sight is "the vainest of all the senses; it takes extreme delight to be coozened; one of the pleasures of the eye is the deceit of it." It is only once his subject's eyes "sufficiently testified her godly sorrow" that she can be considered at all saintlike.[101] Mary's blindness is conventionally glossed in Hodson as indicative of her desire to search for holiness in material things. Only when Christ speaks her name, thereby driving her gaze inward, does she in fact "see" him with any degree of clarity. Here again, the Magdalene's method for seeing holy things involves the turn to memory and spiritual interiority. What is intriguing about Hodson's work, however, is the way in which he chooses to frame the Magdalene for the reader's gaze. Despite her reformed—and apparently Protestant—condition, she remains an object of *visual* scrutiny. Hodson writes:

> Have you not seen some artificiall pictures drawn by the pencill of a skilfull optick, in the same part of the frame or table, according to divers sights and aspects, represent divers things? Such an admirable piece with a double resemblance hath Saint Luke (an excellent limner, as the ancients write) here delineated in the most lively colours. Look on the one side, you shall see a lascivious wanton setting her self to sale in the most tempting fashion; step on the other side, you may behold an admirable convert attended by a retinue of graces.[102]

The passage alludes to the figurative painting that reads differently depending upon the perspective of the beholder: the most famous example of the technique is Hans Holbein's *The Ambassadors* (1533).[103] The use of the term *limner*—illuminator, painter, illustrator—may gesture toward the imagistic style of Luke's text, or it may actually suggest that Luke is a painter, the Gospel a painting, and Hodson's own work a print copied after the work of the greater master. If Luke is the master, then Hodson promises that he will be the engraver; he will "imitate the most curious gravers" who look "upon green flies to recollect their scattered sight again," and he will fix his "eyes through the glasse of contemplation on the picture of this penitent woman."[104] Hodson's responsibility, in other words, is to reproduce or copy the figure of the Magdalene, as Luke has painted her. Lewalski writes that the Bible afforded a "literary model" for Protestant poets who could imitate its genre, language, and symbolism, "confident that in this model at least the difficult problems of art and truth are perfectly resolved."[105] Hodson suggests that one of the literary models on offer is visual in impact. If Luke asks his readers to behold a scene as he paints it, it becomes the imperative of latter-day poets to copy this scene, as an engraver does, in order to assure that others with less privileged access to the original have immediate and material contact with its content. "To see a convert come home to God," concludes Hodson, "is both happy and wonderous to men and angels."[106]

Hodson's figurative mode is neatly anticipated by the image that precedes the frontispiece to his text (fig. 31). The print is a rather rough illustration of Luke 7, accompanied by a Latin title and English caption. The title, "Despicit at coelum sic tamen Illa videt," and the caption,

> Upon the ground this Weeper casts her eyes
> So cunningly that Heaven she there espies:
> No word she spake, yet granted was her sute,
> Her tears were Vocall, though her tongue was mute,

essentially say the same thing. The reader is told to acknowledge the Magdalene's silent meditation and to recognize that her eyes look inward and thus toward heavenly rather than earthly matters. This is the Magdalene to which Andrewes alludes. And yet simultaneously the image obliges the reader to acknowledge the picture on the page as if it provides the only route to the interiorized meditation that the passage advocates. In order to see what the subject sees, we must first see her graven image. Hodson worries, like many of his time, that "the eye is the first part that is over come in any battel; upon the first assault it yeelds up our strongest fort," and yet he is prepared to risk "the

FIGURE 31. William Marshall, frontispiece from William Hodson, *The Holy sinner, a tractate on some passages of the storie of the penitent woman in the Pharisees house* (London, 1639). © The British Library Board. All Rights Reserved. RB.23.a.9369.

pleasures of the eye" and justly "take up an *Ecce*" because only then will the reader see what it means to be touched by Christ.[107]

Hodson's awareness of the risk involved in positioning the Magdalene at the center of the image-word debate proves to be quite prescient as, over the course of the next two decades, it becomes more and more difficult to distinguish devout executions of Luke from fashionable renderings that appeal to the eye of the connoisseur. As Counter-Reformation aesthetics become of greater interest to patrons and collectors, the distinctions between devotional art and secular art on religious subjects become more difficult to discern. What is evident, however, is that treatments of the Magdalene, visual and verbal, participate in the formulation of a Counter-Reformation aesthetic or style that produces a taste for religious art, particularly in printed form.

In the body of his work, Hodson makes reference to a contemporary Latin epigram by Jacobus Zevecotius (1596–1642), "De lacrymis Madalenae." Of this poem, Hodson says: "I will therefore take her picture as it is exquisitely drawn by him, and set it in my own frame; I will be bold to borrow some characters from his presse, the better to imprint them in my own and my readers memorie."[108] Hodson confirms yet again that the making of the Magdalene and the making of prints are imaginatively linked activities. Together, the two forces constitute a poetics of portraiture that seems to forge a kind of imaginative community. Writers borrow and elaborate upon each other, they write to and for each other, in stylish games of wit that often prevail over religious matters. Nowhere is this more evident than at the end of Hodson's book, where there appears a collection of clever epigrams praising not Mary Magdalene but Hodson's ingenious rendition of her. William Moffat of Canterbury, for instance, writes:

> The Jeweller that made her, knew her worth,
> And told thee, when first he sent it forth
> Into thy heart inspir'd; and thou hast took
> This precious gemme, and put it in a book,
> In leaves of gold; so that each eye may gaze
> At that, which did the God of heaven amaze.

Simon Jackman of Oxford contributes:

> Let your bold critick judge, condemn, repreue,
> Or what he will; thy Magdalene must live:
> Christ did foretell it should be so, and we
> Find it exactly now perform'd by thee.

Referring specifically to the engraving at the beginning of the book, Jackman remarks that Hodson's Magdalene is both pleasing to "the understanding and the sight," while Reuban Bourn, also of Canterbury, writes:

> This thou
> Hast drawn from sacred beams of holy writ,
> Which though no specious glosse can better it,
> Yet thou euen to those glorious lamps so bright
> Hast added lustre, whence thou borrowedst light.

Thomas Draper calls Hodson's work "rare Alchymie," and William Wimpew argues that "to the last sand of time shall live her glory, / while such an herald doth display her story." And finally, superlatively, John Wimpew, once again of Canterbury, writes:

> A Sinner turn'd a saint! what change is this?
> 'Tis none of Ovid's Metamorphosis:
> No, 'tis a sacred Sinner, who thinks meet
> By thee to do her penance in a sheet.
> Now is she bound for heaven, and by thy dresse
> Thou mak'st her well deserve both praise and press.[109]

In displays of *sprezzatura* that thoroughly elide the political and theological controversies that lie at the core of the Magdalene story, these tributes both recognize and strive for a kind of grace that is more reminiscent of Castiglione than of Gregory or Calvin. For these Magdalene critics (most of them signing *in artibus magister*), the ideal, artful dressing of the saint necessitates the alchemical transformation of the figure's scriptural messiness into a perfectly precise print. As the engraver needs to distill the nuance of a painter's brushstrokes into the simplicity of etched lines, so the poet must discern and articulate the Magdalene's most salient features, first rendered by that master limner, Luke. The figure of the Magdalene, as Hodson's reference to print reminds us, is infinitely reproducible, and that is part of her new appeal. She is now a collectable subject for the age of art wherein the value of any given manifestation lies in skillful reiteration rather than in controversial investment in affective immediacy or presence.

FIVE

She's a Nice Piece of Work

This posture's loose and negligent,

The sight on't would beget a warm desire

In souls whom impotence and age had chilled.

—Aphra Behn, *The Rover* (2.1.211–13)

In 2.2 of Aphra Behn's play *The Rover*, three portraits, one large and two smaller, of the famous courtesan Angellica Bianca are mounted against her balcony facing the public piazza. The portraits immediately draw the attention of prospective clients who comment upon Angellica's extraordinary beauty and, with great regret, her exorbitant price. Angellica herself briefly appears upon the balcony, provoking comparison between the original and its painted representations. Willmore, Royalist exile, English Cavalier, and the rakish hero of the play, removes one of the images, thereby incurring the wrath of Angellica, who chastises him for his insolence. Willmore responds by accusing her of setting the image "to tempt poor amorous mortals with so much excellence[,] which I find you have but too well consulted by the unmerciful price you have set upon't."[1]

The portrait scene has been the subject of considerable critical commentary. Most importantly, Elin Diamond has argued that

> Angellica's portraits represent the courtesan in the most radical sense. They both produce an image of her and reduce her to that image. Notwithstanding her passionate addresses, Angellica cannot exceed her simulacra. When Willmore gestically appropriates the courtesan's painted image, he makes visible the patriarchal and homosocial economy that controls the apparatus as well as the commodity status of the paintings, their model, the painted actress and the painted Scenes.[2]

There is no question that Angellica's representation in the painting does, in fact, establish the courtesan as an art object to be looked upon, to be coveted, and ultimately to be collected. This chapter, however, will attempt to dislodge the portraits from their complicity in what Diamond calls the "patriarchal and homosocial economy" of the Restoration, in order to reconsider them as central to the play's critical investigation of the Magdalene iconographic tradition as reconfigured in poetry and art after 1660.[3] When viewed in this context, Behn's use of the portraits becomes not so much a critique of a culture that habitually looks at women as rarefied *objets d'art,* than a complex investigation of the politics of looking in a culture in which the Magdalene image had become separated from the evangelical task assigned to it by Matthew 26:13. No longer bound to the preaching of the Word and no longer tied to imaginative attempts to convey an idea of Christ's presence, literary and visual representations of Mary Magdalene become, by the end of the seventeenth century, ironic iterations of medieval iconography. For the most part, Restoration Magdalenes, divested of their legitimacy, nod their heads in mock piety, lifting a tearful eye in coy acknowledgment of their enraptured beholders. Their hands reach for their hearts, not to point to the image of Christ lying therein, but to reveal a hint of a nipple framed in the exquisite folds of rich fabrics tailored into the latest fashions.

The genealogy of the Magdalene's Restoration decadence can be traced to her medieval past and to the legendary apparatus that denotes her lineage as aristocratic and her youth as profligate. The first of these attributes also surfaced in post-Reformation treatments in which the saint was refigured as a pious patron; the examples of the countesses of Pembroke and Cumberland are most notable. The previous chapter explored the entrance of the Magdalene into the splendid consumer culture of the pre–Civil War period by showing how the image appealed to a generation of collectors who had learned to appreciate, in her, the beauty of holiness. In this period, religious art continued to be of interest to a culture both enthralled and vexed by clever executions of the Magdalene's radiant contrition. However, the post–Civil War Magdalene is considerably less rarified than the earlier manifestations. Copies of the image, both literary and visual, circulated more liberally, and in these later treatments the taint of the figure's profligate past is reinvigorated and superimposed upon an artful and more or less artificial penance shaped to appeal to the discriminating tastes of the pleasure-seeking Cavalier. And yet even in this context, certain iterations of the figure, Behn's amongst them, serve as sites of memory whereupon the vestigial contours of the saint's scriptural persona are traced. As was the case in chapter 1, this chapter keeps one text, *The Rover*, at its center, digressing only occasionally to explore other works set in play by Behn's narrative. I argue that the portraits in *The Rover* avail themselves of "a tenuous, intangible, almost ineffable bond" with a discarded image, and that they are evidence of what remains of an "inexpugnable, intimate attachment" to a faded, almost forgotten symbol that modeled a way of seeing both the Word and the world.[4]

The Rover *and Restoration Portraiture*

No absolute conclusions can be drawn upon the style and manner of the portraits in act 2 of *The Rover*. However, as he removes the smallest of the three images, Willmore speaks the ekphrastic words that form the epigraph to this chapter:

This posture's loose and negligent,
The sight on't would beget a warm desire
In souls whom impotence and age had chilled.
This must along with me.

(2.1.211–14)

Behn provides no further description of the portraits, but Willmore's comment allows one to conclude that the sitter appears *en chemise* or in loose undergarments as was common in the contemporary court portraiture of van Dyck, Lely, and Sir Godfrey Kneller. The most celebrated examples of this painting tradition are the "Windsor Beauties," a series of portraits of the ladies of the court of Charles II (including several of his mistresses) commissioned of Lely by Anne Hyde, the eldest daughter of Edward Hyde, Earl of Clarendon, and wife of James, the Duke of York.[5] These pictures display what Anne Hollander has described as a "masculine spirit of easy disdain" that reflects an "aggressive *déshabillé*" that reads as "less erotic than aristocratic—or, rather, erotic *because* aristocratic, that is, a little depraved and more than a little contemptuous."[6]

Though not of the "Windsor Beauties" series, Lely's portrait of Barbara Villiers, Countess of Castlemaine (c. 1662; fig. 32) is a typical example of Lely's work in its illustration of *leggiadria* and of *grazia*, or the effortless grace of the sitter.[7] In keeping with Lely's style is the appropriately ostentatious background and the billowing fabric that drapes Villiers's body. These qualities connote a careless romance or informality suggestive of privilege and status, while the unstructured form of the dress itself draws attention to the body beneath. The face is representative of an English type or portrait aesthetic: the heavy brows and hooded, almond-shaped eyes, which were allegedly based on Villiers's own features but which came to stand for Lely's personal construction of beauty—"a transaction between artist, specific sitter and a reinterpretation of earlier conventions."[8] However, as Diana Dethloff observes, while Lely and his contemporaries were working in a continuing visual tradition, their pictures were being read differently, to a purpose much less invested in convention than in the pleasures of the moment:

FIGURE 32. Sir Peter Lely, *Barbara Villiers, Countess of Castlemaine* (1662). Knole, The Sackville Collection (The National Trust). Photograph: Photographic Survey, Courtauld Institute of Art, London.

The underlying principles of Neoplatonism, which had idealized physical beauty as an index of spiritual qualities, had permeated life in the Italian courts and that of Charles I, where they had strongly affected early Caroline literature and drama and influenced the way women were treated and perceived. There it had been the Queen, Henrietta Maria, who set the standard. In its atmosphere of cynicism, skepticism and sexual freedom, the court of Charles II was very different. Here the role models were the King's mistresses, whose outward beauty was unlikely to have suggested a corresponding inner virtue; and Neoplatonism was relegated to ridicule by the libertine poets.[9]

Portraits like Lely's, of the Countess of Castlemaine, or those of Angellica Bianca, were on display in the public spaces of the palace or marketplace, and, as Dethloff concludes, "learned and unlearned alike appear to have focused more openly on sensual appeal for its own sake. . . . The anticipated pleasure of hair brushing against soft skin, of fabrics concealing/revealing the body beneath, and the desire to possess the woman herself through her portrait" were of immediate consequence as pious postures acquired an aura of disheveled decadence.[10] Samuel Pepys suggests as much in a diary entry for 8 March 1666:

> After dinner I took coach and away to Hale's, where my wife is sitting; and endeed, her face and neck which are now finished, do so please me, that I am not myself almost, nor was not all the night after, in writing of my letters, in consideration of the fine picture that I shall be maister of.[11]

The execution of the portraits and the artistic lineage they commemorate are overlooked in readings like this one as images of royal courtesans are seen as soliciting desire through a polished display of both availability and scornful exclusivity that can, as Behn puts it, "tempt poor amorous mortals with so much excellence" (2.2.2–3). The Comte de Gramont, in yet another instance of this kind, found his "tender feelings" for one of Lely's sitters, Elizabeth Hamilton, particularly agitated when the Duke of York became so mesmerized by her painting that he began "ogling the original."[12] The distinction between painted likeness and living presence is one that becomes, under these circumstances, increasingly difficult to make.

Within this particular painting tradition, the iconographic model that most firmly associates aristocracy with illicit sexuality was, without question, Mary Magdalene, whose past—her noble birth and sexual profligacy—made her an ironically suitable patroness for elite courtesans.[13] Lely painted at least one obvious tribute to the subject (fig. 33). However, Julia Marciari Alexander suggests Lely's Countess of Castlemaine (fig. 32) is almost certainly a Magdalene-inspired image as well—one that makes specific reference to Guido Reni's *The Penitent Magdalen*, one of the most famous images of the Magdalene in circulation in Europe in painted and print forms. Through its allusions to the Magdalene, Alexander argues, "Lely's portrait implied a flattering link between Barbara Villiers and the king, positing him as Christ to her Mary."[14] There are other Restoration Magdalene portraits to turn to as well: Lely's portrait of Mary Banks, *Lady Jenkinson* (1660), features the sitter with a jar of oil; and Kneller painted several ladies of the English court *à la Madeleine*, including a portrait of Elizabeth Villiers, Countess of Orkney, which is specifically after Titian (fig. 34, fig. 5). Much less restrained is Lely's portrait of another royal mistress, Louise de Kéröualle, Duchess of Portsmouth, painted as the Magdalene reclining in her grotto (fig. 35).

These pictures are not exactly cynical, nor do they question the sitters' morals or fashion them as the trashy products of court decadence. Rather, they capture an "aesthetic of pleasure" shaped "by earlier ideas of femininity and beauty, and underscored by appropriate attributes and allegorical disguises." These portraits are fully secularized examples of a continuing visual tradition of Magdalene iconography; they are examples of the enduring appeal of the image as "handed down from Renaissance Italy through van Dyck's work and tempered by Lely's particular style and interests."[15] A similar use of the Magdalene can be observed in contemporary literature in which

FIGURE 33. Sir Peter Lely, *The Penitent Magdalen*. Kingston Lacy, The Bankes Collection (The National Trust). Photograph: Photographic Survey, Courtauld Institute of Art, London.

FIGURE 34. Sir Godfrey Kneller, *Elizabeth Villiers, Countess of Orkney* (1698). Marston Hall, Grantham. Photograph: The National Portrait Gallery, London.

FIGURE 35. Sir Peter Lely, *Louise de Kéröualle, Duchess of Portsmouth, as Mary Magdalene* (c. 1670). Catalogue of the Rosenthal Sale (Colville-Hyde Collection). Sotheby's, London. Photograph: Photographic Survey, Courtauld Institute of Art, London.

the patterning of an aristocratic life after the Gospel penitent was, by this point, a well-established practice. A rather stunning example is to be found in a sermon preached by George Ashe in 1693/4 at Trinity College, University of Dublin. The text is a justification of the importance of university education—a response to the criticism that instruction fosters atheism—which provides occasion for reflection upon the founder of the university, Queen Elizabeth:

A Princess the most eminent for Piety, Learning, Chastity, and Happy Government that ever blessed these Kingdoms, having enlightened our neighbouring Nation with the brightnes of the Reformation and fenc'd it in by Laws and just Authority against all the open force and secret contrivances of Popery or Schism; took into Her Royal Thoughts also the care and concerns of our poor Island, almost quite over-run with Barbarity and Superstition, and as the most effectual means to polish the one and reform the other, Founded this Seminary . . . whence true Religion, and Virtue, sound Learning and ingenious Education, might always spring up and issue forth to Plant and Cultivate the rest of the Land. She *pour'd this Box of Pretious Ointment upon the Head* or Capital of our Kingdom, whence it might stream or descend to the most distant parts, and refresh the whole with its excellent *savour;* She laid in here such lasting Supplies of Piety and Literature, which like *Ointment,* might smooth the natural roughness of our Temper, supple our morosest Passions, make us of a cheerful Countenance, render us active & fit for any Employment to which Church or State should call us; . . . we and all who are benefitted by this Auspicious Foundation, must ever gratefully join with our Blessed Saviour in my Text, *Verily we say unto you, wheresoever the Gospel* (whose Holy Doctrine we have here suck'd in, and to the understanding and declaring of which we have been here train'd up and educated) *shall be preach'd* by any of us *in the whole world, there also this, that this Woman has done* for us, *shall be told as a memorial of her.*[16]

The memory of the Magdalene invokes, in this instance, the memory of a glorious humanist as the body of the nation replaces Christ's body and Mary's oil becomes the soothing balm that turns mercenary profiteers into stalwart citizens. While the text does suggest how secular, how disassociated from Scripture and from the discussion of Christ's enduring presence, the image had become, the Magdalene is, nevertheless, positioned "against all the open force and secret contrivances of Popery or Schism." By polishing barbarity and reforming superstition, she is marshaled in the service of English civility.

William Perse, preaching in 1669 on Matthew 26:13, provides another relevant literary portrait upon the occasion of the death of Mary of Modena (1669). Perse requests his readers' patience as he presents "a small free-will offering of the Sweetest Oyle I can pour out of my shallow and narrow Cruse, mixed with a few graines of Frankincense for a memoriall of another *Mary*, our late most gracious Queen, now of Glorious, and happy memory."[17] As does Ashe, Perse extols his subject in the terms of Christ's praise of the Magdalene: fervent love, true devotion, and great charity. However, the comparison seems to derail slightly when, in the privacy of her chamber, the thoughts of this noble wife stray from Christ to her absent husband:

> In her own retir'd apartment she could pay her homage to the King of Kings, to her Saviour, to her Redeemer: Here it was that she so often mourned like a disconsolate Turtle the Absence of her deare Consort whilst he was exposing himselfe to all the hazards of warr, to all perills both at sea and Land for our sakes; Here she put up her constant, and ardant prayers, where she Sent up her most fervent Wishes for his safety, his success, and his happy Return.[18]

As with the tributes of Breton, Lanyer, and Donne, both of these sermons are in keeping with the 1549 Book of Common Prayer in its anticipation of a healthy lineage of well-dressed and properly pious Magdalenes whose memories would be "patterns" for English gentlewomen. But the too easy slippage from the sacred to the secular witnessed in these later texts suggests the topos was, like the English paintings on the subject, becoming divested of spiritual content. What is remarkable about these latter-day lady-Magdalenes is just how worldly they had become.[19]

The resonances of the piazza paintings in *The Rover* are, nevertheless, deeper than their links to real-life court mistresses and to secularized, aestheticized treatments of Luke's sinner. The reference to the Italian baroque tradition, though not explicit in Behn's play, is clearly present in Thomas Killigrew's play *Thomaso*, upon which Behn based much of *The Rover* and from which she explicitly borrowed the character and treatment of Angellica Bianca. Killigrew has one of his rakes identify the painter of Angellica's image as van Dyck ("a great Master, and a Civil Pencil"), remarking further that the sitter's smile has "a grace and sweetness in it Titian could never have catch'd."[20] The reference to van Dyck in concert with Titian is important. Van Dyck had been the court painter for Charles I and Henrietta Maria, and Killigrew's reference to him is a reminder of the long-standing tradition of Stuart patronage of the visual arts. Moreover, it is not inconsequential that Behn alters the location of *The Rover* from Spain, in Killigrew's play, to Venice. Italy was the ultimate destination for the Grand Tourist–turned–art collector, the prototype of which was the English Catholic or, during the Commonwealth period, the Royalist patron in exile.[21]

Over the course of the Civil War, many of the great collections, including that of Charles I, were dispersed, and the individual works went on to enrich the collections of France, Spain, and imperial Russia.[22] But the Restoration of the monarchy brought with it a return to art collecting, and Charles II, upon the advice of his courtiers and significantly his Catholic wife and mistresses, brought many of Europe's finest painters to London. In his early years in England, Lely was mentored by van Dyck and was the natural successor to the post of principal painter to which he was appointed in 1661. Angellica's piazza paintings, in correlation with the specifically pro-Royalist politics of *The Rover*, do, I think, make reference to this newly invigorated tradition of court portraiture. Moreover, the paintings that invoke the Magdalene image serve as a return to the rich visual culture of the time of Charles I—a return to Italy and thus a return to baroque art. *The Rover* portraits therefore constitute an attempt to pay homage, as do the "Windsor Beauties," to English court patronage of the visual arts and, by way of van Dyck, to Titian and to Italian Renaissance art. The Royalist Cavaliers are here presented as indulging in the liberties offered by Italian Carnival and also as reveling in the cultural distinction afforded by the consumption of Continental art. Angellica Bianca is, incidentally, the only Italian character in the play despite its Venetian setting.

One could point out that Behn, like the allegedly secular court painters, gets away with the invocation of the Magdalene by assuring that her sitter is stripped of the sacred iconography that typifies Renaissance Magdalenes. In other words, in *The Rover* the holy connotations of the Counter-Reformation models are abandoned in favor of a rich sensuality that exoticizes Catholic motif. But then if this is so, the portraits risk invoking the specter of anti-Catholicism and the public distrust of Catholic court ladies emulating Henrietta Maria—a "popish brat" who always got her own way.[23] Moreover, it is well known that Protestant and parliamentarian satirists made the connection between aristocratic fine taste and pornography crystal clear in their attacks upon the decadence, sexual profligacy, and thus the Catholicism of the court of Charles II. As Rachel Weil has argued, "It was largely through narratives of sexual excess that satirists were able to establish an identity between absolutism and Catholicism. . . . A debauched king was, potentially, a Catholic king, and Charles's embrace of his Catholic whores—the countess of Castlemaine, the duchess of Portsmouth and the duchess of Mazarin—ominously pointed to his embrace of the Whore of Rome."[24] Precisely because of the currency of these contemporary associations, any image that risked debasement to the pornographic would be dangerous in a play attempting to link cultural distinction and high art to libertine court values.

In literature at least, the Magdalene had become an easy model for political lampooning of the sort that Weil describes. Richard Brathwaite, in his satire of the court of Charles II, *The chimney's scuffle*, provides a fit illustration:

> Clear that *Augean Stable;* Let no strain
> Darken the Splendor of our *Charlemain,*
> Nor his *court-gait:* May th' *Ladies* of this time
> Be Aemulators of our *Katherine*
> Late come, long wish'd: whose Princely fame shall be
> A living Annal to posteritie.
> To whose pure judgement, then which none more *strong*
> Being *Stranger* to the *world* and so *Young*
> Nought can detract more from a knowing Nation
> Then making a meer *Idol* of a *Fashion;*
> Or in resemblance unto *His Asse*

To sacrifice the *Morning* to their *Glasse:*
Such *atoms of lost honour* SHE esteems
For wandring Fancies or Phanatick Dreams:
"This *Royal Pattern* may, no doubt, re-gain
Our *Albyon* Halcyon days and *Saturns*-Raign.
The World's new-moulded: —SHE who t'other day
Could Chant and Chirp like any Bird in *May*,
Stor'd with *Caresses* of the Choicest sort
That Art could purchase from a Forreign Court,
Limn'd so by Natures Pencil, as no part
But gave a wound, where e'r it found an heart.
"A Fortresse and Main-Castle of Defence
"Secur'd from all *Assailants* saving *Sence*.
But SHE's a *Convert* and a *Mirrour* now
Both in her *Carriage* and *Profession* too;
Divorc'd from Strange Embraces: as my Pen
May justly style Her *Englands Magdalen*.
Wherein She's to be held of more esteem
In being fam'd a *Convert* of the *Queen*.
And so from relapse that She secure'd might be
SHE *wisely* deigns to keep her Companie.[25]

The Katherine in question is Catherine of Braganza, the Portuguese infanta wed to the king in 1662, the year the satire was published. This "royal pattern" is praised for her modest style and reasonable judgment, as well as for the decorum and sobriety she brings to the English court. The world is apparently "new-moulded" after her for the other "She," the king's mistress, the Countess of Castlemaine, is allegedly transformed by the new queen's presence. Castlemaine is here described as the king's "Main-Castle," restyled "England's Magdalene" converted, as it were, by the arrival of the pious new queen. Brathwaite's tongue is, no doubt, planted firmly in cheek as Catherine would never be able to challenge Castlemaine's favor, and by the following year, the countess was appointed lady to the queen's bedchamber. While the marriage lasted all of Charles's life, it was the countess's taste for foreign art (and artifice) that had the greatest influence over court culture, and it was the countess's patronage that drew prestigious artists, like Lely, to England. The passage, therefore, sets up precisely the kind of atmosphere that I see operating in *The Rover*, wherein the "art" of the Magdalene ("the Choicest sort / . . . purchase[d] from a Forreign Court, / Limn'd so by Natures Pencil") now fully divorced from its holiness, becomes a satiric model for a courtly aesthetic that defined the sumptuous lifestyle of pleasure-seeking aristocrats.

Another example of the degree to which representations of the Magdalene become at this point a vehicle for sensational social commentary is provided by Thomas Robinson's peculiar epic, *The soules pilgrimage to heavenly Hierusalem. In three severall dayes journeyes, by three severall wayes: purgative, illuminative, unitive. Expressed in the life and death of saint Mary Magdalen.* A manuscript version of this text was discussed in chapter 1, but the poem acquired a new life when it was revised and published anonymously in 1650. The Magdalene psycho-machia plot, first observed in the Digby play and then reformed by Wager in *The Life and Repentaunce*, becomes, in this later iteration, an allegorical reflection of midcentury aristocratic decadence. As noted earlier, the Magdalene is first discovered as a courtier in the palace of Aphrodite:

> Among the wanton traine of Luxurie,
> That to her Palaces themselves addrest:
> One was more beautifull unto the eye,
> More faire, more delicate, then all the rest
> In colour, and just symmetry so blest,
>   That were she but with softer sleepe allaid
>   Of Virgins waxe you would suppose her made,
> A Damsel faire without, but inwardly decaid.[26]

The heroine's sinfulness lies in the fact that her "colour" is truer and her "symmetry" more just. She looks like an icon carved from the purest wax. Like the delicate denizens of English high society, this Magdalene is nothing but art. The 1650 printing, however, does substantially depart from the original. The following stanza, for instance—a continuation of the standard Magdalene blazon—is not in the later published text:

> Next her *debared* brests *bewitch mine* eyes,
> And with a Lethargy *my* sight appall;
> But *by and by the selfe-wild heauy spies*
> *Vnto y^e* centre of her nauell fall,
> From whence they starte, awaked at the call
>   Of her *depurpur'd* things, heere at a stand.[27]

Also missing is the manuscript's extraordinary description of Mary's encounter with Christ, a scene that takes the pastoral imagery first used to depict Mary's prurient bower of bliss and reconfigures it in the holy tradition of the Song of Songs to create the poetic equivalent of the more florid engravings of the buff half-naked gardener and his kneeling mistress:

> Wonder it is, y^t this accursed crue
> Should knowe ye Sauiour, whom but few could knowe;
> Sure, they obseru'd his white and ruddy hue,
> That made him cheefest of 10 thousand showe,
> His lockes as blacke as rauen, and ye snowe
>   Of his faire Doue-like eyes. His cheekes beneath
>   Bedight with flowers, like beds of Spices breath;
> His lily lippes, pure myrrhe vnto his spouse bequeath.
>
> His hands, gould ringes beset with Chrysolite;
> His mouth, with sweetnesse fraught, and odours newe;
> His belly vnder, like ye Iu'ry white,
> All interchast with veins of Sappheirs blewe:
> His pleasant countenance like Hermons dewe,
>   His leggs and feete, like marble pillers rare
>   On goulden sockets, yet by farre more faire:
> His vestures, with y^r Casia perfum'd ye aire.[28]

The aestheticized sensuality of Mary's encounter with Christ the gardener is still a feature of the 1650 text, but here the emphasis falls on politics rather than the scene's pleasing pastoral encounter. The larger-than-life, fantasy quality of the manuscript is subsumed in social commentary on the dire state of the nation as Mary Magdalene's journey through hell to repentance is reconfigured in English allegory. The murky underworld in this interregnum configuration is populated by the likes of Harry Hotspur and "Richard Crookback":

> Is't not a Bedlam, or the lowest Hell?
> Where murther, contumely, clamour, braule,
> Blasphemy, hate, and threats together dwell,
> One able to make strongest Cities fall,
> Combinde sufficient to demolish all
>   The Universe, these lately did resort
>   To ENGLAND and here kept their frantike Court,
> And we to murder Citizens to make it our sport.[29]

Even the recent regicide—here blamed entirely on the Scots—is figured through Mary's encounter with Judas:

> Here Judas hung, who Iesus had betray'd
> For thirty pence, and to the Synod sold.
> The crafty SCOTS a wiser bargain made,
> When for two hundred thousand pound in gold,
> They sold their King, the money here was told,
>   Judas recants, and shedding some vain teares,
>   Upon an Elder leaves both life and eares,
> And ever since such fruit the haplesse Elder bears.

> If all the trees in SCOTLAND every yeare
> Should blossome so, and bear such goodly fruit,
> And every JUDAS hang'd some here, some there,
> Would there be trees enough (think you) to do't?
> One tree, one Scot, guud Sir you put one to't.
>   O pray you SCOTS Historians may be dumb.
>   No volumes written in the times to come;
> Else you'll be registered all Nations basest scumme.[30]

This long passage makes the author's Royalist allegiance quite clear. The "bargain" in question refers to the spurious connection between the English Parliament's payment of £200,000 to the Scottish army and the largely unrelated decision to surrender the king then harbored in Scotland.[31] But the author's politics are indeed complex, as his support for the English Crown does not preclude criticism of courtly decadence. Part of Mary's trial is that she cannot leave the court, even after she recognizes its depravity:

> MARY abhors the late delightfull Court,
> Detests the Compay [*sic*] of her old Mates,
> And odious is the very name of sport,
> She loathes choice Viands, and delicious Kates,
> Fine cloths, masks, dancing, revelling she hates:
>   But MAGDALEN must further yet be vext,
>   Her soule with more anxieties perplext,
> As you shall heare in prosecution of our Text.

Her perpetual torture is configured as a warning to the women of English society, those "gentle Ladies Daughters of the light" who "for mirth and jollity too long have been / Within these courts" and now find themselves wandering like doomed spirits along the dingy corridors of their ruined palaces:

> Your joyes like MARIES end at last with paine,
> Though here you feast and boules of gladness drinke
> Else where you must from Kates and boules refraine,
> And quaffe off sorrowes cup fill'd to the brinke,
> Your pampred bodies die here, else-where stinke:
>   For Chamberd deckt, expect a Cobweb'd Roome,
>   For downy Beds, a darke ill smelling tombe,
> For idle complements a Judges serious doome.[32]

The Rover does reflect an awareness of the easy slippage between the Magdalene of high art and the cheap and available images fabricated to please the pundits. Despite the efforts of Moretta (Angellica's bawd) to present the portraits as indicative of Angellica's status as a rarified object destined for the bedroom of only the most prestigious of collectors, the connection between Angellica's person and popular consumption is well established in the play. The English rakes seem to be all too keen to devalue the portraits by discussing them in terms usually associated with cheap print culture. At two separate moments, the men insist that they are no "chapmen" for Angellica's image (2.1.99–100, 2.2.44–45), suggesting that the portraits are not high art but rather mass-produced prints carrying none of the markers of erudition and legitimacy once associated with the engraved image. The print, likely cheapened through its abundance, had lost the gilded allure it acquired in the court of Charles I and here becomes without question the lesser art. After the Restoration, prints of illustrious public figures were easy to come by, and in much the same way that today's tabloids profit from the publication of photographs of royal indiscretions, great commerce was made through the circulation of less than decorous prints of notorious aristocrats and their entourages.

Josias English copied Lely's painting of the Countess of Castlemaine sometime after 1667, adding the iconography that would transform her into what Brathwaite called *Englands Magdalen* (fig. 36).[33] While Lely's paintings of Villiers (as the Magdalene, as St. Catherine, and as the Madonna, among other figures) certainly helped to establish, in court circles, the countess's status as the king's first mistress, the great number of copies of these portraits attests to the larger public success of the countess's program of self-promotion.[34] The second print reproduced here (fig. 37) was apparently sold after 1678 by Thomas Taylor from his book and print shop in Fleet Street. It does not make explicit reference to Magdalene iconography, but the title of the image, "St. Mary Magdalen," tells us how it is to be read. Both the sitter and the print artist are unknown in this instance, though the print is after a painting by Lely in the collection of the Duke of Buccleuch and Queensbury.[35] Catherine MacLeod suggests the sitter may be another royal mistress: the actress Mary Davis, who was painted in a very similar pose by W. P. (possibly William Pawlett, c. 1673). MacLeod observes that the shift from implicit to explicit Magdalene content likely indicates a shift in audience for the image. While the

FIGURE 36. Josias English (after Sir Peter Lely), *Barbara Villiers, Countess of Castlemaine* (1667). © The Trustees of the British Museum, London.

FIGURE 37. *St. Mary Magdalen* (1678). © The Trustees of the British Museum, London.

original paintings were executed with the court in mind, these prints were destined for a broader viewing public, Taylor's Fleet Street customers, whose interests and tastes are much more difficult to define.[36] It is possible, therefore, to imagine that these print references to the Magdalene are supremely ironic; they are, like their literary counterparts, social satire that approaches crude lampoon.

If *The Rover* portraits do refer to Mary Magdalene, all the more intriguing (albeit speculative) is the possibility that the play's print references also take up religious controversy by way of allusion to the underground commerce in print illustrations of Christ and his followers. For instance, in 1652, when Michael Sparke (one of the witnesses summoned to testify against Laud at his trial) wrote *A Second Beacon Fired by Scintilla* in order to expose a series of papist plots, including the sale of Bibles bound with illustrations, his concern was not directed at art enthusiasts purchasing pictures for personal edification and enjoyment, but rather at the swarms of English women who, having purchased any number of these images at London stalls, were now apparently heading to the nunneries of Europe. Sparke even suggests that the allegedly popish images were originally of "Vandikes Draft" and that "proffers" had made of them since.[37] The tension in operation in *The Rover* is precisely that which is reflected in Sparke's blast: the image itself is of less concern than the threat of its immodest reproduction and circulation. A painting of a court mistress hanging in the gallery of a king is one thing; a naughty print at large in society is another.

The Angellica Icon

Why, then, does Behn introduce the portraits? Why establish the Royalist affinity for high art in order to debase it by association with the Magdalene cliché, the marketplace, and possibly even pornography or popery? The fact that *The Rover* was a favorite of both Charles II and his Catholic brother/successor suggests that the paintings were not received in these terms per se.[38] I think that the answer to the play's enduring appeal lies in the paradoxical presentation of Angellica's iconic status. The play, on the one hand, uses Angellica and her portraits to cast a critical eye upon the subjects of image collection and veneration; on the other hand, it simultaneously lends the figure of Angellica, and the actress that portrays her, some of the respect and veneration paid to a previous generation of Magdalene-like women.[39]

The Rover entertains the possibility that Angellica might not live up to her portraits. "A thousand crowns! Had not the painter flattered her, I should not think it dear," extols Antonio, only to be rebutted by Pedro, who insists upon the image's artistic poverty: "Flattered her! By heaven, he cannot. I have seen the original, nor is there one charm here more than adorns her face and eyes; all this soft and sweet, with a certain languishing air that no artist can represent" (2.1.147–52). The argument is never settled, which invites the reading that the relationship between image and original is of little consequence. There is some historical basis for this assumption; consider, for instance, Pepys's reaction to the "Windsor Beauties," which he described as "good, but not like," suggesting that the quality of the image need not be bound to the accuracy of its representation.[40] This last observation can also be made of Lely's works, as the generic quality of the poses makes it nearly impossible to distinguish one decked beauty from another.[41] "All his pictures had an Air one of another," writes one of Lely's critics, "all the Eyes were Sleepy alike. So that Mr Walker Ye. Painter swore Lilly's Pictures was all Brothers and Sisters."[42] The point is that these images appear to be empty of presence; they are vehicles without tenors, beautiful signs that have lost their referents.

Willmore is shamelessly aware of this fact. He agrees with Pedro, Angellica's portrait is "the shadow of the fair substance," but he finds value in it because he can gaze upon it "for nothing" (2.1.19–20). Later in the same scene, he observes to Angellica that her image provides an entirely acceptable substitute for the poor man who cannot afford the original:

> I saw your charming picture and was wounded; quite
> through my soul each pointed beauty ran; and wanting a
> thousand crowns [Angellica's price] to procure my remedy,

I laid this little picture to my bosom, which, if you cannot
allow me, I'll resign.

(2.1.234–37)

The image is not only capable of "wounding" this beholder, it is also,
suggestively, able to sooth those wounds with its physical proximity.
The picture is, apparently, a bargain—an effective stand-in for the
over-priced real thing. Moreover, there is no danger that Willmore
will confuse portrait for sitter (as Pepys does in his description of his
wife's picture); in fact, quite the opposite seems to be true. When Willmore looks upon the real Angellica he speaks of her as *art*. Though
he is initially compelled to acknowledge that there is "something so
divinely powerful" in her person that his stare is transfixed, when she
demands his money he replies,

Oh, why dost thou draw me from an awful worship,
By showing thou art no divinity?
Conceal the fiend, and show me the angel!
Keep me but ignorant, and I'll be devout
And pay my vows forever at this shrine.

(2.2.70, 147–51)

Willmore does not want to pay Angellica's price, and his strategy is
to point to the distinction between the sinner who stands before him
and her artfully holy image. Needless to say, it is the image he prefers.
Willmore tells the Venetian courtesan that his "awful" worship is interrupted when the surface cracks and its unholy artifice is revealed. If
presented with nothing but the dazzling surface of the shrine, he will
languish pleasurably in his idolatry, corrupt though it may be.

Willmore is an anti-Catholic stereotype. He is living proof of the
cynical decadence of Catholic art appreciation. Not only is he obsessed
by his collection of images and relics, but he knows they are empty
signs and meaningless containers and he wants them anyway. And yet,
astonishingly, there is nothing of the scathing satire, evident in Brathwaite's lampoon of the Duchess of Castlemaine, in Behn's portrait of
Angellica. To begin with, this icon looks back:

she's now the only adored beauty of all the youth in
Naples, who put on all their charms to appear lovely in her
sight: their coaches, liveries, and themselves, all gay as on
a monarch's birthday, to attract the eyes of this fair
charmer, while she has the pleasure to behold all languish
for her that see her.

                                                (1.2.314–18)

Moreover, Angellica's power resides not just in her charming look
or her "unmerciful price," but also in her witty, unsentimental view of
her commodified sexuality. "I have had no time for love," she says to
her bawd, "the bravest and noblest of mankind have purchased my
favours at so dear a rate, as if no coin but gold were concurrent with
our trade" (2.1.142–43). Angellica, like the famously self-interested
and also famously popular mistresses of Charles II, is absolutely
unapologetic about her commodity status in Cavalier consumer culture because it allows her to exert influence in the best possible social
circles. Even when she has lost everything, she reflects upon her demise with an acuity that exceeds the self-awareness of any other character in the play. And thus, when Willmore switches his affection to
the virtuous Hellena, Angellica's devastation is poignant:

> I should have thought all men were born my slaves,
> And worn my power like lightning in my eyes,
> To have destroyed at pleasure when offended:
> But when Love held the mirror, the undeceiving glass
> Reflected in all the weakness of my soul, and made me know
> My richest treasure being lost, my honour,
> And the remaining spoil could not be worth
> The conqueror's care or value.

                                                (5.1.284–291)

Angellica knows that her painted eyes are powerful only if she remains
a rarefied thing—beyond the reach of all but the most discriminating
of collectors. And when she falls, when she ceases to be treated as an

exquisitely executed paragon of beauty and becomes a cheap replica, sullied with misuse, the audience is, without a doubt, on her side.

Most significantly, despite Willmore's rather loathsome account of his idolatrous worship of Angellica's image, the language of Catholic devotion is most consistently used to foster sympathy for the courtesan's character:

> Oh, how I fell, like a long worshipped idol,
> Discovering all the cheat.
> Would not the incense and rich sacrifice,
> Which blind devotion offered at my altars
> Have fall'n to thee?
> Why wouldst thou then destroy my fancied power?
>   (5.1.292–97)

Behn was not one to use religious imagery glibly. Her own religious sympathies are the subject of much speculation, but there can be no question that her Royalist politics and public friendships with known Catholics assured that her work was never above scrutiny. Moreover, any suggestion of Catholic sympathy would have been audacious and controversial in the months before the exposure of the Popish Plot.[43] The devotional terms that decide the reception of the "famous courtesan" are thus not to be disregarded. As her name suggests, Angellica is not depicted solely as a fallen woman or as a tainted idol reminiscent of the decadence of Rome; her status is much more paradoxical. Her fall is lamentable—more lamentable than the unions of the favored couples are cause for celebration. The demise of Angellica seems to signal the end of a sensibility that recognizes that rich and sensual worldliness is not incompatible with virtue and honorability. Angellica's treatment is, in fact, reminiscent of Behn's rather melancholy defenses of the stage which lament the intolerance and narrow-mindedness of radical reformers who positioned themselves against the alleged profanity of the theater. Why is it, Behn wonders, that the "pious work of Reformation" arms itself against players for "our small Religion sure can do no harm."[44]

Behn's sense that there is something holy, or at the very least miraculously transformative, about the theatrical enterprise constitutes a further point of connection between her play's meditation upon the vulgarization of visual art and the treatment of Angellica. When Pedro refers to Angellica as an original that exceeds representation, his words seem ironic in the context of Behn's theater since representing Angellica is precisely what the actress is doing. And yet if the portrait-props were representations of the actress playing Angellica, as I am proposing they might have been, the actress can also be understood as the original, the real thing, that the audience, familiar with the popular print images, has come to see. Furthermore, the actress becomes, by virtue of her professional skill and the sacramental magic of the theater, the true likeness of Angellica, a figure whose living presence has the power to inspire wonder in her audience. Under such performance conditions, Willmore's refusal to venerate the person of Angellica stands opposed to the experience of actual playgoers moved by an actress, transformed before their very eyes, from image into icon.[45]

Is it possible, then, that the misuse of "the sign of Angellica" is emblematic of the fate of the theater in a world where two of its principal affects, wonder and beauty, carry with them baggage of both Protestant iconophobia and Cavalier irreverence?[46] Is it possible that Behn is using Angellica, and the theater for that matter, to provide an alternative to anti-Catholic and Royalist readings of women and the theater, positioning both in what Frances Dolan calls "new roles, to tell other stories."[47] If it is imaginable that Behn's play seeks to make this conceptual leap, it is significant that Angellica is not the only figure in Behn's writing to receive such sensuous and even devotional rhetorical treatment. To Nell Gwyn, for example, Behn wrote the following:

> Tis no wonder that hitherto I followed not the good example of the believing Poets, since less faith and zeal than you alone can inspire, had wanted power to have reduc't me to the true worship: Your permission, *Madam*, had inlighted me, and I with shame look back on my past Ignorance, which suffered me not to pay

an Adoration long since, where there was so very much due, yet even now though secure in my opinion, I make this Sacrifice with infinite fear and trembling, well known that so Excellent and perfect a Creature as your self differs only from the Divine powers in this; the Offerings made to you ought to be worthy of you, whilst they accept the will alone; and how Madam, would your Altars be loaded, if like heaven you gave permission to all that had a will and desire to approach'em, who now at a distance can only wish and admire, which all mankinde agree to do; as if, Madam, you alone had the pattent from heaven to ingross all hearts.[48]

The first printed versions of *The Rover* (1677) note that the part of Angellica Bianca was played by "Mrs Gwin" at the Duke's Theatre, and the second edition of the play (1697) also attributes the role of "the famous courtesan" to Gwyn, this time in performance at Little Lincoln's Inn Fields. Theater historians concur, however, that Gwyn retired from the stage in 1671 when she became mistress to the king, and it is generally conceded Anne Marshall (aka Anne Quin) played the part.[49] I would like to suggest, however, that the likeness of Gwyn would have been very apparent in Behn's treatment of Angellica and that the early printers' errors are, in this respect, understandable. It also seems possible to speculate that the Magdalene reflection, discernable in the court portraiture and in the commodified images of Angellica in *The Rover*, is reinvigorated in the person of Gwyn, to whom Angellica is a tribute.

If this proposition is all too provisional, it can be said more generally, and thus more confidently, that Behn's portraits of both courtesans and actresses seem to beg their audiences to reflect upon the aesthetic work that the Magdalene enables. As I hope to have shown in previous chapters, the Magdalene is, for the postmedieval artist, a maker of memory: she facilitates the creative processes by which the longing born of absence (the physical absence of Christ; the loss of the doctrine of transubstantiation; the destruction and desecration of religious art; or, more generally, the loss of a sense of history) is transformed into commemorative work that allows its readers to see and feel at least an idea of past presence in aesthetic terms.

The vulgarization of the Magdalene in pictures and in literature, like the demise of the person of Angellica, suggests that the consumers of Restoration art, highbrow and popular alike, were unable to acknowledge the melancholic grace the Magdalene posture should have afforded to the "Windsor Beauties"—Gwyn, Villiers, and de Kéröualle among them. *The Rover,* rather than dwelling solely upon a politics of looking that firmly establishes certain classes of women as commodities or as objects of exchange passed between charming rakes and irresistible libertines, is more precisely scrutinizing a social economy so transfixed by the surface of its images that it failed to acknowledge the tradition—the rich and varied compendium of Scriptures, legends, homilies, meditations, poems, dedications, sermons, plays, and pictures—which stood behind those images, constituting their history and informing their meaning. And without this sense of the past, or more precisely this sense of rupture with the past (a feeling that the Magdalene's grief enacts so exquisitely), the fear is that there will be neither need nor will to remember anything. For Behn, however, it seems that the merry Magdalenes of the Restoration court and stage were, like the "chaste prostitute" who inspired their public presentation, paradoxical figures—blessed sinners and beguiling penitents— whose unsettling image spurred readers and viewers to think again upon all the riches now lost to them. As Willmore says, "The sight on't would beget a warm desire / In souls whom impotence and age had chilled."

A Something Else Thereby

There are more early modern Magdalenes than are accounted for here. Some of them, like Elizabeth Cary's life of the saint, now lost, lie beyond my reach.[1] Others were simply set aside: the anonymous and aptly titled "Another on the Same Subject" (1601), for instance, which is a meditation on the heavenly Jerusalem wherein Magdalene is no longer maudlin, having forever "lost her moane." Also left for another day is Thomas Jordan's "On Mary Magdalen's coming to the Tomb" (1643), a protogothic poem set against a dark, "sad night" ("An Apparition, t'was she came to see"). I could have written about Owen Feltnam's "The Reconcilement" (1661), in which the speaker begs his wayward lover to return as a penitent Magdalene:

> So Convert Magdalen
> Excell'd more after her Conversion, then
> Before she had offended: slips that be
> 'Twixt friends from frailty, are but as you see
> Sad absence to strong lovers; when they meet,
> It makes their warm imbraces far more sweet.

But even this verse, sweet as it is, adds little to the account as it stands. The same is true of Thomas Cranley's *Amanda, or the Reformed Whore* (1635), a tediously long, moralizing treatise that maps Mary Magdalene's *vita* upon the life of a London prostitute. Samuel Speed's syrupy tribute "Delights of the Minde" (1677), Joseph Beaumont's ode to that "noble smell," Mary's precious nard (c. 1652), as well as Hugh Crompton's epigram, a poem that can be praised only for its brevity, are similarly ignored. And there are doubtless more than these.[2] To account for these texts now, even in this cursory fashion, risks bathos, which is, at the end of the day, part of my point. William Lithgow, in another poem that I have overlooked, observes that Mary Magdalene's "memorie should last, / From age to age, till all ages be past"; it should be evident by now that the writers of early modern England took this charge seriously—though some did so with greater skill, and to greater effect, than others.[3]

I began this book with reference to Pierre Nora's discussion of memory as an evolving phenomenon of the present. The same can be said of the literary manifestations of the Magdalene. Whether she is found writhing in fits of demonic possession, somber in modest penitential attire, or half naked, bathed in the light of holy rapture, her image is never fixed, sacred, or impervious to all manners of manipulation. Part of her enduring appeal is that she can always be reinvented. She is, in every instance, a pliable, malleable medium of feeling and enchantment that accommodates those who make her a surface upon which to trace the phantom lines of something else more remote and much more inaccessible. She is also, however, a creature of history. Sometimes she recalls a Protestant penitent, sometimes a Catholic mystic, and even, upon occasion, a dead duchess or an aristocratic whore, but in every manifestation her form becomes a measure of just how much has been lost between then and now. She recalls for us a past that is always, in some way, in dispute, under revision, or on the verge of being entirely forgotten. And for this reason, she is not simply memory embodied but rather the perfect manifestation of the *lieu de mémoire* that mitigates the amnesia of history by materializing something of the past.

We are not done with Mary Magdalene, not by any means. Her image is tirelessly reinvented in the literature, film, and art of post-modernity. This book itself is a manifestation of this phenomenon, and its working title, "I don't know how to love him," a testament to my own affection for *Jesus Christ Superstar* and the other popular re-workings of the topos. In *Godspell* Mary Magdalene prays for three things: to "see Thee more clearly, love Thee more dearly, and follow Thee more nearly." These words have been at the back of my mind, as has been Barbara Hershey's stirring interpretation of Mary Magdalene in Scorsese's film adaptation of Kazantzakis's controversial novel *The Last Temptation of Christ.* I can't forget Catherine Wilkening's unadulterated and yet sweet take on the Magdalene as redeemed fashion model in Denys Arcand's *Jésus de Montréal.*[4] And the list could go on. If Michèle Roberts's *The Wild Girl* (1984) and Angela Carter's "Impressions: The Writsman Magdalene" (1992) were enough to persuade me of the importance of the figure to a generation of writers who found marvelous possibilities for magic realism in the vestiges of Catholic iconography, it was Nino Ricci's *Testament* (2002), Margaret George's historical novel *Mary Called Magdalene* (2002), and, most obviously, Dan Brown's best seller *The Da Vinci Code* (2003) that bore witness to our enduring infatuation with the spiritual influence and ecclesiastical authority of this saint.[5] In all of this contemporary Magdaleneia, the figure is brought to mind for the same reason she was in early modern England: she knew a man who is, for everyone else, unknowable. Mary Magdalene is today what she has always been: a repository of memory who effects a crucial transition between a living and present Christ and a Christ who exists in historical memory, and in the shapes and forms that commemorate him or seek to make him present.

Before I leave this subject once and for all, I want to turn to one last poem, a genuinely moving piece of writing that impressed itself upon my mind at the very beginning of the project but did not find a place in this book until now. The text is from John Donne's "The Relique," and it prods so many of the pressure points in the Magdalene story that it seems right to finish with it:

If this fall in a time, or land,
Where mis-devotion doth command,
Then, he that digges us up, will bring
Us, to the Bishop, and the King,
    To make us relics then
Thou shalt be'a Mary Magdalen, and I
    A something else thereby;
All women shall adore us, and some men;
And since at such time, miracles are sought,
I would have that age by this paper taught
What miracles wee harmlesse lovers wrought.[6]

Between 1550 and 1700, Mary Magdalene found herself in both a time and a land in which religious turmoil (some would call it "mis-devotion") did command. She was dug up and readdressed in homilies, meditations, sermons, poems, dedications, plays, and pictures. She was then brought before many, including at least one bishop and a number of kings. As a relic—or site of memory—the Magdalene resurrects an old idea of presence and generates a new idea of beauty, with unforeseeable consequences. She limits forgetting when there are no pictures to look at, and she recalls something more transcendent when pictures proliferate and the heart of the matter feels lost. But always, and in every manifestation, she effects change in those who look upon her. "And I a something else thereby," writes Donne's speaker, perhaps implying that he becomes Christ-like in his lover's presence or, more evocatively, that he finds himself at a rare loss for words when it comes to proclaiming his lover's transformative power. The only certainty is this: when and wherever "miracles are sought," there shall also be this, what this woman hath done, be told for a memorial of her.

NOTES

Acknowledgments

1. Badir, "To allure vnto their loue," 1–20; Badir, "Medieval Poetics," 205–19.

Introduction: Creeping After the Cart

1. Marbeck, *Lyues of holy Sainctes*, A3. For Marbeck's biography, see Mateer, "Marbeck, John (c. 1505–1585?)."
2. Marbeck, *Lyues of holy Sainctes*, A5.
3. The panorama of the English Protestant Reformation continues to spark debate in scholarly circles. Influential recent studies include: Bossy, *The English Catholic Community*; Duffy, *The Stripping of the Altars*; Haigh, *English Reformations*; Marshall, *Reformation England*; Pettegree, *Reformation*; Questier, *Conversion, Politics, and Religion in England*; Tyacke, *England's Long Reformation*. Much of this work has challenged the orthodoxy of a Protestant master narrative (see Dickens's *The English Reformation*) and posited in its place successive "reformations" producing competing and often unstable systems of belief, institutional structures, and subject positions. One of the most significant products of this revisionist thinking, for my purposes, has been an increase in sensitivity to the vestiges of Catholicism in post-Reformation English culture (see in particular Duffy, *The Stripping of the Altars*). On the related subject of English anti-Catholicism, see Lake, "Anti-Popery," 72–106; Weiner, "The Beleaguered Isle," 27–62; and Clifton, "The Popular Fear of Catholics," 23–53; as well as the essays in Marotti, *Catholicism and Anti-Catholicism* and *Religious Ideology*. For a more nuanced sense of how the Reformation impacted the

development of Protestant culture, see the essays collected in McClendon, Ward, and MacDonald, *Protestant Identities*. On the subject of iconoclasm, particularly in England, see Aston, *England's Iconoclasts*; Collinson, *From Iconoclasm to Iconophobia*; Duffy, *The Stripping of the Altars*; Eire, *War Against the Idols*; Michalski, *The Reformation*; Phillips, *The Reformation of Images*.

4. *Canons and Decrees of the Council of Trent*, 216.

5. Nora, *Realms of Memory*, 7.

6. Nora, *Realms of Memory*, 15.

7. Marbeck, *Lyues of holy Sainctes*, 223–24.

8. Marbeck does not mention the Mary Magdalene from whom Christ expelled seven devils (Luke 8:2).

9. Matthew 26:6–13 describes a woman of Bethany, in the house of Simon the leper, who came to Jesus "with a boxe of very costly oyntment, and powred it on his head as he sate at the table." Mary Magdalene is named in Matthew 27:56 and 28:1–8 as present at the crucifixion and at the sepulcher. Mark 14:3 notes that while Jesus was at Bethany "in the house of Simon the leper . . . there came a woman hauing a boxe of oyntment of spikenard, very costly, and shee brake the boxe and powred it on his head." Mark also notes the presence of Mary Magdalene at the crucifixion and at the sepulcher (15:40–47 and 16:1–11) and acknowledges her to be the first witness of the resurrection. Luke 7:37–50 recounts the events in the home of Simon the Pharisee (not the leper) where "a woman in the citie, which was a sinner, when she knewe that Iesus sate at table in the Pharises house, shee brought a boxe of oyntment." Luke, in the next chapter, mentions Mary Magdalene by name as the woman "out of whom went seven devils" (8:2). Mary of "a certaine towne," who in Luke's Gospel (10:38–42) is a sister of Martha and who "sate at Iesus feete, and heard his preaching," is, in John 11:1–46, the sister of Lazarus whom Christ raises from the dead. Mary Magdalene appears again in Luke at the cross and at the sepulcher (23:55 and 24:10–12). John's Mary of Bethany "anoynted Jesus feete with her heare, and the house was filled with the sauour of oyntment" (12:3); his Mary Magdalene is present at the crucifixion (19:25), and it is she who speaks to the resurrected Christ before the empty tomb (20:1–18).

10. Gregory the Great's homily on Luke's Gospel was probably delivered in 591 at the Basilica di San Clemente in Rome on the Friday after Holy Cross Day (14 September). The homily firmly consolidated the composite identity of the Magdalene—an identity that, despite ongoing theological intervention, remains largely intact today. See Gregory the Great, "Homilia 33." See also Haskins, *Mary Magdalen*, 95–97; Saxer, *Le culte de Marie Magdaleine*, 33; de Leeuw, "Gregory the Great's Homilies," 855–69. For the first English translation of Jacobus's recounting of the Magdalene legend see *Legenda aurea* (1487).

11. For a comprehensive discussion of the taint of Mary's birthplace as well as the attendant Magdalene legends, see Haskins, *Mary Magdalen*, 15, 98–133, and the chapter on the representation of Mary Magdalene as "Beata Peccatrix" (134–91).

12. More English churches were dedicated to Mary Magdalene than to any other Christian saint, with the exception of the Virgin Mary. See Arnold-Foster, *Studies in Church Dedications*, 3:19. Magdalene College, Oxford, was dedicated in 1448. The Cambridge Magdalene College was not dedicated until 1542. The hospital count is provided by Jansen, *The Making of the Magdalen*, 111.

13. Saxer's survey, *Le culte de Marie Magdaleine*, was the first comprehensive effort to compile a representational history of the saint. This work continues to be an invaluable resource cited by all Magdalene scholars as foundational and, in many respects, unsurpassed. Haskins's *Mary Magdalen* is a compendium of Magdalene material which itemizes manifestations of the saint from her appearance in the Gospels of the New Testament to her modern image in art, music, and literature. My own work remains very much in debt to this capacious volume, particularly for its pan-European bibliography and its exhaustive coverage of art history. Jansen, in *The Making of the Magdalen*, has captured and revealed the importance of the *apostola apostolorum* to mendicant culture, arguing convincingly that it is in her capacity as *nucia*, or preacher, that Mary Magdalene became "the most important female saint of the period." Her cult, Jansen illustrates, "exemplified, reflected, and refracted some of the most important social issues, theological questions, and pressing politics of the later Middle Ages" (17). Thimmes has also written a useful biographical essay on Magdalene scholarship ("Memory and Revision"). See also Malvern, *Venus in a Sackcloth*.

14. Shuger, *The Renaissance Bible*, 191.

15. Coletti, *Mary Magdalene*, 230.

16. The most comprehensive study of Lefèvre's influence upon the Magdalene is Hufstader, "Lefèvre d'Étaples," 31–60. My reporting of the controversy paraphrases this work. Lefèvre's work is called *De Marie Magdalena* (1517). See also Rex, *The Theology of John Fisher*.

17. Hufstader, "Lefèvre d'Étaples," 44.

18. Fisher, *De unica Magdalena, Libri tres*, A3v, trans. Hufstader, "Lefèvre d'Étaples," 44. Fisher's writings on the Magdalene are described by Surtz, *The Works and Days*, 5–7, 157–60, 274–89.

19. Coletti, *Mary Magdalene*, 220–21.

20. Lefèvre also had his defenders. The most significant of these was Dutch theologian Josse Clichtove whose interpretation of Lefèvre's purpose provides immediate access to the postmedieval role the Magdalene would come to play. Clichtove argued that "through the contemplation of wisdom (the mind must) be joined to the most transcendent, divine, and praiseworthy aspects of

being, to which indeed the mind is not joined by nearness or presence in space, but by inward consideration and the raising of the mind to meditating heavenly things." Contemplative happiness of this sort is not found in the saint's nonscriptural vocation as a preacher and mystic but rather is expressed by the figure found "sitting at the Lord's feet." It is of course ironic that Clichtove makes precisely the conflation that Lefèvre railed against. See Hufstader, "Lefèvre d'Étaples," 59. Marc de Grandval (an Augustinian Canon of St. Victor) also lent his voice to the debate, as did the Nuremberg humanist Willibald Pirckheimer. Finally, in October 1519, Erasmus weighed in, in a letter to Fisher in which he laments "that such good men should oppose each other." For summaries of the positions of all the contributors to the debate, see Hufstader, "Lefèvre d'Étaples."

21. Simpson, "The Rule of Medieval Imagination," 10–12, 22–24.

22. The Geneva Bible.

23. For instance, MacCulloch, in *The Reformation*, 80–184, draws attention to radical Protestants' preference for the theological genius of Origen over Augustine, particularly in relation to the problem of the Trinity and Jesus' place within it. McCulloch shows that Protestant radicals generally favored older Christologies that were Unitarian rather than Trinitarian. Some affirmed that Christ was fully divine (and it was therefore blasphemous to assume he had any element of humanity within himself), while others argued that the unity of God demanded that Christ the Son could not be considered as fully God in the same sense as God the Father was fully God. In any case, as ancient and reformist theology converged to deny Christ's humanity in favor of his divinity, the central object of focus was the mass, specifically the Eucharist. Zwingli denied the possibility of real corporeal or physical presence in the Eucharist by following Erasmus's gloss of Christ's affirmation that it is the spirit that gives life while the flesh profits nothing (John 6:63). For further discussion of the differences among post-Reformation Protestants and Catholics with respect to the subject of presence, see Radner, *The End of the Church*, particularly the chapters on the visibility of the saints and the corporeality of the Eucharist, in which he argues that the justification of contradictory answers to the question of Christ's presence in the elements was essentially the sole interest of eucharistic theology. See also B. Marshall's review of Radner's book, "The Divided Church," 377–95.

24. *Glossa Ordinaria*, Matthew 26:6–12, in the works of Walafrid Strabo (d. 849). Strabo's gloss is an extensively annotated presentation of Jerome's Vulgate Bible with marginal and interlineal annotations on the readings of the Latin Fathers as well as references to writings of Strabo's master, Rabanus Maurus. The *Glossa Ordinaria* was considered an authoritative reading of the Gospels until well into the seventeenth century. Here is the full gloss (verse 13 is not glossed):

VERS. 6.—*Cum autem.* Habito consilio ordo narrationis illuc transit, *tunc abiit unus de duodecim*, ut factum Judae conjungatur ad consilium sacerdotum. Redit autem ad eum diem, qui erat ante sex dies paschae dicens: *Cum autem*, etc. *Simonis.* Permanet pristinum nomen ut virtus curantis appareat. Per eam domum accipe illam partem populi quae credidit Domino et curata est. *Simon*, id est obediens.
VERS. 7.—*Accessit.* Diligenter observa, quae de duabus super caput. Siquidem peccatrix, super pedes, et ea quae dicitur non fuisse peccatrix, super caput. *Mulier habens.* Maria Magdalena soror Lazari modo justa et familiaris, quae quondam peccatrix venit et pedes lacrymis lavit, nunc caput et pedes unxit, pedes nunc, ut Joannes dicit. *Unguenti pretiosi.* Marcus: nardi spicati, id est, de spicis et foliis confecti, quod pretiosius est. Joannes nardi pistici, id est, fidelis, non adulterati aliis herbis: πίστις Graece, fides Latine. *Mystice.* Haec devotio Mariae fidem significat Ecclesiae, quae dum deitatem Christi praedicat, caput ungit: dum humanitatem, pedes. De hoc unguento in domo Simonis leprosi in Bethania dicunt, et Matthaeus et Marcus et Joannes. Lucas vero aliud dicit simile huic factum ante in domo alterius Simonis pharisaei non leprosi, neque in Bethania, sed de eadem muliere quae tunc accessit peccatrix.
VERS. 8.—*Discipuli indignati.* Joannes dicit haec Judam locutum, et hoc gratia cupiditatis: alii potuerunt verbis ejus consentire, vel etiam idem dicere, sed propter curam pauperum.
VERS. 11.—*Me autem*, etc. Corporali praesentia, alioquin dicit alibi: *Ecce ego vobiscum sum omnibus diebus usque ad consummationem saeculi.*
VERS. 12.—*Mittens enim.* Officium est sepulturae quod vos perditionem esse putatis. Nec mirum, si mihi dat fidei odorem, pro qua mox fusurus sum sanguinem.

25. Rheims-Douay Bible.
26. Calvin, *Harmonie*, 679–80. Despite Tridentine attempts to segregate the individual figures that make up the composite sinner-saint of the Middle Ages, Calvin assumes that the woman with the alabaster box is indeed Mary Magdalene.
27. Ward, *Theological Questions*, 338.
28. Calvin, *Harmonie*, 680.
29. Trapp, *Commentary*, 310.
30. Erasmus, *Paraphrase*, n.p.
31. Collins, *Reading the Written Image*, 71–74.
32. D'Étaples, *Disceptatio prima, Secunda emissio*, f. 36 v. As cited in Hufstader, "Lefèvre d'Étaples," 59–60.
33. Nora, *Realms of Memory*, 15.
34. Shuger, *The Renaissance Bible*, 5.

35. See Hill, *The English Bible*; Hammond, *The Making of the English Bible*; Herbert et al., *Historical Catalogue*; Pelikan et al., *The Reformation of the Bible*; Levi, *The English Bible*; Mandelbrote, "The Authority of the Word," 135–56; Nicholson, *God's Secretaries*; O'Sullivan, *The Bible as Book*; Walsham, "Domme preachers?" 72–123; Walsham, "Unclasping the Book," 141–66; Walsham, "Jewels for Gentlewomen," 123–42.

36. In other words, I take for granted Mazzola's assertion that it is not just that "the Renaissance imagination was sharply defined by ideas that reformers forced it to repudiate," but that "sacred symbols and practices still powerfully organized the English moral imagination in the sixteenth and seventeenth centuries, continued to orient behaviors and arrange perceptions, and persisted in specifying to believers and non-believers alike the limits of the known world" (*Pathology*, 3). See also Collins, *Reading the Written Image*; Diehl, *Staging Reform*; Dimmick et al., *Images*; Gilman, *Iconoclasm*; Tassi, *The Scandal of Images*; Luxon, *Literal Figures*; O'Connell, *The Idolatrous Eye*; Pinkus, *Picturing Silence*. For recent work in postmedieval English Catholicism that assumes formal and aesthetic continuities between the Catholic past and the largely Protestant present, see contributions by Dawson and Yachnin in *The Culture of Playgoing*; Greenblatt, *Hamlet*; Kuchar, *Divine Subjection*; Lupton, *Afterlives of the Saints*; Shell, *Catholicism*; Tumbleson, *Catholicism in the English Protestant Imagination*; Dolan, *Whores of Babylon*; Sullivan, *Dismembered Rhetoric*. See also the essays collected in McMullan and Matthews, *Reading the Medieval*.

37. Martz, *The Poetry of Meditation*; Lewalski, *Protestant Poetics*.

38. See, for example, Barbour, *Literature and Religious Culture*; Corns, *Uncloistered Virtue*; Doerksen and Hodgkins, *Centered on the Word*; Gregerson, *The Reformation of the Subject*; Orlin, *Private Matters*; Rambuss, *Closet Devotions*; Schoenfeldt, *Prayer and Power*; Shuger, *The Renaissance Bible*; Skerpan-Wheeler, *The Rhetoric of Politics*; Targoff, *Common Prayer*. While generally historicist in methodology, these studies are notably different from explicitly New Historicist scholarship, which tended to consider matters of religion in terms of ideology and politics and in the process to misrecognize religious subjectivity as a kind of false consciousness; see, for example, Sinfield, *Literature*; or Gallagher and Greenblatt, *Practicing New Historicism*. For a discussion of the shortcomings of New Historicism with respect to religion, see Aers, "New Historicism"; Aers and Beckwith, "Introduction"; Beckwith, "Greenblatt's *Hamlet*."

39. Mitchell, *Iconology*, 43–44.

40. For further discussion of the "religious turn" in early modern studies and its origins in continental philosophy, see Jackson and Marotti, "The Turn to Religion," 167–90.

Chapter 1.   The Look of Love

1. Harim White, *The Ready Way*, 2.

2. For a discussion of the medieval Magdalene as an exemplar of perfect penance, see Jansen, *The Making of the Magdalen*, 199–244; and Coletti, *Mary Magdalene*, 51–189.

3. Harim White, *The Ready Way*, 46–47.

4. Harim White, *The Ready Way*, 33–34.

5. Harim White, *The Ready Way*, 31.

6. The poem exists in two manuscripts, Harleian 6211 (British Library) and Rawlinson 41 (Bodleian Library). Sommer claims that the manuscripts are from the latter half of the sixteenth century, though it seems likely that their dates are somewhat later. Sommer also argues that the author of the manuscripts was Thomas Robinson, dean of Durham (fl. c. 1520–61). This Thomas Robinson was a member of the committee that prepared the 1549 Book of Common Prayer, but he fell out of favor under Elizabeth because of his Catholicism. The other possible author is the pamphleteer Thomas Robinson (fl. 1622), who is best known for his account of the scandalous activities of the English Bridgettine convent in Lisbon, *An Anatomy of the English Nunnery at Lisbon* (1622). See Parish, "Robertson, Thomas (fl. ca. 1520–1561)," and Sheils, "Robertson, Thomas (fl. 1622)." The poem was printed in 1650, anonymously and under the title *The Soules Pilgrimage to Heavenly Hierusalem*. See chapter 5 for further discussion of this poem's afterlife.

7. Robinson, *The Life and Death*, 39.

8. Robinson, *The Life and Death*, 56.

9. Robinson, *The Life and Death*, 5.

10. Rogers, "The Penitent Citizen," 137–39.

11. Rogers, "The Penitent Citizen," 189.

12. Robinson, *The Life and Death*, 4.

13. Robinson, *The Life and Death*, 64.

14. Simpson, "The Rule of Medieval Imagination," 11.

15. The play's full title is *A new Enterlude, neuer before this tyme imprinted, entreating of the Life and Repentaunce of Marie Magdalene; not only godlie, learned and fruitefull, but also well furnished with pleasaunt myrth and pastime, very delectable for those which shall heare or reade the same.* References here are from Paul Whitfield White's old-spelling critical edition, *The Life and Repentaunce of Mary Magdalene and The Story of Jacob and Esau*. All line references to the play will appear in parentheses in the body of the text. White assumes that though the play was first entered in the Stationers' Register in 1566, the reference to "the Kyng" (as opposed to "the Queen") as well as its obvious indebtedness to Calvin's *Institutes* point to an Edwardian date (*Reformation Biblical Drama*, xxii–iii).

16. L. King, *Sacred Eroticism*, 336–38.

17. Paul White notes that, along with other Reformation publicists, Wager was principally and actively "involved in the dissemination of Protestantism" (*Theatre and Reformation*, 7). The Reformation's use of theatricality has been discussed at length: Strong's ground-breaking study *The Cult of Elizabeth* was an early work in this field. Breightenberg's "Reading Elizabethan Iconicity" argued convincingly that text and icon (word and theater) rather than oppositional binary terms are, rather, "isomorphic categories which opposing political and religious ideologies sought to appropriate and govern" (217). John King has illustrated that early evangelicals, contrary to common stereotypes of the Puritans, approved of drama, and that scriptural themes are the "hallmark of Edwardian drama" (*English Reformation Literature*, 277–80). Comprehensive studies of Reformation drama have been undertaken by Kendall (*The Drama of Dissent*), who argues that "repeatedly, in the non-conformist canon, the reader encounters the products of an inherently theatrical imagination" (8); and by White (*Theatre and Reformation*), who proves that "from the 1530s, playwrights and players, both amateur and professional, contributed to the formation of an emerging Protestant culture" (3). Particularly relevant to this chapter is Diehl's influential *Staging Reform*, which suggests that while England's Protestant reformers invoked antitheatricalist sentiment in their denunciation of the images, spectacles, rituals, and ceremonies of the Roman Catholic Church, they nevertheless "imagine[d] their struggle to wrest the English Church from Rome as a grand heroic drama, staging their defiant acts of iconoclasm in highly theatrical ways and constructing Protestant martyrdoms as powerful theater" (14). Pettegree, in his recent book *The Reformation and the Culture of Persuasion*, considers Protestant theater as a public and communal process of commitment by means of which individuals and communities were encouraged to convert to the new church (see, in particular, 88–91).

18. Jansen, *The Making of the Magdalen*, 147, 169, 194. For more detail on the medieval treatment of the Magdalene's preconversion story, see the section of Jansen's book, "The Wages of Sin," 145–96.

19. Jacobus, "Seynt Marie Magdalene," CCxvi (v).

20. Herzfeld, *The Old English Martyrology*, 127.

21. *The Northern Passion*, 12.

22. *The Early South-English Legendary*, 462–64.

23. Bokenham, *Legendys*, 149.

24. *Saint Mary Magdalen*, 44.

25. Erasmus, *Paraphrase*, 86–87.

26. Calvin, *Harmonie*, 367.

27. Dolan, *Whores of Babylon*, 8.

28. Weil, "Sometimes a Scepter Is Only a Scepter," 147.

29. Scott, "Against the praying to Saintes," C5v. For a recent discussion of Wager's treatment of the diabolical/Catholic femininity of the preconversion Magdalene, see Hill-Vásquez, *Sacred Players*, 168–85.

30. "Against the Peril of Idolatry," 2:2:3, 2820–50.

31. Dolan, *Whores of Babylon*, 43.

32. Wager's Infidelitie appears to be modeled upon Bale's Infidelitas, from *A Comedy Concernynge thre lawes*, 64–124. Bale's character controls the vice figures Idolatria and Sodomismus, and together this unholy trinity sets about corrupting Natural Law (see 357–92, 77–78).

33. Penetrability is, incidentally, characteristic of bodies other than Mary's. As Infidelitie "enters" the Magdalene, he himself is entered by the seven deadly sins described as "impes," which press upon him. Pride of Life further remarks that "In vs foure without faile be contained / As many vices as euer in this world raigned" (125; 377–78). Furthermore, the contents of each body of vice are enumerated in abhorrent detail: within Carnal Concupiscence lie lechery, fornication, whoredom, adultery, rape, incest, sacrilege, softness, bestiality, blindness of mind, inconstancy, headiness, and inconsideration (389–93); in Cupiditie lurk theft, fraud, perjury, dissimulation, lying, rapine, inhumanity, inquietude of mind, falsehood, vanity, vengeance, envy, rancor, ire, murder, war, treason, greedy desire, and usury, as well as dice and card playing (407–14); in Pride of Life lie idolatry, boasting, arrogance, and vainglory, not to mention obstinacy, disobedience, idleness, and negligence (427–32). The vices are both willing corrupters of Mary's body and labile, pregnable spaces themselves, apparently effeminized through their proximity to a libidinous and promiscuous woman. To borrow from Orgel's important discussion of Renaissance sexuality, "in an age in which sexuality itself is misogynistic," Mary is dangerous to men because sexual passion for Mary renders men effeminate. By extension, the Catholic Church is also effeminizing in that those lured into its sphere of influence become weakened and corrupted by the predatory power of its idols (Orgel, *Impersonations*, 11, 26).

34. Simpson, "The Rule of Medieval Imagination," 12.

35. For a full discussion of iconoclasm in England, see Aston, *England's Iconoclasts*; Collinson, *From Iconoclasm to Iconophobia*; Duffy, *The Stripping of the Altars*; Phillips, *The Reformation of Images*.

36. "Against the Peril of Idolatry," 2783–84. Aston, in *England's Iconoclasts*, writes, "Protestant disparagement (which turned ousted church images into a new sort of toy) was conveniently able to subsume its disdain for the falsities of little popes—'popetry'—into the deluding manipulations of carved and jointed images—'puppetry'" (403).

37. The Rood was brought into the marketplace in Maidstone in 1538, where its mechanics were exposed to public view. Aston argues that in the

context of late medieval devotional culture the eyes of statues were thought to gaze at worshipers with a frontal directness that invited effective communication (*England's Iconoclasts*, 1:25, 401). For a description of the Boxley Rood, see Duffy, *The Stripping of the Altars*, 403; Aston, *England's Iconoclasts*, 1:234; Paul White, *Theatre and Reformation*, 36–37. The destruction of the Rood is chronicled by Wriothesley, *A Chronicle of England*, 2:75–76, 78–81, 83. For further discussion of the veneration of statues, see Foresyth, "Magi and Majesty," 215–22; Baxandall, *Limewood Sculptors*, 166. The exhibition of the Boxley Rood was followed by a sermon from the bishop of Rochester, and it was then destroyed and burned on a bonfire. Paul White suggests Bale's iconoclastic treatment of Catholic ceremonies works in a fashion analogous to the rood burning in that both demystify the object of veneration by displacing it from its original holy context. White's argument applies directly to Wager's play, wherein the once venerated saint's statue is vigorously debased by its relocation in a morally and physically corrupted universe (*Theatre and Reformation*, 36–37).

38. "Against the Peril of Idolatry," 2:2:3, 2792. Also cited in Aston, *England's Iconoclasts*, 129.

39. Wager's fashion-conscious Magdalene is drawn from medieval sources, in particular the *Legenda aurea* and the Digby Mary Magdalene play, where she appears as noble from birth, descended from a line of kings. In these stories, Mary's fall and her expensive taste in clothing are inherited legacies. See Haskins, *Mary Magdalen*, 157–58. For references in the play to Mary's predisposition to sartorial excess, see Wager, 143–90. For a Protestant take on the excesses of dress, particularly in women, see "Against Excess of Apparel" in *The Elizabethan Homilies*, as well as Gosson's *Pleasant Quippes*. The concern over the potency and allure of fashionable femininity extends beyond Mary to the effeminate vice figures who are themselves "dressed up" as Catholic clergymen. This dissembling is further evidence of Mary's corruption—Carnall Concupiscence becomes Pleasure, "that pretie Marie loueth beyond all measure." Moreover, the vices' ability to make artifice pass for virtue ensures that the duplicity of Catholicism remains associated with the affectations of femininity (Wager, 32, 33, 51, 466). Stallybrass provides evidence that the church, having no further use for its Catholic garments, sold or rented the items, on occasion, to players. Thus, memories of Catholic ceremony are literally set against representations of the feminized priest and the virile, overdressed monk made popular in medieval literature. See Stallybrass, "Worn Worlds," 305–6, 312.

40. See Cunnington and Cunnington, *The History of Underclothes*, 27, 32–37. See also Cunnington and Cunnnington, *Handbook of English Costume*, 53–86, 149–89; Ewing, *Dress and Undress*, 21–34; Ewing, *Fashion in Underwear*, 20–31.

41. Kunzle, working through Michel Foucault, has concluded that it is not a historical accident that waist confinement and décolletage remained

fashionable from the fourteenth century down to World War I, for these are "the primary sexualizing devices of Western costume, which arose when people first became sexually conscious, and conscious of sexual guilt in a public and social way." Thus, Mary's underwear signals both her own deviance and her society's desire to control it ("Dress Reform," 578–79).

42. Thomas adds that Puritan writers "shared the widespread notion that there was something effeminate and undesirable about excessive cleanliness" ("Cleanliness," 66). Infidelitie further describes Mary as "a pretie mynion, / Feate, cleane made, wel compact, and aptly lymmed" (193–94).

43. St. Mary Magdalene's girdle "sent to women travailing" was shipped from Burton in Somerset. See Duffy, *The Stripping of the Altars*, 384.

44. Calvin, *A very profitable treatise*, B1r, cited in Diehl, *Staging Reform*, 16.

45. *Letters and Papers* 4, no. 42. Cited in Duffy, *The Stripping of the Altars*, 384.

46. Haskins notes that most visual and literary representations of Mary Magdalene, from the fourteenth century onward, depict the figure with red or fair hair, conforming to contemporary ideals of feminine beauty. Loose hair was a moral indicator and as such was suitable only for young girls and virgins. Upon marriage, women were to wear their hair up, a custom that survived until the Victorian period. As for color, Firenzuola's treatise on feminine beauty, *Del Dialogo*, 91v, remarks that a woman's hair, ideally "fine and blond," was a principal factor in determining beauty. See Haskins, *Mary Magdalen*, 246–48, for a further discussion of the semiotic connotations of blonde hair.

47. The *bon grâce*, a decorated cap headdress, is mentioned at 670–71 as coming "farre ouer [her] face." See Cunnington and Cunnington, *Handbook*, 74.

48. For a discussion of how this moment is worked out in medieval drama, see Coletti's discussion of the exorcism of Mary Magdalene in the N-Town play (*Mary Magdalene*, 90–91).

49. *Statutes of the Realm*, 3 and 4 Edward VI, c.10, 4:110–11. The statute was a more forceful articulation of Edward's third set of injunctions issued in 1547. Hughes and Larkin, *Tudor Royal Proclamations* 2, no. 460, 123. See also Frere and Kennedy, *Visitation Articles*, 2:116. These resolute pronouncements ordered visitors to "take way, utterly extinct, and destroy all shrines, covering of shrines, all tables, candlesticks, trindles and rolls of wax, pictures, paintings, and all other monuments of feigned miracles, pilgrimages, idolatry, and superstition, so that there remain no memory of the same in walls, glasses, windows or elsewhere within their churches and houses." Aston notes that these injunctions betray the adoption of extreme principles by means of which "England seemed to be aligning with the *ne plus ultra* iconoclasts" (*England's Iconoclasts*, 258). Further discussion of Edwardian iconoclasm can be found in Phillips, *The Reformation of Images*, 82–100; Duffy, *The Stripping of the Altars*, 448–77; Simpson, "The Rule of Medieval Imagination," 13.

50. Cranmer, *Cathechismvs*, C5–v; also referenced in Aston, *England's Iconoclasts*, 431. *Three Chapters of Letters*, 143, 224. See also Duffy, *The Stripping of the Altars*, 385.

51. For a discussion of the chemise, see Cunnington and Cunnington, *History of Underclothes*, 32–34. The use of the word *sad* is also reminiscent of the sumptuary laws wherein the term was equated with a suitable kind of modesty. For a discussion of the same moment in the Digby play, see Coletti, *Mary Magdalene*, 181–82. Painted images of the penitent Magdalene will be discussed in chapter 4.

52. Crawford has noted that within the more masculine deity of the Reformation, where emphasis fell on the omnipotence rather than the suffering of Christ and where the denigration of images left only the masculine Trinity and an all-male ministry before the eyes of believers, modest piety was the only legitimate feminine expression of faith. Women could not become priests or theologians, and with the closure of the monasteries and abbeys, a religious vocation was no longer a possibility for unmarried women (*Women and Religion*, 37). Calvin seems to grant certain apostolic vocations to New Testament women; however, his overall position on women is still disputed by scholars: some have argued that his writing is steeped in hierarchy and hostile to sixteenth-century defenses of women, while others have gestured to his protofeminist tendencies. To the exceptionally pious woman, it appears that Calvin, and Wager, accord certain ministerial or apostolic functions ("I shall declare his mercy in towne and citie" [Wager, 1951]), but this freedom to speak is considerably limited. For discussions of Calvin and feminism, see Douglass (who defends him), *Women, Freedom and Calvin*; Thompson (who writes on his hierarchical view of women's role in faith), *John Calvin*.

53. Kronenfeld, *King Lear*, 27–28.

54. The history of the nude Magdalene is a long one. In *The Old English Martyrology*, Mary retreats into the desert following the resurrection and lives there both penitent and naked. The earliest visual images of the naked Mary appear in the second decade of the thirteenth century; in these portraits her hair generally covers from head to foot what is evidently a nude figure. By the fifteenth century the hair tends to be drawn back to reveal the full body of the figure, though the nakedness of the subject suggests its innocence. Haskins draws attention to Bonamicus's fresco dated 1225 in the chapel of the Church of St. Prospero in Perugia, in which Mary's body is covered from head to toe by her hair. The altarpiece of the Apocalypse in the Victoria and Albert Museum (Haskins notes it was probably made for the Franciscan Magdalene Cloister in Hamberg, c. 1400) represents the figure entirely naked except for a strategically placed frond. In the panel of Quentin Metsys (1466–1530; Philadelphia Museum of Art), Mary kneels facing Mary of Egypt: both are naked and yet appear innocent and sexless. Renaissance paintings of the penitent Magdalene fre-

quently portray an entirely or partially naked figure. Titian's rendition (c. 1530; fig. 27) and Correggio's reading penitent (d. 1522; fig. 3) are but two examples that present a truth that is entirely stripped of its coverings. Other nude Magdalenes roughly contemporary to Wager's play include Tintoretto's (c. 1598; Musei Capitolini, Rome) and Annibale Carracci's (c. 1600; Fitzwilliam Museum, Cambridge) penitent Magdalenes. For a thorough discussion of these nude Magdalenes, see Haskins, *Mary Magdalen*, 232–36. For a full treatment of the use of drapery in the representation of the female body, see Hollander's chapter on "undress" in *Seeing Through Clothes*, 157–236. See also Nead, *The Female Nude*.

55. Kendall, *Drama of Dissent*, 110. Beckwith argues that in Bale's plays "a theater of epistemological doubt in a signifying language of appearance and reality replaces a theater of acknowledgment that uses the play of presence and absence as its signifying idiom, a presence and absence understood through and achieved by means of the community's availability to and presence to itself" (*Signifying God*, 152).

56. Diehl writes that "the breaking of familiar and well-loved images necessitates the making of new ones," and that these "new ways of seeing" were more "skeptical, more self-reflexive, and more attentive to what lies beyond visual representations" (*Staging Reform*, 46).

57. Wager has his robust Calvinism absolutely straight by this point. Mary re-enters the stage accompanied by the character of Justification, who righteously reminds the audience that salvation is by no means the direct result of the love of Christ; it is by virtue of Christ's mercy alone that Mary is granted grace. Only after this postulate is fully understood, can Divine Love enter the stage. Finally, the lines of the play spoken by Love himself resume the progress of Mary's repentance in explicitly Calvinist terms:

> By the word came faith, Faith brought penitence,
> But bothe the gyft of Gods magnificence.
> Thus by Faith onely, Marie was iustified,
> Like as before it is playnly verified,
> From thens came loue, as a testification
> Of Gods mercy and her iustification.
>
> (2129–34)

For more detail on Wager's Calvinist agenda see Paul White, "Lewis Wager's *Life and Repentaunce*," 508–12; *Theatre and Reformation*, app. B, 181–85. See also Happé, "The Protestant Adaptation," 205–40.

58. Shaxton, for example, felt that the contemplation of a picture, when accompanied by appropriate textual interpretations, encouraged "men's minds be stirred and kindled sometimes to virtue and constancy, in faith and love towards God, and sometimes to lament for their sins and offenses" (*Church of*

England Visitation Articles, 2:57). For a further discussion of the relationship between books and images, see Diehl's useful study of Foxe's *Book of Martyrs* in *Staging Reform*, 22–39. For a discussion of the defense of images in the later Middle Ages, see Simpson, "The Rule of Medieval Imagination," 16–19.

59. Koerner, *The Reformation of the Image*, 20.

60. As Womack has argued, theater is "idolatrous in its essential nature because it works by setting up false images with the intention that they should be taken for truths . . . however assiduously it proclaims Protestant doctrines, theater is still a *Catholic kind of thing* in its suspect reassigning of substance: a brown paper effigy is a dragon; some base fellow is Christ; wine is blood" ("Shakespeare," 177). See also Coletti, *Mary Magdalene*, 200–204.

61. This sequence from John 20 is not dramatized in Wager's play. Harvey, "Introduction," 15.

62. Shuger, *The Renaissance Bible*, 188. Wager's representation of Christ on stage resonates powerfully against medieval debate on the uses and abuses of the body of Christ for entertainment purposes. The Lollard (or Wycliffite) *Tretise of Miraclis Pleyinge* (1380–1425) argues that the playing of the Passion is a "scorning of Crist," whose own body never laughed but was the source of "penaunse, teris and scheding of blod." The spectator, it follows, should never derive recreational pleasure (associated with carnal pleasure) from the representation of the corporeal suffering of Christ; instead, the response to Christ's Passion should be "in disciplining of oure fleyssh, and in penaunce of adversite." The greatest source of anxiety in the *Tretise*, however, is not just the tension between diversion and devotion, but also the issue of visual representation itself. The most vitriolic antitheatricalism is, in fact, concerned precisely with the question of mimesis, wherein actors' bodies reconstitute sacred events for a viewing public. The use of the disguised body to replace that of Christ and the use of the staged voice to replace the words of the sanctioned Gospel were understood as travesty and as corrupting the "earnestness" of the original holy deeds (*A Tretise of Miraclis Pleyinge*, 113, 95–96).

63. Erasmus, *Paraphrase*, n.p.

64. Erasmus, *Paraphrase*, n.p.

65. Erasmus, *Paraphrase*, n.p.

66. Erasmus, *Paraphrase*, n.p.

67. Calvin, *Harmonie*, 368–69.

68. *Life and Repentaunce* was written for a troupe of "four men and a boy." The casting chart on the printed title page indicates that the child actor played Mary Magdalene and the adults doubled the vice/virtue roles. See Paul White, *Reformation Biblical Drama*, xxiii.

69. "The argument against transvestite actors," Orgel notes, warns that male spectators "will be seduced by the impersonation, and losing their reason will become effeminate, which in this case means not only that they will

lust after the woman in the drama, which is bad enough, but also after the youth beneath the woman's costume" (*Impersonations*, 27). See also Levine, *Men in Women's Clothing*.

70. Interestingly, the medieval Digby play seems to be more self-aware in this respect. Coletti writes, "The Digby saint play articulates an alternative conception of a deity who is recognized principally not by his corporeal signs but his divine power, intimating that its own spectacular visual and material resources are susceptible to critique as conduits of sacred knowledge" (*Mary Magdalene*, 192–93).

71. See Diehl, *Staging Reform*, 26; Simpson, "The Rule of Medieval Imagination," 23–24.

72. Nora, *Realms of Memory*, 1, 3, 6. Nora writes that "unlike historical objects, *lieux de mémoire* have no referents in reality; or, rather they are their own referents—pure signs. This is not to say that they are without content, physical presence, or history—on the contrary. But what makes them *lieux de mémoire* is precisely that which allows them to escape from history" (19).

73. Simpson, "The Rule of Medieval Imagination," 22.

74. The song at 870 ff. repeats the blazon.

75. Gregorius I, "Homilia 33," *Patrilogia Latina*, 76, col. 1239. Translated and cited in Haskins, *Mary Magdalen*, 96.

76. Jacobus, "Seynt Marye Magdalene," CCxvii; Bokenham, *Legendys*, 158.

77. Jansen writes that tears "represented the state of contrition—sorrowful, painful, and bitter" and that they "denote woman per se, since they were a form of water, an archetypal emblem gendered female" (*The Making of the Magdalen*, 194, 209).

78. *Saint Mary Magdalen*, 94.

79. Coletti, *Mary Magdalene*, 213.

80. Belting, *Likeness and Presence*, 15–16, 459.

81. Erasmus, *Paraphrase*, n.p.

82. J. C., *Saint Marie Magdalens Conversion*, A1v.

83. J. C., *Conversion*, A4, B1v.

84. J. C., *Conversion*, C1.

85. Katherine Hastings (née Dudley) was Robert Dudley's sister and aunt to Mary and Philip Sidney. Katherine's husband, Henry Hastings, Earl of Huntingdon, was entrusted with the keeping of Mary Queen of Scots. After his death in 1595, Katherine remained in the close company of the queen. A number of theological works were penned under her patronage.

86. T. Collins, *Penitent Pvblican*, C3.

87. J. C., *Conversion*, C1.

88. Drummond, "For the Magdalene," 145–46.

89. Sweetnam, *S. Mary Magdalens Pilgrimage*, 17.

90. Sweetnam, *S. Mary Magdalens Pilgrimage*, 24, 36, 139, frontispiece.

Chapter 2.   Touch Me Not

1. Walkington, *The Optik Glasse.*
2. Walkington, *Rabboni,* 132.
3. Walkington, *Rabboni,* 15–16.
4. Walkington, *Rabboni,* 8. The courtly motif is also very much part of the medieval tradition. See, for example, Bokenham's *Legendys,* which reads the Magdalene's privilege and distinction as a function of her ardent love:

> See now þan how þis perfyth creature
>   Conioynyd was on-to her creatur,
>   Of trewe loue þorgh affeccyoun pure,
>   And eek he to hyr in syngulere amour;
>   For nere of hys lyf in þe last our,
>   Euen by a lytyl beforn hys passyoun,
>   Of hyr he made þis specyal commendacyoun.
>   (155–56)

5. Walkington, *Rabboni,* 33–34.
6. Walkington, *Rabboni,* 38.
7. Walkington, *Rabboni,* 39, 42.
8. Walkington, *Rabboni,* 56–58.
9. Nora, *Realms of Memory,* 12.
10. Walkington, *Rabboni,* 89, 93.
11. See, for instance, Sullivan, "The Physiology of Penitence," 31–47. Sullivan has observed that the literature of tears tends to reverse the expectations raised in the secular sonnet: "Far from the gaze defining the poet by affording him a coherent view of an ideal object," she suggests, "the poet becomes the object of his tears' attempts to cleanse him" (31). See also Kuchar, *The Poetry of Religious Sorrow,* and Sullivan, *The Rhetoric of the Conscience,* both of which were published just as this book went to press.
12. Phillippy, *Women, Death, and Literature.* See in particular 30–39.
13. Belting, *Likeness and Presence,* 484.
14. Walkington, *Rabboni,* 42.
15. Scarry asks, "Why, when the lights go out and the storytelling begins, is the most compelling tale (most convincing, most believable) a ghost story?":

> Since most of us have no experience of ghosts in the material world, this should be the tale we least easily believe. The answer is that the story instructs its hearers to create an image whose own properties are second nature to the imagination: it instructs its hearers to depict in the mind something thin, dry, filmy, two-dimensional, and without solidity. Hence the imaginers' conviction: we at once recognize, perhaps with amazement, that we are picturing, if not with vivacity, then with exquisite correctness,

precisely the thing described. It is not hard to imagine a ghost successfully. What is hard is successfully to imagine an object, any object, that does not look like a ghost. (*Dreaming by the Book*, 23–24)

16. The homily's medieval and early modern editors assumed its author was Origen, though it now seems likely that the homily was of Cistercian origin. It is also associated with Chaucer's prologue to *A Legend of Good Women*, in which Alceste reminds Cupid that Chaucer's praise of women is made manifest in his translation of "Orygenes upon the Maudeleyne." See McCall, "Chaucer and the Pseudo Origen," 491–97; Delasanta and Rousseau, "Chaucer's *Orygenes*," 319–42. Saxer's tally of 185 manuscripts replaces McCall's earlier count of 130. Saxer has identified at least 24 fourteenth- and fifteenth-century manuscripts of English provenance. He provides an account of these (including locations and provenance) in "L'homilie latine," 667–76.

17. The Latin text was printed in London by William Menyman for Richard Whitington under the title *Omelia orige[n]is de beata maria magdalena*. The 1555 English translation, entitled *An Homelie of Marye Magdalene, declaring her ferue[n]t loue and zele towards Christ. Newly Translated*, was printed for Henry Sutton. The second edition was printed for Reginald Wolfe in 1565.

18. "Dulcis magister," the narrator implores, "ad quid provocas spiritum huius mulieris et animum eius [que] tota pendet in te, tota manet in te, tota sperat in te, tota desperate de se." *Omelia origenis*, 334.

19. *Omelia origenis*, 340.

20. The figure of the angel asks, "Quem quaeritis?" and the three respond, "Ihesum Nazarenum." The angel replies, "Non est hic. Surrexit sicut praedixerat. Ite, nuntiate quia surrexit a mortuis," and the three turn to the choir, singing, "Alleluia. Resurrexit Dominus." The angel calls the women back, speaking the antiphon "Vinite et videte locum," and then the angel shows them the empty sepulcher and the discarded linen. The three then take up the linen and show that the Lord has risen as they sing the antiphon "Surrexit Dominus de sepulchro." The source of the Quem quaeritis is the *Regularis concordia*. The relevant page is reprinted in Kobialka, *This Is My Body*, 78. The translation used here is roughly Kobialka's (77–79). There is a simpler (though not earlier) version of the trope that functioned as the Introit to the Easter mass found in a manuscript in the Monastery of St. Gall (c. 950). This version does not include the angel's request that the Marys examine the sepulcher.

21. Kobialka, *This Is My Body*, viii, 32–33, 35–39, 198, 217–18.

22. I am moving from the Latin original to an English translation for convenience and because, for the moment, the differences between the two have no bearing on my argument. I will return to these differences shortly at the point where they begin to matter.

23. *An Homelie*, A4, C1v.

24. The work of medievalists such as Beckwith, Bynum, and Rubin has done much to articulate the corporeal substance of late medieval piety and thus to cement the bond between the physical body and any location or place that might be called the soul. Moreover, recent work by early modern scholars such as Paster, Maus, and Schoenfeldt has solidified the early modern interest in an increasingly dichotomized, and yet frustratingly inconsistent, discourse on the relationships between bodies and souls, and between reason and the passions or senses. See Beckwith, *Christ's Body* and *Signifying God*; Bynum, *Fragmentation and Redemption* and "Why All the Fuss About the Body?"; Rubin, *Corpus Christi*; Paster, *The Body Embarrassed*, "The Body and Its Passions," 44–50, and *Humoring the Body*; Maus, *Inwardness and Theater*; Schoenfeldt, *Bodies and Selves*, especially chapter 1, "Bodies of Rule," as well as "That Spectacle of Too Much Weight," 561–84.

25. *An Homelie*, A5v.

26. *An Homelie*, A5v.

27. *An Homelie*, B4v, B8, C1, C2.

28. Southwell, *Funeral Teares*, 48.

29. For further discussion of the loss of affect as a sign of separation from God, see Kuchar, *Divine Subjection*, 22–23. Kuchar has recently expanded upon his earlier reading of the "radical self-division" of Southwell's Magdalene, arguing that the split she suffers "between the inward conscience and the outward ceremonial that should be its expression is precisely the antagonism that characterizes the recusant's dilemma as Southwell describes it. And it is this antagonism that the work as a whole seeks to symbolically mitigate" ("Gender and Recusant Melancholia," 141).

30. Both Magdalene poems were first published as companion pieces to Southwell's *S. Peters complaint*, 35–36, 37–38.

31. *An Homelie*, A6v.

32. *An Homelie*, C4v–C5. The homilist's description of the Magdalene's need for holy sustenance is an allusion to one of the legendary aspects of the Magdalene's life, largely excised from her *vita* by the Council of Trent in 1563. I return to the desert legend in the next chapter in the context of the contemplative life of early modern Magdalenes.

33. Beckwith, *Signifying God*, 31, 73–74.

34. *An Homelie*, C6.

35. *An Homelie*, A3.

36. Southwell, *Funeral Teares*, 5, 17.

37. Kuchar, *Divine Subjection*, 38–39, 56, 70. Kuchar's reading also considers how the "excessive nature of the Magdalene's passion for Christ is simultaneously celebrated and contained" in order to demonstrate how the figure's "passion for Christ betrays long-held anxieties about the devotional power of women" (39, 55–71). See also Kuchar, "Gender and Recusant Melancholy,"

149–51. McClain has also suggested that "Mary Magdalene resonated with English Catholics of the sixteenth and seventeenth centuries because she shared a common trial of faith—the loss of Christ's body." Strong devotion to the saint thus reflected English fear over losing access to the mass, and Southwell's work (as well as that of other English Catholic writers) represents an effort to comfort the laity over this loss ("They have taken away my Lord," 77–78).

38. *The Passion Play*, 154.

39. Jacobus, "Seynt Marye Magdalene," CCxvi.

40. *The Towneley Plays*, 318.

41. Julian of Norwich, *A Revelation of Love*, 3.

42. Southwell, *Funeral Teares*, 12v–13, 29.

43. On the subject of literary ghosts in relation to the doctrine of purgatory, see Greenblatt, *Hamlet in Purgatory*. In particular, see his discussion of means by which Christians could distinguish between good and evil ghosts (103–5) and his apropos treatment of Aristotle, memory, and the perception of likeness: "For Aristotle, this perception is the way one knows, when one is contemplating a mental image or *phantasm* that it is in fact a memory—the remembrance of something that belongs irrevocably to the past—and not something that fully exists in the present. The mind is aware of a ratio between what actually once existed: a memory is grasped as a likeness, as he puts it, 'relative to something else'" (215). Greenblatt is citing Aristotle's *On Memory*, from *The Complete Works of Aristotle*, edited by Jonathan Barnes, 2 vols. (Princeton: Princeton University Press, 1984), 1:716.

44. In his discussion of the figure of Doubting Thomas, who also features in John 20, Most argues that the prohibition upon Mary's touch exists primarily to prepare for the Thomas sequence in the second half of the chapter, "in which the question of touching Jesus' body will be the central issue—but in which, so far from prohibiting a woman from touching him, Jesus will invite a man to touch him" (*Doubting Thomas*, 41). Most's point is that Thomas doesn't, in the end, touch Christ even though he is invited to do so. This detail would appear to confirm sight as a viable form of knowledge; however, Most argues that Jesus' treatment of Thomas suggests that he dismisses "such belief as second-rate in comparison with the faith of those people who only hear a verbal message but can nonetheless succeed in believing on that basis alone . . . it is on the sole basis of these verbal messages that those people whom Jesus praises for believing will be able to do so" (60).

45. Coletti, *Mary Magdalene*, 83. Jansen shows that the prohibition was used in the fourth century to argue that women were forbidden to teach in the church; see *Making of the Magdalen*, 54.

46. Beckwith, *Signifying God*, 85–86.

47. Southwell, *Funeral Teares*, 63.

48. Southwell, *Funeral Teares*, 68–68v.

49. Erasmus, *Paraphrase*, PPp 6v–7v.

50. Erasmus is not alone in this reading. Calvin's commentaries on John 20 focus predictably on the *noli me tangere*, with reference to Matthew 28:9 and Luke 24:39. When Christ saw his disciples embracing "his feete too busily, he did moderate and correct that rash zeale." Of Mary's prohibition in John, Calvin concludes, "We must persuade our seules that they were not forbidden to touch him vntil such time as Christ had see[n]e y^t he was retained and kept in the worlde with their foolish and unseasonable desires." Zwingli goes even further by arguing that Christ's refusal to be touched by Mary Magdalene constitutes a prohibition on all forms of three-dimensional representation of his person. Christ's encounter with Mary teaches us that "we ought to be taught by the word of God externally, and by the Spirit internally, those things that have to do with piety, and not by sculpture wrought by the artist's hand." Zwingli's treatment of the Magdalene suggests that her function is to show us "that we worship a God who is invisible and who forbids us to make any visible representation of him." Calvin, *Harmonie*, 439; Zwingli, *Commentary*, 332.

51. Kessler, *Spiritual Seeing*, 136. Kessler's articulation of spiritual seeing is essentially Augustinian. The Augustine references are from *De Genesi ad literam* and are as follows:

> Tunc enim cogitarent Deum, si ab illis et ab eorum oculis homo auferretur, ut amputata familiaritate quae cum carne erat facta, discerent vel absente care divinitatem cogitar. Sermo 264, *Patrologia Latina* 38, 1214. (As cited in Kessler, *Spiritual Seeing*, 236n117)

> Siue cum absentia corpora iam nota cogitamus, ut ex eis formetur quidam spriritalis aspectus. 12, 23, *Corpus Scriptorum Ecclesiasticorum Latinorum*, 414. (As cited in Kessler, *Spiritual Seeing*, 236–37n118)

Beckwith connects the form of sight made possible at the sepulcher with Lollard anti-clericism by citing Wycliffite sermons in which the guarding of Christ's body in the tomb "is made analogous to the retention of Christ as word" (*Signifying God*, 78–80). Lewalski's contention that a new poetics, both Protestant and specifically biblical, shaped the aesthetics of the sixteenth- and seventeenth-century devotional writers also needs to be acknowledged at this point. Specifically relevant to the Magdalene literature is Lewalski's suggestion that, in accordance with Luther, Protestant paradigms of sin and salvation hold that at the time of *justification* a process of *sanctification* is begun. "Sanctification," she argues, "involves the actual but gradual repairing of the defaced image of God in the soul, whereby it enjoys a 'new life.'" The final stage of salvation, *glorification*, is "the perfect restoration of the image of God in man" that "may begin in this life but is fully attained only after death" (*Protestant Poetics*, 18).

52. Nora, *Realms of Memory*, 12.

53. Southwell, *Funeral Teares*, 63v–64.

54. Martz, *Poetry of Meditation*, 185. For further discussion of Southwell's literary theory as reflected in the "Epistle," see Janelle, *Robert Southwell*, 170–72.

55. Martz, *Poetry of Meditation*, 78–79.

56. Harvey, "Introduction," 1–2, 21.

57. Merleau-Ponty, *The Visible and the Invisible*, 133–34. For discussion and critique of Merleau-Ponty's work on touch, see Butler, "Sexual Differences as a Question of Ethics," 68–72, and Grosz, *Volatile Bodies*, 97–111.

58. Susan Stewart, *Poetry*, 2–3, 15, 162, 194.

59. Southwell, *Funeral Teares*, 68v.

60. Kuchar's reading of *Funeral Teares* makes helpful use of Paul Ricoeur's work in order to suggest that the Magdalene's excessive grief posits "disorientation as a means for reorientation." Kuchar writes, "Through a loss of one's claim to self-possession, one is reoriented to 'new possibilities,' to a discovery of another more counterintuitive way of seeing" (*Divine Subjection*, 21). For further discussion of the relation between the lyric and the social, see Adorno's seminal essay, "On Lyric Poetry and Society."

61. Southwell, *Funeral Teares*, A3v, A6.

62. Verstegan, "A Complaint of S. Mary Magdalene," 89–90. Verstegan was a Catholic publicist and spy for the English Mission abroad. He arranged for passports, smuggled books, and oversaw the printing of Catholic books in Antwerp. He wrote polemical and martyrological works as well as devotional translations and religious verse. See Arblaster, "Verstegan, Richard (1548–1640)."

63. Alabaster, "Upon Christ's Saying to Mary," 11.

64. Alabaster, "A Morning Meditation [2]," 39. It appears as though Alabaster converted to Catholicism in 1597. During that summer Alabaster began to write his religious sonnets, including those to Mary Magdalene. He was deprived of his orders and benefices on 20 February 1598. He was imprisoned but escaped and traveled to Rome where he authored a manuscript account of his conversion. In 1599 he was captured by English agents and committed to the Tower, and his testimony surfaced at Essex's trial in 1601. He regained the king's favor, was absolved of his crimes, and was created D. D. at Cambridge in 1614. See Bremer, "Alabaster, William (1568–1640)."

65. Constable, "To St Mary Magdalen" [4], 187, 191–92. Constable was an early convert to Protestantism. While his commitment to the Reformation was initially uncompromising, he would later return to Catholicism. He died in exile in France after a period of imprisonment in the Tower of London for heresy. See Sullivan, "Constable, Henry (1562–1613)."

66. Kuchar argues that by comparing Constable to Southwell, "we can better grasp Constable's unique synthesis of medieval devotional traditions and Counter-Reformation poetic forms." Of particular relevance here is

Kuchar's observation that the apostrophic structure of the poems "makes it possible to unfold a meditation in which the male speaker imagines himself transforming into the female saint." This means of expressing the experience of repentance is, Kuchar suggests, "much more akin to late medieval mysticism than it is to Southwell's Counter-Reformation accounts of Magdalen as ideal penitent" ("Henry Constable and Catholic Poetics," 70, 73).

67. Nora, *Realms of Memory*, 20.

68. The first edition was printed by John Wolfe for Gabriel Cawood in 1591. The second edition was printed by Adam Islip for Gabriel Cawood in 1594. The 1596 edition was printed by James Roberts, also for Cawood. The 1602 and 1609 editions were printed by Roberts and by T. Snodham for William Leake. The text was also published with *S. Peters Complaint* in 1616, 1620, 1630, and 1636 by the Jesuit press, the English College Press. This evidence works to dismantle the long-standing association of Catholicism with spectacle as opposed to literacy—a project that Dolan undertakes in *Whores of Babylon*, where she argues that Catholics "never really inhabited this fantasyland. Like everyone else in the period, Catholics existed in the midst of a sloppy transition from image to word, a transition that, of course, can never be complete" (27–29).

69. The Stationers' Register for 1591 records the following entry for 8 November: "Master Cawood. Entered for his copie under the hand of the Lord Archbishop of Canterbury. A booke entituled, *Mary Magdalen's Funerall teares . . . Vid.*" Cited in Janelle, *Robert Southwell*, 146. Devlin suggests that Cawood may have had Catholic sympathies; see *The Life of Robert Southwell*, 234. For an extensive discussion of the popularity and influence of Southwell's Catholicism, see Shell, *Catholicism*, 60–63. Sullivan also argues for the significance of Catholic influence in *Dismembered Rhetoric*, 20–21.

70. Markham's religious convictions are uncertain. McClain seems to be convinced of his Catholic allegiances ("They have taken away my Lord," 84–85). However, Steggle's entry in the *ODNB* identifies Markham's work with the Essex faction, and Markham's prose adaptation of Philip Sidney's *Arcadia* also links him to more radical Protestantism. It is not clear to me how Markham's name originally became associated with the versification of the Southwell text. A note in the 1604 edition of the Markham text in the British Library says that the text is rare and supposedly by Nicholas Breton. Poynter argues that it is the companion poem to Markham's *The Teares of the Beloved*, published a year earlier (see *A Bibliography of Gervase Markham*, 47). A collation of *Marie Magdalens Lamentations* with Southwell's *Funeral Teares* reveals that the former is, at least in part, a versification of the latter, for its author borrows entire conceits verbatim from Southwell's prose. I concur with Shell's conclusion that the attribution is provocative but not definitive (*Catholicism*, 79–80).

71. Markham, *Marie Magdalens lamentations*, F1.

72. Markham, *Marie Magdalens lamentations*, F2, F3.
73. Markham, *Marie Magdalens lamentations*, F1.
74. Markham, *Marie Magdalens lamentations*, D3v, D5v.
75. See Wall, "Renaissance National Husbandry," 767–85.
76. One could make the same argument for Markham's poetic rendering of the Song of Songs. See Lewalski, *Protestant Poetics*, 66–67.
77. Markham, *Mary Magdalens lamentations*, A3–A3v.
78. Susan Stewart, *Poetry*, 11–12.
79. Shell, *Catholicism*, 80–81.
80. Susan Stewart, *Poetry*, 11.
81. Markham, *Marie Magdalens lamentations*, A3v–A4.
82. Markham, *Marie Magdalens lamentations*, A4v. The complete passage is:

> If you will deigne with favour to peruse
> *Maries* memoriall of her sad lament,
> Exciting *Collin* in his graver Muse,
> To tell the manner of her hearts repent:
>   My gaine is great, my guerdon granted is,
>   Let Maries plaints plead pardon for amisse.

83. Skelton's use of the Colin Clout figure predates Spenser's. Both inherited Colin from "Lamentation for Madame Louise of Savoy," by Clement Marot (1496–1544). I would like to thank Rachel Abramowitz-Tripp for her assistance with this reference. See also Shell, *Catholicism*, 76–77.
84. Susan Stewart, *Poetry*, 2.

Chapter 3.   The Task of Beauty

1. Donne, "To the Lady *Magdalen Herbert*," in *The Complete Poetry*, 333.
2. See Doebler and Warnicke, "Magdalen Herbert Danvers," 5–22.
3. Jansen, *The Making of the Magdalen*, 149–55, 307–32. See also Coletti, *Mary Magdalene*, x.
4. My account of works in which a patron is fashioned as a Magdalene is not exhaustive. See, for instance, Martin, *Mary Magdalen's Tears wip't off* (1659). I have selected for consideration here only the most exquisite examples.
5. Susan Stewart, *Poetry*, 194.
6. Breton dedicated *Pilgrimage to Paradise, Ioyned with the Countess of Penbrookes loue* (1592) and *Auspicante Jehoua. Maries Exercise* (1597) to Pembroke. *The Passions of the Spirit*, once attributed to Pembroke, may also have been originally written for her. See Brennan, "Breton, Nicholas (1554/5–ca. 1626)."

7. See, for example, Breton, *Auspicante Jehoua*, A3–A3v.

8. [Breton], *Marie Magdalens Loue*, D8v. The attribution of the work to Breton remains speculative. For many years, the text's investment in the Magdalene figure allowed biographers to conclude that Breton was an ardent Catholic. However, since we now know that the Magdalene topos was widely used by conformist writers, and given the author's association with Mary Herbert, the possibility of Catholic allegiance seems unlikely. For the most recent account of Breton's life, see Brennan, "Breton, Nicholas (1554/5–ca. 1626)."

9. [Breton], *Marie Magdalens Loue*, A5.

10. [Breton], *Marie Magdalens Loue*, B2v, B5–B6, E2v–E3.

11. Breton, *Auspicante Jehoua*, 6v–7.

12. Jansen, *The Making of the Magdalen*, 116.

13. Jacobus, "Seynt Marye Magdalene," CCxviii.

14. The stage instructions read as follows:

Here xall to angyllys desend into wyldyrnesse, and other to xall bring an oble, opynly aperyng aloft in þe clowddys; þe to benethyn shall bring Mari, and she xall receyve þe bred, and than go aȝen into wyldrynesse. (*Saint Mary Magdalen*, 91)

15. Brown, *The Southern Passion*, 72.

16. For further discussion of Rimini's painting as well as the Magdalene's affinity with St. Francis and the Virgin Mary, see Jansen, *The Making of the Magdalen*, 137–42, 286–306.

17. "Siluer tongu'd Smith, whose well tun'd stile hath made thy death the generall teares of the Muses, queintlie couldst thou deuise heauenly Ditties to *Apolloes* Lute, and teach stately verse to trip it as smoothly, as if *Ouid* and thou had but one soule" (Nashe, *Pierce Penilesse*, 192–93). See Jenkins, "Smith, Henry (ca. 1560–1591)."

18. H. Smith, "Mary's Choice," 330.

19. H. Smith, "Mary's Choice," 321, 323–24, 325.

20. Calvin, *Harmonie*, 371–72.

21. See the provisions for the feast of St. Mary Magdalene, *The boke of the common praier* (1549), Cxxxx–Cxlii.

22. Jansen, *The Making of the Magdalen*, 295.

23. The most accessible account of the Magdalene's travails with/for the King of Provence and his family is found in Jacobus's "Seynt Marye Magdalene." See also Jansen, *The Making of the Magdalen*, 294–303.

24. Peters, *Patterns of Piety*, 237.

25. Breton, "The blessed Weeper," A2.

26. Breton follows in the tradition of Southwell and the pseudo-Origenist homily here.

27. Breton, "The blessed Weeper," F1–F1v.

28. Breton, "The blessed Weeper," F3–F4.

29. Breton, *The Countesse of Penbrookes loue*, 92.

30. Breton, *The Passions of the Spirit*, 40. The poem is dedicated to Mary Houghton. Brennan conjectures that the circumstances surrounding Breton's eventual falling-out with Pembroke may have involved this tactless dedication initiated by the book's printer, Thomas Este. Brennan, "Nicholas Breton's," 221–25.

31. Breton, "The blessed Weeper," F3v.

32. Beckwith, *Christ's Body*, 91–94.

33. Pierre Bersuire (Petrus Berchorius), for example, argues that "Christ is a sort of book written into the skin of the Virgin . . . That book was spoken in the disposition of the Father, written in the conception of the mother, exposited in the clarification of the nativity, corrected in the passion, erased in the flagellation, punctuated in the imprint of the wounds, adorned in the crucifixion above the pulpit, illuminated in the outpouring of the blood, bound in the resurrection, and examined in the ascension" (cited in Gellrich's *The Idea of the Book*, 17). For further discussion of medieval paintings of reading women, see the essays collected in Smith and Taylor, *Women and the Book*. In particular, see L. Smith, "*Scriba, Femina*," 21–44; Driver, "Mirrors of a Collective Past," 75–93; Penketh, "Women and Books of Hours," 266–81.

34. Tintoretto's Magdalene is in the Pinacoteca Capitolino, Rome.

35. The sculpture dates to 1511. The legend associated with this statue is that anyone able to land a coin on the Magdalene's back will soon have a new set of clothes (see Peter, *The Story of the Church*, 15).

36. The authorship of *The complaynt* is uncertain. It was initially assumed to be Chaucer's translation of the pseudo-Origenist homily discussed in the previous chapter. The connection between Chaucer and *The complaynt* likely originates with the sixteenth-century printings of Chaucer's *Book of Fame* which include *The complaynt* in the same volume. The text cited here is from the volume published by Richard Pynson entitled *Here begynneth the boke of Fame, made by Geffray Chaucer: with dyuers other of his workes* (1526), E6, F3v. The British Library Catalogue entry comments that the text is "from Origen" and possibly by Lydgate. The text is the same as that printed by Wynkyn de Worde entitled *The complaynte of the louer of Cryst Saynt Mary Magdaleyn* (1520?). Charles Edward Tame's edition (*Our Lady's Lament and the Lamentation of St. Mary Magdalen*) attributes the poem to Lydgate. There is another nineteenth-century edition, Skeat, *The Lamentatyon of Mary Magdalyn*, which further discusses the authorship question. For further discussion of the Chaucerian question, see McCall, "Chaucer and the Pseudo Origen," 491–509; and Delasanta and Rousseau, "Chaucer's *Orygenes*," 319–41.

37. Bokenham, *Legendys*, 144. This lesson is reinforced in Bokenham's gloss of Mary's weeping at Simon's house in which maudlin display is reconfigured as private confession communicated wordlessly to Christ. "Rendered as a private communication with Christ, rather than public contrition," concludes Sanok, "Magdalene's tears can stand as a model for the legend's patron, Lady Bourchier, ensuring that she does not follow her countrywoman Margery Kempe in a more literal imitation of the story." Sanok, *Her Life Historical*, 126–31.

38. Hooker, *Of the lawes of Ecclesiastical Politie* (fig. 8). The engraving was designed to appeal to James I, pictured in the top left-hand corner. The State (the edifice) descends from God (the Tetragrammaton). Power comes from God to the king as well as to a woman (Mary Magdalene) holding a book (the Scriptures) and to the church (a cathedral). The State itself is supported by two women: Charity and Justice.

39. Shuger, *The Renaissance Bible*, 190–91. Peter Lake's recent discussion of *The Lawes* has questioned the text's canonical status as a "continuation of a variety of (often mutually exclusive) Anglican or English Reformed businesses as usual." Lake argues that, to some readers, the work stated a position at odds with the altogether too hot Protestant mainstream of the post-Reformation English Church. In such readings, Lake finds "the origins of later *avant-garde* conformist and Laudian polemical and pietistic styles of anti-Puritanism." See Lake, "Business as Usual?" 82.

40. Breton, "The blessed Weeper," D4.

41. Breton, "The blessed Weeper," D4v.

42. Breton, "The blessed Weeper," D4v.

43. The problem of propriety between author and patron is differently resolved by Trill, who notes that in *The Countess of Penbrooke's loue* as well as in other Breton texts dedicated to the countess, Pembroke achieves the same "loss of subjecthood" that Luce Irigaray sees as the "core of mysticism." Trill's point is that the speaker in Breton's poems (increasingly identified with Breton himself) "can only achieve the ecstasy of this 'denial' by appropriating a female voice." Breton's ventriloquism of the Magdalene figure in a poem dedicated to Pembroke is ultimately "an acknowledgment of the significance of the 'feminine' in Christianity and his recognition of his exclusion from the privileged intimacy with Christ that both Mary Magdalene and the countess of Pembroke, by different means, were able to obtain." Trill, "Engendering Penitence," 39–40.

44. Breton, "The blessed Weeper," F3v. The correlation between my reading of Breton's and Lanyer's Magdalene poetry and Mary Sidney's self-fashioning as the reader and memorializer of Philip Sidney is very apropos here. See Wall, "Our Bodies/Our Texts?" 131–59; Hodgson, "Prophecy and Gendered Mourning," 111–12.

45. Scarry, *Dreaming by the Book*, 23–24.
46. Breton, "The blessed Weeper," F3v.
47. Breton, "The blessed Weeper," D4.
48. Lanyer, *Salve Deus*, 139.
49. Lanyer, *Salve Deus*, 107.
50. Lanyer, *Salve Deus*, 108.
51. Lanyer, *Salve Deus*, 109.
52. For a discussion of Lanyer's treatment of "the contract of shared grief and sympathy" between women and Christ, see Hodgson's "Prophecy and Gendered Mourning," in which she argues that this unique bond authorizes the female prophetic voice (101–16). See also Kuchar's recent formulation of Lanyer's poetic authority as derived from Marian iconography ("Aemilia Lanyer and the Virgin's Swoon").

Chapter 4.   *Penance in a Sheet*

1. Andrewes, "A Sermon" [1620], 13–14.
2. Andrewes, "A Sermon" [1620], 20–21.
3. Andrewes, "A Sermon" [1621], 28.
4. The appeal is to Chrysostom, Gregory, and Augustine. According to Andrewes, Chrysostom's reading of the passage suggests that the Magdalene's love is both too impassioned and too of this world to be an appropriate means to address her Lord. When "her passion is over," she will then be admitted to his person. Thus the *noli* is considered instruction to all Christians who essentially need "better manners":

> It was but to Mary Magdalene; and to her but till she had learned a little better manners. Not to any, but such as she, or worse than she, that in unbeseeming manner press and proffer to touch Him—the only cause of her repulse. But at another time, when she was on her knees, fell down at His feet, then did she touch Him without any check at all. Be you now but as she was then, and this *noli Me tangere* will not touch you at all. ("A Sermon" [1621], 35)

Andrewes reads Gregory as arguing that Christ prohibits Mary's touch because he has more important things for her to do, namely the preaching of his resurrection ("A Sermon" [1621], 35). And finally, according to Andrewes, Augustine argues that the prohibition is a check on sensual pleasure. Christ is teaching Mary "another touch" that will serve when "the body and bodily touch were taken from us" ("A Sermon" [1621], 37).

5. Andrewes, "A Sermon" [1621], 24.
6. Andrewes, "A Sermon" [1622], 44.

7. The Gospel of Mary Magdalene is part of the collection of works called the Nag Hammadi Library, so named for its discovery in 1945 in Nag Hammadi, Egypt. This finding renewed interest in another text, also a Gospel of Mary, found in Egypt in 1896. For further information, see *The Gospel of Mary Magdalene*, and Pagels, *The Gnostic Gospels*.

8. Lake, "Lancelot Andrewes," 124. Lake is citing Andrewes's sermon preached at Hampton Court before Elizabeth, 6 March 1594.

9. Parry, *Glory, Laud and Honour*, 20–22; and Lake, "Lancelot Andrewes," 113–14, 130–31. See also McCullough, "Making Dead Men Speak," 401–24. For more discussion of Hooker's influence upon Andrewes, as well as for consideration of both Hooker's and Andrewes's contributions to the development of Laudian sensibilities, see Parry, *Glory, Laud and Honour*, 14–19.

10. Parry, *Glory, Laud and Honour*, 21–23. In the preface to his book, Parry refers to the difficulty of finding appropriate terminology to describe the movement that produced the ceremonial aesthetics of the 1620s and 1630s. He argues that the term *Arminianism* is too narrow and perhaps too derogatory. The word *Anglicanism* was not in common usage at the time, and *High Church* is a Victorian anachronism. *Sacramentalism* and *Ceremonialism* are possibilities but are less capacious terms than *Laudianism*, which Parry uses to describe the increased emphasis on "ceremony, liturgy and ornament in the services of the Church from the middle of the second decade of the seventeenth century." Moreover, Parry does not hesitate to use the term to describe individuals espousing Laudian values before the age of Laud. I too acknowledge the difficulty of terminology and deploy all of the above terms in full recognition of their limitations (see Parry, *Glory, Laud and Honour*, xi).

11. The phrase "the bewtie of holiness" was given new life in the 1590s by Hooker (*Of the Laws*, 5, 16:61). Lake argues that Andrewes's approach was heavily Christocentric—that is, for Andrewes it was important for people to *see* Christ's passion (the crucifixion, the resurrection, the harrowing of hell, the triumph over death and the Pentecost) so that they would see their sins as responsible for Christ's death, be moved to repentance and good works, and be reminded of the spiritual gifts bestowed upon them ("Lancelot Andrewes," 120–21).

12. It does not seem likely that van Dyck was present at the preaching of either of Andrewes's Easter sermons. The most recent account of the painter's stay at the court of King James I suggests that he was "newly come to the towne" in October 1620 and that he departed in February 1621. See Howarth, "The Arrival of van Dyck," 709–10. The painter would eventually take up residence in London, at the request of the king, in 1632.

13. Nora, *Realms of Memory*, 12, 20.

14. Huston Diehl's *Staging Reform* is an important example of recent attempts to understand the appeal of the visual to Protestant culture.

15. G. Herbert, "Marie Magdalene," in *The Works of George Herbert*, 173.

16. "The Thanksgiving," in *The Works of George Herbert*, 35. Of these lines, Schoenfeldt writes, "Although imitating the sacrifice of God entails for Herbert a misguided mode of devotion, imitating the words of God, making them your own, entails the ultimate sacrifice—that of the self and its language. In the self-immolation of a fully biblical stylistics, Herbert points to what it might mean to 'copie thy fair though bloudie hand'" ("That Spectacle of Too Much Weight," 577).

17. The most influential proponents of Herbert's Protestant poetics have been Strier ("George Herbert") and Lewalski (*Protestant Poetics*), as well as Veith (*Reformation Spirituality*), Hodgkins (*Authority, Church, and Society*), and Doerksen (*Conforming to the Word*). The challengers include Young (*Doctrine and Devotion*), Guibbory (*Ceremony and Community*), and Clarke (*Theory and Theology*), all of whom argue for more critical flexibility and historical nuance in the assessment of Herbert's political and religious affinities. Whalen provides a useful synopsis of the debate in "George Herbert's Sacramental Puritanism," 1273–77.

18. Martz, *The Poetry of Meditation*, 203; Slater, *The Complete English Works: George Herbert*, xxii; Strier, "Changing the Object," 24, and *Love Known*, 134. See also Strier, "George Herbert and Tears," 229–39.

19. Lewalski, *Protestant Poetics*, 6; Schoenfeldt, *Prayer and Power*, 237–39. See also Vendler, *The Poetry of George Herbert*, 161. Both Vendler and Schoenfeldt find the source of the conflict in Herbert's inability to incorporate religious sentiment in a poem that on some level honors his mother, Lady Magdalene Herbert.

20. Lewalski, *Protestant Poetics*, 13.

21. G. Herbert, "Jordan (I)," in *The Works of George Herbert*, 56. Netzley makes a similar argument in his discussion of Herbert's rendering of sacramental physiology. "The connective or unifying 'experience' that dominates Strier's or Guibbory's, and, to a certain extent, Schoenfeldt's analysis," writes Netzley, "assumes that one can possess an experience of union. However, it is precisely this experience as possession that seems under contestation in *The Temple*" ("Take and Taste," 206). Targoff, in her discussion of the liturgical elements in Herbert's poetry, also notes a commitment to formalized language which suggests that the critical binaries that separate the personal lyric from communal liturgical verse need to be re-evaluated (*Common Prayer*, 99–111).

22. Martz, *From Renaissance to Baroque*, 29. Martz is arguing that Herbert's work shows "the high consciousness of artistry characteristic of the Mannerism of elegance."

23. The south face of the cross shows scenes from the Gospels, all apparently identified by inscriptions from the Vulgate *textus receptus*. The main panel shows Mary Magdalene bending over the feet of Christ and presumably washing them. The inscription from Luke 7:37–38 surrounding this reads AD[TULIT ALABA]STRUM UNGUENTI & STANS RETRO SECUS PEDES EIUS LACRIMIS COEPIT RIGARE PEDES EIUS & CAPILLIS CAPITIS SUI TERGEBAT (She brought an alabaster box of ointment and standing behind His feet she began to wash His feet with her tears, and she wiped [them] with the hairs of her head).

24. *Complaynt of Mary Magdalene.* The image is on f. EV.

25. Osborne, "A Newe Ballad."

26. For further discussion of Oliver's position at court see Edmond, "Oliver, Isaac (c. 1565–1617)."

27. Oliver apparently began work on a painting of the burial of Christ which featured Mary Magdalene "sitting upon the ground wringing both hands agrieving," but he died before it could be finished. Charles I had Oliver's son, Peter, complete the painting, but of it no trace can be found. See Holms, "English Miniature Painters," 25.

28. Parry, *Glory, Laud and Honour*, 23, 105.

29. Villiers flirted with Catholicism in the early 1620s, but Laud persuaded him to remain loyal to the Church of England. See Parry, *Glory, Laud and Honour*, 13.

30. Parry, *Glory, Laud and Honour*, 108–9. Parry asserts that while the queen's chapel was "a well-maintained Catholic establishment," the Chapel Royal at Whitehall "seems to have been characterized by Protestant plainness" (108).

31. For discussion of this window see Parry, *Glory, Laud and Honour*, 66.

32. For further general discussion of art collecting in England and on the contact between the English court and Continental masters, see Peck, *Consuming Splendor*, 162–87; Roston, *Renaissance Perspectives*, 317–18; and Swann, *Curiosities and Texts*, 2. See also the articles collected in Howarth, *Art and Patronage*, and Orgel, "Idols of the Gallery," 251–83.

33. Parry, *Glory, Laud and Honour*, 105–6.

34. Watt, *Cheap Print*, 131–32, 168–77. Watt's study addresses the growing market for woodcut prints citing the "Christus natvs est" (1631) image registered with the Stationers' Company in 1637. See also Aston, *England's Iconoclasts*, 1:92, and S. O'Connell, *The Popular Print in England*, 68–81. O'Connell has observed that while there was no "native English tradition" to speak of, "biblical narratives were less problematic than images of saints and [cheap prints on biblical subjects] even appeared from time to time in the seventeenth century" (68, 80, 156).

35. Parry, *Glory, Laud and Honour*, 118–19.

36. Another print, entitled *The Crucifixion* (1631), engraved by Bolswert after a painting by Rubens, appears also to have been in fairly wide circulation (S. O'Connell, *Popular Print*, 80, 153–56).

37. See Henderson, "Bible Illustration," 175–76.

38. Witnesses summoned at Laud's trial, including Mr. Walley and Michael Sparke, Sr., clerks of Stationers' Hall, would testify that the printed Bibles were indeed publicly sold. A Master Willingham would likewise attest that the pictures sold by Peake were printed under the direction of Laud and his chaplain. Walley further observed that the pictures so offended him that he and his colleagues went to Lambeth to ask Laud whether they should seize them or allow them to be sold. For extensive discussion of these events, see Henderson, "Bible Illustration," 178.

39. See, for instance, the Edinburgh edition of the New Testament printed by Robert Young in 1636. The images reproduced here are from the 1638 Barker printing (ESTC 2329.4). See Griffiths, *The Print in Stuart Britain*, 22.

40. Peake's emendations included alterations to the images that originally included some pictorial representations of God, making what Henderson has described as "a clear distinction between the attitude to the representation of God in England and the attitude not only in Catholic countries but also in Protestant Germany" ("Bible Illustration," 179). See also Aston, "The Bishop's Bible Illustrations," 267–85.

41. Koerner, *The Reformation*, 20.

42. Henderson, "Bible Illustration," 179.

43. Blaise also finds images in Herbert's sensuous signs, though she sees them as extensions of the incarnation, arguing "that words, in Herbert's poetry, really become a new verbal equivalent of icons as defined by Byzantine patristics" ("Sweetnesse redie penn'd," 12).

44. Miller, "Scribal and Print Publication," 14–34. See also Targoff, who points to dedications by Bacon, Harvey, Crashaw, and Vaughan (*Common Prayer*, 95–96).

45. The Little Gidding household numbered about thirty persons. Provisions were made for a regular round of prayer, and a school was established for local children as well as an almshouse for elderly widows.

46. At least twelve Gospel harmonies were produced at Little Gidding, along with one compilation of the books of Kings and Chronicles, one compilation each of the Acts of the Apostles and the book of Revelation, and two compilations of the Pentateuch.

47. The title of the volume is *The Actions & Doctrine & other Passages touching our Lord & Sauior Iesus Christ*. For an inventory and description of all the extant Little Gidding harmonies, see Ransome, "Monotessaron," 22–52.

48. See Blaise, "Sweetnesse redie penn'd," 14.

49. *Materials*, 76.

50. Stanley Stewart, "Herbert and the 'Harmonies,'" 9.

51. Dyck, "So rare a use," 76.

52. *Materials*, 76.

53. "Prayer-Book Protestantism" is Judith Maltby's term (*Prayer Book and People*).

54. Mitchell, *Iconology*, 43.

55. Whalen argues in a similar vein in his article "George Herbert's Sacramental Puritanism." Whalen suggests that Herbert's commitment to Protestantism need not be seen as incompatible with "an avant-guarde fondness for ceremony," and he finds Herbert making a place for the "material integrity of sacramental grace" without compromising the genuinely introspective quality of *The Temple* (1293).

56. Malcolmson, *Heart-Work*, 211.

57. *Materials*, 77–79. The king was so pleased with his new book that he ordered a second harmony of the books of Kings and Chronicles. His wish was granted and the presentations of this "second treasure," as he called it, apparently provoked the king to exclaim, "How happy a prince were I if there were many such virgins in my kingdom that would employ themselves as these do at Gidding" (*Materials*, 79). It has been conjectured that another volume, bound in purple velvet and now in the collection of Lord Salisbury, was received by Prince James, and it is known that John's son, young Nicholas, made a unique polyglot version for Prince Charles after the death of Nicholas senior.

58. Ferrar, *Nicholas Ferrar*, 118.

59. Once he was made aware of the existence of the picture book, Laud claims he sent for one himself and then acquainted the Lords of the Council with it, who resolved they should not be "sold publickly, nor laid upon stalls, for feare of giving scandall"; rather, they should be sold privately and then only "to learned and Discreet Men." When accused of authorizing the "Englishing" and the republication of the images on native soil, Laud again affirmed his innocence by testifying that he first learned of the Bibles when he saw one in a woman's hand (Mistress Kirkes) in the chapel in Whitehall; at this point he ordered one and further asked that they be sold only to those who asked for them. He advised "that they might doe well not to lay them out publickly upon their stals to be sold as yet, lest they should give offence; but if any come to ask for them or to buy them in your shops, in Gods name sell them freely to them, without any scruple; adding the second time, sell them to such in Gods name, but lay them not upon your stals in publick view." Here again, Laud's attitude toward the pictures is that they are dangerous only if they fall into the hands of those unable to read them properly (Prynne, *Canterburies Doome*, 109–10, 491). See also Henderson, "Bible Illustration," 176–78. For further discussion of the "peril" of the images within the rhetoric of antipopery,

see Lake, "Anti-Popery," 74, 96–97. Also, see Lake with Questier, *The Anti-Christ's Lewd Hat*.

60. Wells-Cole, *Art and Decoration*. The first chapter in this book is an informative introduction to the circulation of prints in early modern England, with particularly useful discussions of the presence of Continental prints in private libraries. Griffiths's book *The Print in Stuart Britain* provides the most extensive treatment of the subject, including a comprehensive discussion of printing practices, censorship, and licensing and copyright issues.

61. Bardon describes the print as exemplary of the baroque "open" style (*style ouverte*) which would dominate French impressions of the Magdalene between 1625 and 1660 ("Le thème de la Madeleine," 275). The coat of arms in the bottom right-hand corner belongs to Dominique Seguier (d. 1659), brother to the chancellor of France and bishop of Meaux. Mellan was a presence in England after accepting an invitation to come to London in 1637. His plans apparently fell through, though it is clear from the invitation that the English court was interested in his work. Griffiths suggests that Mellan's influence in England can be gauged by the fact that the English engraver William Faithorne copied his work in the 1640s (*The Print in Stuart Britain*, 71).

62. These prints are featured, alongside those by Bolswert, in the Royal Harmony. Ferrar seems to have bought most of his prints abroad and then brought the prints back to Little Gidding, where his nieces did their scissor work (*Materials*, 77–78). The style of most of the pictures is high Renaissance or mannerist, after Rubens and Raphael. There are no Italian or French images in the collection, and the Peake engravings are the only English images. The rest, with one exception (a Dürer), are from the Netherlands. Griffiths suggests this is "striking proof" of the extent to which the Netherlands supplied the London print market; however, it is likely only evidence of the extent to which the Netherlands served Ferrar (see Griffiths, *The Print in Stuart England*, 22). Along with the work of Bolswert, the harmonies preserve images engraved by (or after engravings or paintings by) Boethius's brother Schelte, Martin de Vos, Johannes Stradanus, Maarten van Heemskerck, and Gerard de Jode. I have not been able to identify the engravers of the images of the feast at the house of Simon the Pharisee. Similar works, engraved by Raimondi (*Christ at the table of Simon the Pharisee*, after Raphael's design for a lunette fresco for S. Trinite dei Monti, Rome) and Visscher (after Rubens's *Supper in the House of the Pharisee*, in the Hermitage, St. Petersburg), seem to have been ubiquitous. The Raimondi can be viewed in the Fine Arts Museums of San Francisco ImageBase; and a copy of the Visscher can be found bound in a collection of images from the Old and New Testament, produced in Amsterdam in 1583 (British Museum Print collection, catalogue no: 157* b.25). For further discussion of the prints in the Little Gidding harmonies, see Henderson, "Bible Illustration," 193–94.

63. Peck, *Consuming Splendor*, 162, 180–86. An example of the presence of prints in court collections is provided by the plate of Carracci's *The Agony in the Garden*, made at the command of Charles I, who owned the original. Vorsterman presented another print of the entombment to Queen Henrietta Maria; it appears in the inventory of the collection of Charles I. For further discussion of the circulation of prints through the court of Charles I, see Griffiths, *The Print in Stuart Britain*, 71–104.

64. Stradling, *Diuine Poemes*, 271. The volume is divided into seven "classes." The Magdalene stanza cited here is from the sixth class, which deals with "the Passion, with all circumstances traced." For other stanzas dedicated to the Magdalene, see 232 and 262.

65. Sherburne, *Poems and Translations*. The Magdalene poems fall into the fourth section of the book (*Sacra*): "Draw me, and I will follow Thee" (162); "And she washed his Feet with her teares, and wiped them with the Hairs of her Head" (167). There is also a third Magdalene poem ("Mary Magdalene weeping under the Cross") in the collection; it is only two lines long: "I Thirst, my dear, and dying Saviour cries: / These Hills are dry: O Drink then from my eyes" (169).

66. Bancroft, "To penitent Magdalen," G; Owen, "Upon Mary Magdalen," 89.

67. Swann, *Curiosities and Texts*, 8. Also Swann's fourth chapter, in which she explores the way in which seventeenth-century authors developed new forms of writing indebted to collecting practices.

68. Many of the characteristics I am attributing to the Magdalene epigrams are also attributable to mannerism. Martz has made this equation (*From Renaissance to Baroque*, 29), as has Semler, who argues in *The English Mannerist Poets* that in mannerist art (painting and poetry) "the subject becomes object; body becomes ornament." The figures of the Florentine mannerists, Semler explains, express "not feelings but a precision of elegant art in their faces" (21–24, 37). The same can be said of the Magdalene epigrams. I have not pushed the analogy because I have not come across a mannerist Magdalene portrait that fits comfortably within this exclusively English discussion. The best approximation I know of is Girolamo Savoldo's *Magdalen at the Sepulcher* (c. 1530), London, National Gallery. For further treatment of the relationship between early modern poetry and mannerist painting, see Roston's chapter on George Herbert in *Renaissance Perspectives*.

69. Marvell, "Eyes and Tears," 52.

70. Nigel Smith, *The Poems of Andrew Marvell*, 50.

71. Kuchar, "Andrew Marvell's Anamorphic Tears," 347, 371.

72. Hartwig, "Tears as a Way of Seeing," 73, 77, 80.

73. Marvell, "Eyes and Tears," 53.

74. Semler cites Freedburg in making this observation of mannerist painters (*The English Mannerist Poets*, 24). See also Freedburg, "Observations on the Painting of the Maniera," 187–99, 188.

75. See Fisher, "Whitehall, Robert (bap. 1624, d. 1685)."

76. Herrick, "Observation," in *The Poems of Robert Herrick*, 384. The poem belongs to a collection of epigrams recalling biblical scenes, entitled *His Noble Numbers*, first published as an appendix to *Hesperides* in 1648.

77. *Ekphrasis* is also to be distinguished from the Renaissance *paragone*, the term used to describe a competition between the arts. See Hurley, *John Donne's Poetry*, 25.

78. Mitchell, "Ekphrasis and the Other," in *Picture Theory*, 158–59, 163.

79. Vaughan, "St Mary Magdalen," 343–44.

80. Wells-Cole has discovered that another collection of biblical illustrations, also by de Vos, published in Antwerp by Adriaen Collaert under the title *Vita, Passio, et Resurrectio Iesu Christi, variis Inconibus a celeberrimo pictore Martino de Vos expressa, ab Adrianon Collart nunc pirmum in aes incisa*, was used as a basis of decoration in England (*Art and Decoration*, 103–15). Parry also discusses the importance of Flemish prints to the redecoration of churches under Laud's direction (*Glory, Laud and Honour*, 62).

81. See Martz's discussion of Vaughan and Rembrandt and the Protestant baroque in *From Renaissance to Baroque*, 218–45.

82. Crashaw, "The Weeper," in *Steps to the Temple*, 1–5. I am using the early printed editions of Crashaw's work, rather than L. C. Martin's edition, *Poems, English, Latin and Greek*, because the differences between the 1646 and 1652 printings of "The Weeper" are relevant to my discussion of the poem. For a synopsis of criticism of "The Weeper" and for a discussion of its "place within the canons of taste," see Rambuss, "Sacred Subjects," 497–501; Roberts and Roberts, "Crashavian Criticism"; and Parrish, "Crashaw's Two Weepers," 47–48. Parrish's study of Crashaw's connection to the Little Gidding community, and of his devotion to Mary Collet, provides a relevant discussion of the poet's interest in feminine spirituality ("Richard Crashaw," 187–200). For a recent discussion of Crashaw's negotiations of eucharistic theology, see Netzley, "Oral Devotion," 247–72.

83. Rambuss, "Sacred Subjects," 501.

84. Rambuss, "Sacred Subjects," 506, 522. Kuchar also finds the poem "profoundly Eucharistic in nature." The Magdalene's "transubstantiated tears" speak, announcing "the real presence of Christ's body": "In what is surely one of the most vividly liturgical moments in the history of the English poetry of tears, Crashaw seeks to harness the animating force within prosopopoeia as a way of realizing what we might call a Eucharist effect, a stepping out from representation to reality" ("Andrew Marvell's Anamorphic Tears," 371).

85. Crashaw, "The Teare," 84–85.

86. Martz, *From Renaissance to Baroque*, 203, 213. Parrish finds Crashaw's poetry to be, "as a whole, undeniably feminine—emphasizing intimate and emotional experiences and pointing us beyond the rhetorical gods of logic, argumentation, and analysis" ("O Sweet Contest," 128). For further discussion of the treatment of gender in "The Weeper" see Parrish, "Moderate Sorrow," 217–41.

87. Schwenger, "Crashaw's Perspectivist Metaphor," 70–71.

88. Examples include Paolo Farinati, *The Magdalen* (sixteenth century); Giulio Carpioni, *The Penitent Magdalen* (seventeenth century); Pieter de Jode, *Magdalen in Wilderness* (sixteenth to seventeenth centuries); Jacques Callot, *The Penitents* [*Mors Sanctae Magdalenae*] (1632). All of these images can be found in the ImageBase of the Fine Arts Museums of San Francisco. See also Annibale Carracci, *La Magdaleine repentante* (1591); Charles Le Brun and Jacques Lubin, *La Madeleine allongée* (1658–60); Simon Vouet, *Le ravissement mystique* (1666); Vouet and Michel Dorigny, *La pénitence ouverte* (1651). For a discussion of the various Magdalene postures, see Bardon, "Le thème de la Madeleine," 274–306. The Warburg Institute print archive has a vast repository of photocopies (largely from exhibition catalogues) of Magdalene images, all classified according to the scriptural event.

89. Hollar was associated with Arundel and was eventually appointed royal scenographer to Charles II. He is best known for his celebrated "Views of London," produced after the Great Fire of 1666.

90. Praz, *The Flaming Heart*, 218–19.

91. Southwell, *Funeral Teares*, A8.

92. Krieger, "Ekphrasis and the Still Movement of Poetry," 5, 20, 22; Heffernan, "Ekphrasis and Representation," 298.

93. Mitchell, "Ekphrasis and the Other," 155.

94. The later version of the poem is decidedly more erotic on the subject of Mary's grief: creamy tears trickle down burning cheeks and onto heaving breasts, where they quell the fire of prepenitent lust:

> But can these fair Flouds be
> Freinds with the bosom fires that fill you!
> Can so great flames agree
> Aeternall Teares should thus distill thee!
> O flouds, o fires! o suns o showres!
> Mixt & made friends by loue's sweet powres.
> ("The Weeper," in *Carmen Deo nostro*, 89)

95. Parrish, "Crashaw's Two Weepers," 58. See also Schwenger, who argues that Crashaw's 1648 revisions "are all directed to ordering his metaphori-

cal shifts into a smoother, more unified progression" ("Crashaw's Perspectivist Metaphor," 73).

96. Of this omission, Parrish writes, "One can only speculate why the stanza was dropped since the theme of time remains an important one. . . . Stanza 17 . . . fits comfortably within the image group between 16 and 20; its deletion seems to be less purposeful and its inclusion in the second version would not have marred the poem" ("Crashaw's Two Weepers," 52, 55–58).

97. Bergin, "Pinkney, Miles [Thomas Carre] (bap. 1599, d. 1674)."

98. There is no dedication and very little visual embellishment in *Steps to the Temple*. It may have also been compiled rather hastily, as the poems are prefaced by an apology explaining that some of the poems were mistakenly included.

99. Crashaw, *Carmen Deo nostro*. Lady Denbigh converted to Catholicism in 1651, just before her death in 1652. See Wolfe, "Elizabeth (Tanfield) Cary, Viscountess Falkland, to Susan (Villiers) Fielding, Countess of Denbigh," 211–14. See also Crawford and Gowing, *Women's Worlds*, 249–50.

100. Crashaw, *Carmen Deo nostro*. Carre's reference to Crashaw's abilities as a visual artist echo the preface to *Steps to the Temple*, in which the anonymous "friend" writes: "Amongst [Crashaw's] other accomplishments in Accademick (as well pious as harmlesse arts) hee made his skill in Poetry, Musicke, Drawing, Limming, graving (exercises of his curious invention and sudden fancy) to bee but his subservient recreations for vacant houres, not the grand businesse of his soule" (A4v–A5).

101. Hodson, *The Holy Sinner*, 32, 85.

102. Hodson, *The Holy Sinner*, 11–12.

103. Hans Holbein the Younger, *The Ambassadors* (1553), National Gallery, London.

104. Hodson, *The Holy Sinner*, 56. I can find no source for the reference to green flies. The phrase may be describing a process in which the engraver looks at something small ("green flies" are aphids) in order to focus his eyes for the meticulous task before him.

105. Lewalski, *Protestant Poetics*, 6–7.

106. Hodson, *The Holy Sinner*, 45.

107. Hodson, *The Holy Sinner*, 32, 45.

108. Hodson, *The Holy Sinner*, 83.

109. Hodson, *The Holy Sinner*, E5–E8.

Chapter 5.   She's a Nice Piece of Work

1. Behn, *The Rover*, 2.2.2–5. All subsequent references to the play are to Jane Spencer's edition and will appear in the body of the chapter.

2. Diamond, *Unmaking Mimesis: Essays on Feminism and Theater*, 78.

3. Diamond, "Gestus," 534.

4. Nora, *Realms of Memory*, 20.

5. The "Windsor Beauties" were painted between 1662 and 1665. The paintings, which at one time hung in the White Room at Whitehall, are now at Hampton Court and at the Flagmen in Greenwich. For further discussion of the paintings, see Strong, *The British Portrait*, 83–85. See also Millar, *Tudor, Stuart and Early Georgian Pictures*.

6. Hollander, *Seeing Through Clothes*, 210.

7. See Dethloff, "Portraiture," 26–34. Barbara Palmer (née Villiers, bap. 1640, d. 1709) was Countess of Castlemaine and *suo jure* Duchess of Cleveland. She was a royal mistress between 1660 and 1670. See Wynne, "Palmer, Barbara, Countess of Castlemaine," *ODNB*.

8. Dethloff, "Portraiture," 32.

9. Dethloff, "Portraiture," 34.

10. Dethloff, "Portraiture," 34.

11. Pepys, *The Diary*, 8 March 1666, 7:69, cited in Dethloff, "Portraiture," 34.

12. Upon recognition of the rivalry fused by the painting, a third party, Lady Denham, "took it into her head to renew the negotiations" between Gramont and Hamilton which had been at this point "unfortunately interrupted." Hamilton, *Memoirs*, 190–91.

13. As has been noted, while there is no scriptural reference to Mary Magdalene's social status or to her sexual habits, the *Legenda aurea* describes Mary as descended from kings and thus accustomed to riches and carnal delights. Subsequent treatments fashion the penitent as relinquishing the decadence of her early life in favor of modesty and plain living. See, for example, the Digby play, wherein the heroine features as the owner of the castle of Magdala. For a more contemporary example, see Rogers's "The Penitent Citizen."

14. See MacLeod and Alexander's discussion of the portrait in *Painted Ladies*, 118–20. Reni's *Penitent Magdalen* is in the National Gallery in London.

15. Dethloff, "Portraiture," 33–34.

16. Ashe, *A Sermon*, 2.

17. Perse, *A Sermon*, 3.

18. Perse, *A Sermon*, 16–17.

19. It is worth noting that not all contemporary Magdalenes were so worldly. A third example is provided by the sermon preached upon the occasion of Elizabeth Thomason's funeral in 1657 by the moderate Presbyterian preacher Edward Reynolds, soon-to-be-named bishop of Norwich by the newly restored Charles II. This text draws, in the Counter-Reformation spirit, upon Southwell and Crashaw rather than Lanyer or Donne. Mary's lesson to her followers is that "Love is not overborn with *Sense* and Reason to give over

seeking, what it desires to enjoy, though the eyes and the judgement dictate it to be sought *hic & nunc*, in vaine." Peter and John were satisfied by reason when they abandoned their vigil at the sepulcher. Mary's exemplary status ensues from her determination to persevere in her search for Christ despite the empirical evidence of his disappearance. "She breaks through all difficulties," Reynolds writes; she "digesteth all discouragements, Turnes repulses into Arguments, and by an holy Antiperistasis, the colder her hopes, the hotter are her prayers, till at last she prevaileth for a gracious answer" (*Mary Magdalens Love*, 17–19). I could find no record of Elizabeth Thomason; however, because the sermon was collected by George Thomason, the London bookseller responsible for collecting and preserving many documents relating to the period of the Civil War, I am assuming that there is some family relationship (Thomason's wife was Catherine and his only daughter, according to the *ODNB*, was Katherine). See Stoker, "Thomason, George (ca. 1602–1666)."

20. Killigrew, *Thomaso*, 2.3.333.

21. Recent research on seventeenth-century art-collecting practices has established links among Italian collectors, Flemish painters, and English diplomats whose Catholicism gave them a hearing in Continental art circles. See Chaney, *The Evolution of the Grand Tour*, 203–14. See also Barnes's excellent study of the possible influence of George Gage, a Catholic art agent and diplomat, upon van Dyck's early career ("Van Dyck and George Gage," 1–11).

22. Gaunt stipulates that "the subsequent dispersal of the royal art collections at Whitehall, Hampton Court, and Greenwich was an act of revenge, a means of raising money and, as it can be seen in the perspective of time, a national calamity" (*Court Painting*, 110, 120, 124).

23. Dolan, *Whores of Babylon*, 98.

24. Weil, "Sometimes a Scepter is Only a Scepter," 145–47. See also Dolan's ground-breaking work on anti-Catholicism as used to mobilize misogyny and to discredit women such as Queen Henrietta Maria (*Whores of Babylon*, 97–102).

25. Brathwaite, *The Chimneys Scuffle*, 14–15. Brathwaite (1587/8–1673) is probably best known for his lengthy conduct books, *The English Gentleman* (1630) and *The English Gentlewoman* (1631).

26. *The Soules Pilgrimage*, 9.

27. Robinson, *Life and Death*, 17.

28. Robinson, *Life and Death*, 43–44.

29. *The Soules Pilgrimage*, 49.

30. *The Soules Pilgrimage*, 36.

31. The payment was in partial fulfillment of £1,400,000 in arrears due by the English Parliament to the Scottish army. The House of Commons had agreed to pay £400,000 of the debt, half of which was due immediately. At the same time, the Scots entered into negotiation over the keeping of the king's

person. The English Parliament wanted exclusive rights to him, and this displeased the Scottish Estates; however, the latter were in no position to offer him further protection. Eventually, English Presbyterians induced the Scots to give up the king. While there is no relationship between the salary payment and the surrender of the king, the two events have been inextricably bound in historical memory.

32. *The Soules Pilgrimage*, 30.

33. See MacLeod and Alexander, *Painted Ladies*, 122–24.

34. Wynne, "Palmer, Barbara, Countess of Castlemaine."

35. MacLeod and Alexander, *Painted Ladies*, 155–56, 157.

36. Taylor was a book, print, and map seller in London between 1670 and 1721. His addresses are recorded as "next door to the Beehive on London Bridge," "at the Hand and Bible in the New Buildings on London Bridge," and "at Ye Golden Lyon, over against Serjeants Inn in Fleet Street." For more biographical information see the Thomas Taylor website at the University of Wales: http://www.llgc.org.uk/index.php?id=thomastayloratlas5210.

37. Sparke, a one-time stationer and wholesaler of books, claims to have encountered, when he was an apprentice, one Francis Ash—a West Country bookbinder who was an excellent workman, but also, in his opinion, a papist. Ash allegedly joined pictures of French origin, "of Vandikes Draft," engraved by "Mr. Hollard" (likely Wenceslaus Hollar) and procured by Peake (see chapter 4), who bound them to the pages of the English Bible. Behind Sparke's alarm lies the need to preserve his own livelihood, threatened by stationers whose sale of sensational books was inflating the cost of paper and running the so-called godly stationers out of business (*Second Beacon Fired by Scintilla* [1652], 6–7).

38. *The Rover* was presented at court in 1680, 1685, 1687, and 1690. *The Second Part of the Rover* (1681) was dedicated to the Duke of York, thanking him for "the incouragement Your Royal Highness was pleas'd to give the Rover at his first appearance, and the concern You were pleas'd to have for his second" (*The Works of Aphra Behn*, ed. Todd, 6:228–29).

39. For further discussion of the highly charged use of paintings on the stage in the context of post-Reformation iconoclasm, see Tassi, *The Scandal of Images*.

40. Pepys, *The Diary*, 24 March 1666, 9:284.

41. Gaunt writes, "It might be supposed that the long procession of female sitters in time became merged for Lely into a composite image of Woman. It has never, for instance, been easy to identify among the products of his studio the likeness of Nell Gwyn, though the romantic legend of the Drury-Lane orange girl who became popular on the stage as a comedy actress and was always a favorite with the king, has attached her name to many a canvass" (*Court Painting*, 147).

42. BM Add. MS 22950, f. 41, cited in Dethloff, "Portraiture," 26.

43. Sickened by what Todd calls the "lunatic display of anti-popery" that followed the Popish Plot, Behn wrote:

> For Sport and Pastime, to the brutal Crowd.
> The *World* ran *Mad*, and each distermper'd *Brain*,
> Did *Strange* and *different Frenzies* entertain;
> Here *Politick Mischeifs*, there *Ambition* sway'd;
> The Credulous *Rest*, were *Fool* and *Coward-Mad*.
> The Wiser *few*, who did th'*Infection* shun,
> Were *those* most liable to be *undone:*
> *Honour* as *Breach* of *Priviledge*, was detected;
> And *Common Sense*, was *Popishly affected.*
>   (Quoted in Todd, *The Secret Life*, 266)

For further discussion of Behn's Catholic sympathies, see Todd, *The Secret Life*, 19, 292; and Goreau, *Reconstructing Aphra*, 243.

44. Behn, epilogue (spoken by Lady Desbro) to *The Roundheads*, 424.

45. Erika Lin read and responded to portions of this chapter for a session of the Shakespeare Association of America in 2007. These thoughts on the extent to which actresses might be like art are for the most part hers, and I thank her for them.

46. Behn uses the phrase "the sign of Angellica" in a postscript that defends her play against the accusation that she plagiarized Killigrew's *Thomaso*. In a coy reference to the hanging of Angellica's portraits, Behn here hangs "out the sign of Angellica (the only stolen object) to give notice where a great part of the wit dwelt . . ." (*The Rover*, "Postscript," 11). In truth, Behn's debt to Killigrew is rather more extensive.

47. Dolan, *Whores of Babylon*, 13.

48. Behn, dedication to *The Feign'd Curtizans* (1679), 86.

49. The *ODNB* has Nell Gwyn back on stage in 1677 for the first performances of *The Rover* (8:844). The editors of *A Biographical Dictionary of Actors, Actresses, Musicians, Dancers, Managers and Other Stage Personnel in London, 1660–1800* state that Gwyn could not have played in *The Rover* (12:244). Genest, in *Some Account of the English Stage, from the Restoration in 1660 to 1830*, records Gwyn in the role (1:210). While there is absolutely no evidence, apart from the cast lists, that Gwyn did return to the stage to play the part, there is, to my knowledge, no information that confirms for certain that she did not; nor is there any record of Anne Quin's performance, thereby confirming that it was indeed Quin who assumed the role. Given Behn's affection for Gwyn, it is entertaining to speculate that she might have indeed made a rare appearance at the request of a friend. For further discussion of the Gywn/Quin confusion, see Russell's introduction to *The Rover*, 32; and M. Duffy, *The Passionate Shepherdess*, 147.

Postscript: A Something Else Thereby

1. The poem is mentioned in Cary's biography, *Lady Falkland: Her Life*, written primarily by Cary's daughter, Lucy. The poem was apparently written around the time of the death of Cary's repressive mother-in-law. Cary also wrote verse lives of St. Agnes, St. Elizabeth of Portugal, and the Virgin Mary. See Elizabeth Cary, Lady Falkland, *The Tragedy of Mariam*, 213.

2. "Another," in *The Song of Mary*, 40. The volume also contains another unremarkable reference to the Magdalene in a second poem, "A Sinners Supplication of the Soules Meditation." Jordan, "On Mary Magdalen's coming," in *Piety and Poesy*, B7v. Feltnam, "The Reconcilement," in *Resolves*, 12. Cranley, *Amanda*. Speed, "Delights of the Minde," in *Prison-Pietie*, 139–40. Beaumont, "S. Mary Magdalen's Ointment," in *The Minor Poems of Joseph Beaumont*, 250–51. Crompton, *The Glory of Women*, 30. Crompton's poem is a versification of the English prose translation of Agrippa's *Declamatio de nobilitate & precellentia Fœminei sexus*. The prose text is titled *Female Pre-eminence: Or the Dignity and Excellency of that Sex, above the Male* (1670).

3. Lithgow, *Gushing Teares*, 14.

4. *Jesus Christ Superstar*, directed by Norman Jewison, screenplay by Melvyn Bragg and Norman Jewison (Universal Pictures, 1973); *Godspell*, directed by David Greene, screenplay by David Greene and John-Michael Tebelak (Columbia Pictures, 1973); *The Last Temptation of Christ*, directed by Martin Scorsese, screenplay by Paul Schraeder, based on the novel by Nikos Kazantzakis (Cineplex-Odeon Films, 1988); *Jésus de Montréal*, directed by Denys Arcand, screenplay by Denys Arcand (Centre National de la Cinématographie, 1989); *The Passion of the Christ*, directed by Mel Gibson, screenplay by Benedict Fitzgerald and Mel Gibson (Icon Productions, 2004).

5. Dan Brown's unprecedented success with the *Da Vinci Code* illustrates the influence of popular "conspiracy" theology, including the influential but now largely discredited *Holy Blood, Holy Grail* (Baigent, Leigh, and Lincoln) and Eisler's *The Chalice and the Blade*, both published in the wake of the discovery, translation, and publication of the Nag Hammadi or Gnostic Gospels. The Nag Hammadi Gospel of Mary Magdalene has been recently translated from the Coptic into French by Leloup and then into English by Rowe (*The Gospel of Mary Magdalene*). See also Pagels's classic *The Gnostic Gospels*, or Meyer's *The Gnostic Discoveries*. Studies of the New Testament with the Gnostic Gospels in mind include Brock, *Mary Magdalene*; Hearon, *The Mary Magdalene Tradition*; and Schaberg, *The Resurrection of Mary Magdalene*. Other recent endeavors include: Meyer and De Boer, *The Gospels of Mary*; Picknett, *Mary Magdalene*; K. King, *The Gospel of Mary of Magdala*; and Welborn, *De-Coding Mary Magdalene*. Newspapers, weeklies, and monthly magazines have all weighed in (see

Acocella's article in *The New Yorker* for a sensitive example), and there will certainly be more to account for before this book goes to press.

6. Donne, "The Relique," in *The Complete Poetry*, 142. In 1980 Israeli construction workers building an apartment complex in Jerusalem's East Talpiot district uncovered ten two-thousand-year-old ossuaries. According to the Israel Antiquities Authority, six of these coffins are marked with the names Maria (Mary); Matiah (Matthew); Yeshua bar Yosef (Jesua, son of Joseph); Mariamne (Mary); Josa (or Joseph); and Yehuda bar Yeshua (Judah, son of Jesua). Some contend that the ossuaries contain the relics of Jesus and his family, including those of his wife and lover, Mary Magdalene. The Discovery Channel and Vision TV in Canada produced a documentary on the Talpiot tomb which aired on 4 March 2007. It was directed by Canadian documentary filmmaker Simcha Jacobovici, and produced by Felix Golubev and Ric Esther Bienstock. James Cameron served as executive producer. The film was released in conjunction with the book *The Jesus Family Tomb*, coauthored by Jacobovici and Charles R. Pellegrino.

BIBLIOGRAPHY

Abbreviations

ESTC: English Short Title Catalogue. Pollard and Redgrave, 1475–1640.
ODNB: *Oxford Dictionary of National Biography*.
Wing: English Short Title Catalogue, Wing, 1641–1700.

Primary Materials

*The Actions & Doctrine & other Passages touching our Lord & Sauior Iesus Christ,
as they are related by the foure Euangelists, reduced into one complete body of
historie wherein that, wch is seuerally related by them, is digested in order, and
that, wch is jointly related by all or any twoe or more of them is first expressed
in their own words by way of comparison, and secondly brought into one narration by way of composition, and thirdly extracted into one clear context by
way of collection . . . to wch are added sundry pictures, expressing either the
facts themselues or their types & figures* (1635). Aka The Little Gidding
Royal Harmony, or the "King's Concordance." British Library Shelfmark:
C.23.e.4.
"Against Excess of Apparel." In *The Elizabethan Homilies* (1623). *Renaissance
Electronic Texts*, edited by Ian Lancashire. University of Toronto Library,
1997. Available at http://www.library.utoronto.ca/utel/ret/homilies/
bk2hom2.html.
"Against the Peril of Idolatry." In *The Elizabethan Homilies* (1623). *Renaissance
Electronic Texts*, edited by Ian Lancashire. University of Toronto Library,
1997. Available at http://www.library.utoronto.ca/utel/ret/homilies/
bk2hom2.html.

Alabaster, William. "Upon Christ's Saying to Mary 'Why Weepest Thou'" and "A Morning Medition [2]." In *The Sonnets of William Alabaster*, edited by George Morley Story and Helen Gardner, 11, 39. Oxford: Oxford University Press, 1959.

Andrewes, Lancelot. "A Sermon Preached Before the King's Majesty, at Whitehall, on the Sixteenth of April, A.D. MDCXX [1620], Being Easter-Day." In *Ninety-Six Sermons By the Right Honourable and Reverend Father in God, Lancelot Andrewes Sometime Lord of Winchester*, 3:3–22. Oxford: James Henry Parker, 1841.

———. "A Sermon Preached Before the King's Maiesty at Whitehall on the First of April, A.D. MDCXXI [1621], Being Easter Day." In *Ninety-Six Sermons By the Right Honourable and Reverend Father in God, Lancelot Andrewes Sometime Lord of Winchester*, 3:23–38. Oxford: James Henry Parker, 1841.

———. "A Sermon Preached Before the King's Majesty at Whitehall on the Twenty-First of April, A.D. MDCXXII [1622], Being Easter Day." In *Ninety-Six Sermons By the Right Honourable and Reverend Father in God, Lancelot Andrewes Sometime Lord of Winchester*, 3:39–59. Oxford: James Henry Parker, 1841.

"Another on the Same Subject." In *The Song of Mary the Mother of Christ Containing the Story of his life and passion. The Teares of Christ in the garden: with the description of heauenly Ierusalem*, 38–41. London: E. Allde, 1601. ESTC 17547.

Ashe, George. *A Sermon Preached in Trinity-College Chappell before the University of Dublin, January the 9th, 1693/4.* [Dublin?]: Joseph Ray, 1694. Wing A3933.

Bale, John. *A Comedy Concernynge thre lawes, of Nature Moses & Christ, corrupted by the Sodomytes, Pharysees and Papystes* (1538). In *The Complete Plays of John Bale*, edited by Peter Happé, 2:64–124. Cambridge: D. S. Brewer, 1986.

Bancroft, Thomas. "On Mary Magdalen" and "To penitent Magdalen." In *Two Bookes of Epigrammes, and Epitaphs Dedicated to two top-branches of Gentry: Sir Charles Shirley, Baronet, and William Davenport, Esquire*, G. London: I. Okes, 1639. ESTC 1354.

Beaumont, Joseph. "S. Mary Magdalen's Ointment." In *The Minor Poems of Joseph Beaumont Edited from the Autograph Manuscript*, edited by Eloise Robinson, 250–51. London: Constable, 1914.

Behn, Aphra. "Dedication to *The Feign'd Curtizans*" (1679). In *The Works of Aphra Behn*, edited by Janet Todd, 6:86–87. London: William Pickering, 1996.

———. "Epilogue to *The Roundheads*." In *The Works of Aphra Behn*, edited by Janet Todd, 6:423–24. London: William Pickering, 1996.

———. *The Rover, or the Banished Cavaliers.* In *The Rover and Other Plays*, edited by Jane Spencer. Oxford: Oxford University Press, 1995.

———. *The Works of Aphra Behn.* Edited by Janet Todd. Vol. 6. London: William Pickering, 1996.

The boke of the common praier and administratio[n] of thee sacramentes and other Rytes and ceremonies of the Churche, after the vse of the churche of Englande. 1549. ESTC 16271.

Bokenham, Osbern. *Legendys of hooly wummen.* Edited by Mary S. Serjeantson. Early English Text Society. London: Oxford University Press, 1938.

The booke of Common praier noted. London: Richard Grafton, 1550. ESTC 16441.

Bourghesius, Johannes. *Vitae, passionis et mortis Jesu Christi Mysteria, piis meditationibus, exposita, figuris aeneis expressa per Boetium a Bolswert.* Antwerp, 1622.

Brathwaite, Richard. *The Chimneys Scuffle.* London, 1662. Wing B4259.

———. *The English gentleman containing sundry excellent rules or exquisite observations, tending to direction of every gentleman, of selecter ranke and qualitie; how to demeane or accommodate himselfe in the manage of publike or private affaires. By Richard Brathwaite Esq.* London: Iohn Haviland, 1630. ESTC 3563.

[Breton, Nicholas?]. *Marie Magdalens Loue.* London: John Danter, 1595. ESTC 3665.

Breton, Nicholas. *Auspicante Jehoua. Maries Exercise.* London: Thomas Este, 1597. ESTC 3632.

———. "The blessed Weeper." In *A Diuine Poeme diuided into two Partes: the Rauisht Soule, and the Blessed VVeeper,* D4–F4. London: John Browne, 1601. ESTC 3648.

———. *The Passions of the Spirit.* London: Thomas Este, 1599. ESTC 3682.5.

———. *The Pilgrimage to Paradise, Ioyned with the Countesse of Penbrookes loue.* Oxford: Joseph Barnes, 1592. ESTC 3683.

Calvin Jean (also John). *A Harmonie vpon the Three Euangelists, Matthew, Mark and Luke, with the Commentarie of M. John Caluine: Faithfullie translated out of Latine into English by E.P. Whereunto is added Commentarie vpon the Euangelist S. Iohn, by the same author.* London: George Bishop, 1584. ESTC 2962.

———. *New Testament Commentaries.* Edited by D. W. and I. F. Torrence. Vol. 5. Grand Rapids, Mich.: Eerdmans, 1959–72.

———. *A very profitable treatise made by M. Ihon Caluyne, declarynge what great profit might come to al christendome, yf there were a regester made of all Sainctes bodies and other reliques, which are aswell in Italy, as in Fraunce, Dutchland, Spaine, and other kingdomes and countreys.* London: Rouland Hall, 1561. ESTC 4467.

Canons and Decrees of the Council of Trent. Translated by Henry Joseph Schroe-der. Rockford, Ill.: Tan Books, 1978.

Cary, Elizabeth, Lady Falkland. *The Tragedy of Mariam: The Fair Queen of Jew-ery with The Lady Falkland: Her Life by One of Her Daughters.* Edited by Barry Weller and Margaret W. Ferguson. Berkeley: University of Califor-nia Press, 1994.

Collins, Thomas. *The Penitent Pvblican his Confession of Mouth. Contrition of heart. Vnfained Repentance. An feruent Prayer vnto God, for Mercie and forgiue-nesse.* London: T. Creede, 1610. ESTC 5566.

The complaynt of Mary Magdaleyne. In *Here begynneth the boke of fame, made by Geffray Chaucer: with dyuers other of his workes.* London: Richarde Pynson, 1526. ESTC 5088.

The complaynte of the louer of Cryst Saynt Mary Magdaleyn. London: Wynkyn de Worde, [1520?]. ESTC 17568.

Constable, Henry. "To St Mary Magdalen." In *The Poems of Henry Constable,* edited by Joan Grundy, 187, 191–92. Liverpool: Liverpool University Press, 1960.

Cranley, Thomas. *Amanda: or, The Reformed Whore.* London: J[ohn] Norton, 1635. ESTC 5988.

Cranmer, Thomas. *Cathechismvs, That is to say a shorte Instruction into Christian religion for the synguler commoditie and profyte of childre and yong people. Set forth by the mooste reuerende father in God Thomas Archbyshop of Canterbury, Primate of all England and Metropolitan.* London: Gualterus Lynne, 1548. ESTC 5992.5.

Crashaw, Richard. "The Teare." In *The Poems, English, Latin and Greek of Richard Crashaw,* edited by L. C. Martin, 84–85. Oxford: Clarendon Press, 1957.

———. "The Weeper." In *Carmen Deo nostro, te decet hymnus Sacred Poems, Col-lected, Corrected, Avgmented, Most humbly Presented. To my Lady the Covntesse of Denbigh by her most deuoted seruant. R.C. In heaty [sic] acknowledgment of his immortall obligation to her goodnes & charity,* 84–92. Paris: Peter Targa, 1652. Wing C6830.

———. "The Weeper." In *Steps to the Temple. Sacred Poems, with other Delights of the Muses,* 1–5. London: T. W., 1646. Wing C6836.

Crompton, Hugh. *The Glory of Women or, a Looking-Glasse for Ladies: VVherin they may behold their own Excellency and Preheminence, proved to be greater then mans, by Scripture, Law, Reason & Authority, divine & human. Written first in Latine, by Henricus Cornelius Agrippa, Knight and Doctor both of law and Physick. Afterwards Translated into English Prose, but now turned into Heroicall Verse.* London, 1652. Wing A787.

Donne, John. *The Complete Poetry of John Donne.* Edited by John T. Shawcross. New York: New York University Press, 1968.

Drummond, William. "For the Magdalene." In *The Poetical Works of William Drummond of Hawthorndom*, edited by William B. Turnbull, 145–46. London: John Russell Smith, 1856.

The Early South-English Legendary. Edited by Carl Horstman. Early English Text Society OS 87. London: N. Trübner, 1887.

Erasmus, Desiderius. *The first tome or volume of the Paraphrase of Erasmus vpon the newe testamente*. London: Edwarde Whitchurche, 1548. ESTC 2854.4.

Feltnam, Owen. "The Reconcilement." In *Resolves Divine, Moral, Political*. London, 1661. Wing F655A.

Ferrar, John. *Nicholas Ferrar: Two Lives*. Edited by J. E. B. Mayor. Cambridge: Cambridge University Press, 1855.

Firenzuola, Agnolo. *Del Dialogo . . . Della belleza delle Donne, intitolato Celso*. Florence, 1548.

Fisher, John. *Reverendi Patris Joannis Fisscher [sic] Roffensis in Anglia Episcopi, necnon Cantabrigien. academia Cancellarii dignissimi, De unica Magdalena, Libri tres* (1519).

The Geneva Bible (1587). In *The Bible in English*. Cambridge: Chadwyck-Healey, 1997. Source text: *The Bible: That is, The Holy Scriptvres Conteined in the Olde and Newe Testament. Translated According to the Ebrew and Greeke, and conferred with the best translations in diuers languages. With most profitable annotations vpon all the hard places, and other things of great importance*. London: Christopher Barker, 1587.

The Gospel of Mary Magdalene. Translated by Jean-Yves Leloup (French) and Joseph Rowe (English). Rochester, Vt.: Inner Traditions, 2002.

Gosson, Stephen. *Pleasant Quippes for Vpstart Newfangled Gentle-vvomen*. London: Richard Jhones, 1595. ESTC 12096.

Gregorius I [Gregory the Great]. "Homilia 33." In *Homiliarum in Evangelia Libri Duo*. Patrologiae Cursus Completus, sive bibliotheca universalis . . . omnium S. S. Patrum, Doctorum, Scriptorumque ecclesiasticorum qui ab aevo apostolico ad Innocentii III tempora floruerunt . . . Series Prima, Patrilogiae Tomus 76. Sancti Gregorii Magni, Tomus Secundus. Paris: Venit Apud Editorem, in Via Dicta D'Ambrose, Prope Portam Vulgo D'Enfer Nominatum, Seu Petit-Montrouge, 1849. Patrologia Latina Database. Alexandria, Va.: Chadwyck-Healey, 1996.

Herbert, George. *The Works of George Herbert*. Edited by F. E. Hutchinson. Oxford: Clarendon Press, 1967.

Herrick, Robert. *The Poems of Robert Herrick*. Edited by L. C. Martin. Oxford: Oxford University Press, 1965.

Hodson, William. *The Holy Sinner a Tractate meditated on some Passages of the Storie of the Penitent Woman in the Pharisees house*. London, 1639. ESTC 13555.

An Homelie of Marye Magdalene declaring her ferue[n]t loue and zele towards Christ. Newly translated. London: For Henry Sutton, [1555?]. ESTC 18848.

Hooker, Richard. *Of the Lawes of Ecclesiastical Politie.* Edited by W. Speed Hill. Vol. 5. Cambridge: Cambridge University Press, 1977.

J. C. *Saint Marie Magdalens Conversion.* London: English Secret Press, 1603. ESTC 4282.

Jacobus de Voragine. "Seynt Marye Magdalene." In *Legenda aurea sanctorum, sive, Lombardica historia,* CCxvi–CCxix(v). London: William Caxton, 1483. ESTC 24873.

Jordan, Thomas. "On Mary Magdalen's coming to the Tomb of our Saviour." In *Piety and Poesy,* B7v. London: Robert Wood, 1643. Wing J1054.

Julian of Norwich. *A Revelation of Love.* Edited by Marion Glasscoe. Exeter: University of Exeter Press, 1993.

Killigrew, Thomas. *The First Part of Thomaso.* In *Comedies and Tragedies by Thomas Killigrew* (1664), 313–82. New York: Benjamin Blom, 1967.

The King James Bible (1611). In *The Bible in English.* Cambridge: Chadwyck-Healey, 1997. Source text: *The Holy Bible, Conteyning the Old Testament, And the New: Newly Translated out of the Originall tongues: & with the former Translations diligently compared and reuised by his Maiesties speciall Comandement Appointed to be read in Churches.* London: Robert Barker, 1611.

The Lamentatyon of Mary Magdaleyne. Edited by Bertha Skeat. Cambridge: Fabb and Tyler, 1897.

Lanyer, Aemilia. *Salve Deus Rex Judaeorum: The Poems of Aemilia Lanyer.* Edited by Suzanne Woods. Oxford: Oxford University Press, 1993.

Lefèvre d'Etaples, Jacques. *De Marie Magdalena, & triduo Christi disceptatio, ad Clarissimum virum D. Franciscum Molineum, Christianissimi Francorum Regis Francisci Primi Magistrum.* Paris: Henri Estienne, 1517.

Letters and Papers, Foreign and Domestic of the Reign of Henry VIII. Edited by J. S. Brewer. London: HMSO, 1891.

Lithgow, William. *The Gushing Teares of Godly Sorrow. Containing, The Causes, Conditions, and Remedies of Sinne, Depending mainly upon Contrition and Confession.* Edinburgh: Robert Bryson, 1640.

Marbeck [also Merbeck and Marbeeke], John. *The lyues of holy Sainctes, Prophetes, Patriarches, and others, contayned in holye Scripture so farre forth as expresse mention of them is delyuered vnto vs in Gods worde, with the interpretacion of their names: Collected and gathered into an alphabeticall order, to the great commoditie of the Chrystian reader.* London: Henrie Denham and Richarde Watkins, 1574. ESTC 17569.

Markham, Gervase. *Mary Magdalens Lamentations for the losse of her Maister Jesus.* London: James Roberts, 1604. ESTC 17570.

————. *Marie Magdalens Lamentations for the Losse of her Master Iesus.* London: Adam Islip, 1601. ESTC 17569.

Martin, T. *Mary Magdalen's Tears wip't off. Or The Voice of Peace to an Unquiet Conscience. Written By Way of Letter to a Person of Quality. And Published for the Comfort of all those, who Mourn in Zion.* London: J. C., 1659. Wing M850.

Marvell, Andrew. "Eyes and Tears." In *The Poems of Andrew Marvell*, edited by Nigel Smith, 50–53. London: Pearson Longman, 2003.

Materials for the Life of Nicholas Ferrar: A Reconstruction of John Ferrar's Account of His Brother's Life Based on All the Surviving Copies. Edited by Lynette R. Muir and John S. White. Leeds: Leeds Philosophical and Literary Society, 1996.

Nashe, Thomas. *Pierce Penilesse his Supplication to the Diuell.* In *The Works of Thomas Nashe*, edited by Ronald B. McKerrow, 1:137–245. London: Sedgewick & Jackson, 1904–10.

The Northern Passion. Edited by Francis A. Foster. Early English Text Society OS 145. London: Kegan Paul, Trench, Trübner, 1913.

The Old English Martyrology. Edited by Georg Herzfeld. Early English Text Society OS 116. London: Kegan Paul, Trench, Trübner, 1900.

Omelia orige[n]is de beata maria magdalena. London: Richard Whitington, 1505. ESTC 18846.

Omelia origenis de lamentatione magdalene ad sepulcher domini (14th C.), Corpus Christie College MS. 137 (CUL). In "Chaucer's *Orygenes Upon the Maudeleyne:* A Translation," translated by Rodney K. Delasanta and Constance M. Rousseau. *Chaucer Review* 30:4 (1996): 319–42.

Osborne, M. "A Newe Ballade of a Louer Extollinge his Ladye. To the tune of Damon and Pithias." London: Wylliam Gryffith, 1568. ESTC 18876.

Our Lady's Lament and the Lamentation of St. Mary Magdalen. Edited by Charles Edward Tame. London, 1871.

Owen, John. "Upon Mary Magdalen." In *Parnassi Puerperium: or, Some Well-wishes to Ingenuity, in the Translation of Six Hundred, of Owen's Epigrams; Martial de Spectaculis, or of Rarities to be seen in Rome; and the most select, in Sir. Tho. More. To which is annext A Century of Heroick Epigrams, (Sixty whereof concern the Twelve Caesars; and the Forty remaining, several deserving Persons), By the Author of that celebrated Elegie upon Cleeveland: Tho. Pecke of the Inner Temple, Gent,* 89. London: James Cottrel, 1659. Wing P1040.

The Passion Play from the N. Town Manuscript. Edited by Peter Meredith. New York: Longman, 1990.

Pepys, Samuel. *The Diary of Samuel Pepys.* Edited by Robert Latham and William Matthews. Berkeley: University of California Press, 1983.

Perse, William. *A Sermon Preach'd upon the occasion of the Queen's Death on the 4th Sunday in Lent, being the 3d of March, 1694/5*. York: J. White, 1695. Wing P1655.

Prynne, William. *Canterburies Doome, or, The First Part of a Compleat History of the Commitment, Charge, Tryall, Condemnation, Execution of William Laud, Late Arch-bishop of Canterbury Containing the severall Orders, Articles, Proceedings in Parliament against him, from his first Accusation therein, till his Tryall*. London: John Macock, 1646. Wing P3917.

Reynolds, Edward. *Mary Magdalens Love to Christ. Opened in a Sermon Preached at the Funeral of Mistris Elizabeth Thomason. April. 11. 1659*. London, 1659. Wing R1264.

The Rheims-Douay Bible (1582–1610). In *The Bible in English*. Cambridge: Chadwyck-Healey, 1997. Source text: *The Holie Bible Faithfvlly Translated into English, Ovt of the Avthentical Latin. Diligently conferred with the Hebrew, Greeke, and other Editions in diuers languages. With Argvments of the Bookes, and Chapters: Annotations: Tables: and other helpes, for better vnderstanding of the text: for discouerie of Corrvptions in some late translations: and for clearing Controversies in Religion*. The English College of Douay: 1609–10.

Robinson, Thomas. *The Life and Death of Mary Magdalene: A Legendary Poem in Two Parts* (c. 1620). Edited by H. Oskar Sommer. Early English Text Society, Extra Series 78. London: Paul, Trench, Trübner, 1899.

Rogers, Nehemiah. "The Penitent Citizen." In *A Mirrour of Mercy, and that on Gods Part and Mans. Set out in two Parables, I. The Penitent Citizen, or, Mary Magdalens Conversion, On that Parable, Luke 7. 40, 41, &c. II. The Good Samaritan, On that Parable, Luke 10. 30–38*, 1–279. London: G. M[iller], 1640. ESTC 21196.

Saint Mary Magdalen. In *Late Medieval Religious Plays of Bodleian MSS Digby 133 and E Museo 160*, edited by Donald C. Baker, John L. Murray and Louis B. Hall, Jr., 24–95. Early English Text Society OS 283. Oxford: Oxford University Press, 1982.

Scott, Gregory. "Against the praying to Saintes." In *A briefe Treatise agaynst certayne errors of the Romish Church Very plainly, notably, and pleasantly confuting the same by Scriptures and auncient writers*. London: John Awdeley, 1574. ESTC 21855.

Sherburne, Edward. *Poems and Translations Amorous, Lusory, Morall, Divine*. London: W. Hunt, 1651.

"A Sinners Supplication of the Soules Meditation." In *The Song of Mary the Mother of Christ Containing the Story of his life and passion. The Teares of Christ in the garden: with the description of heauenly Ierusalem*, 42–45. London: E. Allde, 1601. ESTC 17547.

Smith, Henry. "Mary's Choice." In *The Sermons of Mr. Henry Smith, Sometimes Minister of St. Clement Danes,* edited by Thomas Fuller, 2:321–30. London: William Tegg, 1866.

The Soules Pilgrimage to Heavenly Hierusalem. In three severall Dayes journeyes, by three severall wayes: Purgative, Illuminative, Unitive. Expressed in the Life and Death of Saint Mary Magdalen. London, 1650. Wing S4721A.

The Southern Passion. Edited by Beatrice Daw Brown. Early English Text Society OS 169. London: Oxford University Press, 1927.

Southwell, Robert. *Marie Magdalens Funeral Teares* (1591). Intro. by Vincent B. Leitch. Scholars' Facsimiles and Reprints. New York: Delmar, 1975.

———. *Saint Peters Complaint, with Other Poemes.* London: John Wolfe, 1595. ESTC 22955.7.

Sparke, Michael. *A Second Beacon Fired by Scintilla: with his Humble Information and Joynt Attestation to the Truth of his Brethrens former Declaration & Catalogue, that Fired the first Beacon. Wherein is remembred the former Actings of the Papists in their secret Plots: and now discovering their wicked Designes to set up, advance, and cunningly to usher in Popery; by introducing Pictures to the Holy Bible: and by sending many young Gentlewomen beyond the seas to the Nunnes.* London: Privately printed, 1652. Wing S4818BA.

Speed, Samuel. "Delights of the Minde." In *Prison-Pietie, or, Meditations Divine and Moral Digested into Poetical Heads, on Mixt and Various Subjects: Whereunto is added a Panegyrick to the Right Reverend, and most Nobly descended, Henry Lord Bishop of London,* 139–40. London: J. C., 1677. Wing S4902.

The Statutes of the Realm, Printed from Original Records and Authentic Manuscripts. Edited by Alexander Luders, Sir T. Edlyn Tomlins, J. France, W. E. Taunton, and J. Raithby. London: Dawsons of Pall Mall, 1963.

Strabo, Walafridus. *Glossa Ordinaria. Evangelium Secundum Matthaeum.* In *Patrologia Latina,* vol. 114 (1996–2006). ProQuest. Available at http://pld.chadwyck.com/helphtx/htxview?template=basic.htx&content=terms.htx.

Stradling, John. *Diuine Poemes In Seuen Seuerall Classes. Written to his most Excellent Maiestie Charles, by the Grace of God King of Great Britaine, France, and Ireland, Defender of the Faith, &c.* London: William Stansby, 1625. ESTC 23353.

Sweetnam, Joseph. *S. Mary Magdalens Pilgrimage to Paradise. Wherein are liuely imprinted the foote-steps of her excellent Vertues, for Sinners to follow, who desire to accompany her thither.* St. Omer: English College Press, 1617. ESTC 23532.

Three Chapters of Letters Relating to the Suppression of Monasteries. Edited by Thomas Wright. London: Camden Society, 1843.

The Towneley Plays. Edited by Martin Stevens and A. C. Cawley. Vol. 1. Early English Text Society. Oxford: Oxford University Press, 1994.

Trapp, John. *A Commentary or Exposition upon all the Books of the New Testament VVherein the Text is explained, some Controversies are discussed, divers Common places are handled, and many remarkable matters hinted, that had by former interpreters been pretermitted: Besides, divers other Texts of Scripture, which occasionally occur, are fully opened, and the whole so intermixed with pertinent Histories, as will yield both pleasure and profit to the judicious Reader.* London: R. W., 1656. Wing T2039.

A Tretise of Miraclis Pleyinge. Edited by Clifford Davidson. Kalamazoo, Mich.: Medieval Institute Publications, Western Michigan University, 1993.

Tudor Royal Proclamations. Edited by Paul Hughes and James Larkin. 3 vols. New Haven: Yale University Press, 1964–65.

Vaughan, Henry. "St Mary Magdalen." In *Henry Vaughan: Poetry and Selected Prose*, edited by L. C. Martin, 343–44. Oxford Standard Authors. Oxford: Oxford University Press, 1963.

Verstegan [also Rowlands], Richard. "A Complaint of S. Mary Magdalene. At her not Fynding Christ in his Sepulchre." In *Odes In Imitation of the Seaven Penitential Psalmes, vvith Sundry other Poemes and ditties tending to deuotion and pietie*, 89–90. Antwerp: A. Conincx, 1601. ESTC 21359.

Visitation Articles and Injunctions of the Period of the Reformation. Edited by W. H. Frere and W. M. Kennedy. London: Longmans, Green, 1910.

Wager, Lewis. *The Life and Repentaunce of Mary Magdalene.* In *Reformation Biblical Drama in England*, edited by Paul Whitfield White, 1–66. New York: Garland, 1992.

———. *A new Enterlude, neuer before this tyme imprinted, entreating of the Life and Repentaunce of Marie Magdalene: not only godlie, learned and fruitefull, but also well furnished with pleasaunt myrth and pastime, very delectable for those which shall heare or reade the same.* London: John Charlewood, 1566. ESTC 24932.

Walkington, Thomas. *The Optick Glasse of Hvmors. Or The touchstone of a golden temperature, or the Philosophers stone to make a golden temper, wherein the foure complections Sanguine, Cholericke, Phlegmaticke, Melancholicke are succinctly painted forth, and their externall intimates laide open to the purblind eye of ignorance it selfe, by which euery one may iudge of what complection he is, and answerably learne what is most sutable to his nature.* London: John Windet, 1607. ESTC 24967.

———. *Rabboni; Mary Magdalens Teares, of Sorrow, Solace. The one for her Lord being lost. The other for Him being found. In way of Questioning. Wondring. Reioycing. . . . Preached at S. Pauls Crosse, after the Rehearsall, and newly reuised and enlarged.* London: Edw. Griffin, 1620. ESTC 24970.

Ward, Richard. *Theological Questions, Dogmatical Observations, and Euangelical Essays, upon the Gospel of Iesus Christ According to St. Matthew Wherein about Two thousand six hundred and fifty necessary and profitable Questions are discussed, and Five hundred and eighty special points of Doctrine noted, and five hundred and fifty Errors confuted, or Objections answered, together with divers Arguments, whereby divers Truths and true Tenents are confirmed.* London: Peter Cole, 1646. Wing W806.

White, Harim. *The Ready Way To Trve Repentance: or, A Godly, and Learned Treatise, of the Repentance of Mary Magdalen: opened in diuers Sermons at the first; begun in little Alhallowes vpon the Wall, London, the 21. day of Septemb. 1616. and continued in S. Peters Church in Sandwich; contayning doctrine of Faith.* London: 1618. ESTC 25387.

Whitehall, Robert. "The Contrite Heart." In *Exastichon hieron, sive jconum quarundam extranearum (numero 258) explicatio breviuscula & clara . . . being an epigrammatical explanation of the most remarkable stories throughout the Old & New Testament after each sculpture, or cut.* Icon 38. Oxford: Leonard Lichfield, 1677. Wing W1872.

Wriothesley, Charles. *A Chronicle of England During the Reigns of the Tudors.* Edited by W. D. Hamilton. London: Camden Society, 1877.

Zwingli, Ulrich. *Commentary on True and False Religion.* Edited by Samuel Macauley Jackson and Clarence Nevin Heller. Durham, N.C.: Labyrinth Press, 1981.

Secondary Materials

Acocella, Joan. "The Saintly Sinner." *The New Yorker,* 13 February 2006, 140.

Adorno, Theodor W. "On Lyric Poetry and Society." In *Notes to Literature,* edited by Rolf Tiedemann, 1:37–54. Translated by Shierry Weber Nicholsen. New York: Columbia University Press, 1991–92.

Aers, David. "New Historicism and the Eucharist." *Journal of Medieval and Early Modern Studies* 33:2 (2003): 241–59.

Aers, David, and Sarah Beckwith. "Introduction: Hermeneutics and Ideology." *Journal of Medieval and Early Modern Studies* 33:2 (2003): 211–13.

Arblaster, Richard. "Verstegan, Richard (1548–1640)." *ODNB.* Oxford: Oxford University Press, 2004. Available at http://www.oxforddnb.com/view/article 24217.

Arnold-Foster, Frances. *Studies in Church Dedications to England's Patron Saints.* 3 vols. London: Skeffington & Sons, 1899.

Aston, Margaret. "The Bishop's Bible Illustrations." *Studies in Church History* 28 (1992): 267–85.

———. *England's Iconoclasts.* Vol. 1, *Laws Against Images.* Oxford: Clarendon Press, 1988.

Badir, Patricia. "Medieval Poetics and Protestant Magdalenes." In *Reading the Medieval in Early Modern England,* edited by Gordon McMullan and David Matthews, 205–19. Cambridge: Cambridge University Press, 2007.

————. "'To allure vnto their loue': Iconoclasm and Striptease in Lewis Wager's *The Life and Repentaunce of Marie Magdalene.*" *Theatre Journal* 51:1 (1999): 1–20.

Barbour, Reid. *Literature and Religious Culture in Seventeenth-Century England.* Cambridge: Cambridge University Press, 2002.

Bardon, François. "Le thème de la Madeleine pénitente au XVIIème siècle en France." *Journal of the Warburg and Courtauld Institute* 31 (1968): 274–306.

Barnes, Susan. "Van Dyck and George Gage." In *Art and Patronage in the Caroline Courts: Essays in Honour of Sir Oliver Millar,* edited by David Howarth, 1–11. Cambridge: Cambridge University Press, 1993.

Baxandall, Michael. *Limewood Sculptors of Renaissance Germany.* New Haven: Yale University Press, 1982.

Beckwith, Sarah. *Christ's Body: Identity, Culture, and Society in Late Medieval Writings.* London: Routledge, 1993.

————. "Greenblatt's *Hamlet* and the Forms of Oblivion." *Journal of Medieval and Early Modern Studies* 33:2 (2003): 261–80.

————. *Signifying God: Social Relation and Symbolic Act in the York Corpus Christi Plays.* Chicago: University of Chicago Press, 2001.

Belting, Hans. *Likeness and Presence: A History of the Image Before the Era of Art.* Translated by Edmund Jephcott. Chicago: University of Chicago Press, 1994.

Bergin, Joseph. "Pinkney, Miles [Thomas Carre] (bap. 1599, d. 1674)." *ODNB.* Oxford: Oxford University Press, 2004. Available at http://www.oxforddnb .com/view/article/4758.

Blaise, Anne-Marie Miller. "'Sweetnesse readie penn'd': Herbert's Theology of Beauty." *George Herbert Journal* 27:1–2 (2003–4): 1–21.

Bossy, John. *The English Catholic Community, 1570–1850.* London: Darton, Longman & Todd, 1975.

Breightenberg, Mark. "Reading Elizabethan Iconicity: *Gorboduc* and the Semiotics of Reform." *English Literary Renaissance* 18:2 (1988): 194–217.

Bremer, Francis J. "Alabaster, William (1568–1640)." *ODNB.* Oxford: Oxford University Press, 2004. Available at http://www.oxforddnb.com/view/article/265.

Brennan, Michael G. "Breton, Nicholas (1554/5–ca. 1626)." *ODNB.* Oxford: Oxford University Press, 2004. Available at http://www.oxforddnb.com/view/article/3341.

————. "Nicholas Breton's *The Passions of the Spirit* and the Countess of Pembroke." *Review of English Studies* 38 (1987): 221–25.

Brock, Ann Graham. *Mary Magdalene, the First Apostle: The Struggle for Authority.* Cambridge, Mass.: Harvard University Press, 2003.

Butler, Judith. "Sexual Differences as a Question of Ethics: Alterities of the Flesh in Irigaray and Merleau-Ponty." In *Bodies of Resistance: New*

Phenomenologies of Politics, Agency, and Culture, edited by Laura Doyle, 59–77. Evanston, Ill.: Northwestern University Press, 2001.

Bynum, Caroline Walker. *Fragmentation and Redemption: Essays on Gender and the Human Body in Medieval Religion.* Cambridge, Mass.: Zone Books, 1991.

———. "Why All the Fuss About the Body? A Medievalist's Perspective." *Critical Inquiry* 22:1 (1995): 1–33.

Chaney, Edward. *The Evolution of the Grand Tour: Anglo-Italian Cultural Relations Since the Renaissance.* London: Routledge, 1998.

Chilton, Bruce. *Mary Magdalene: A Biography.* New York: Doubleday, 2005.

Clarke, Elizabeth. *Theory and Theology in George Herbert's Poetry.* Oxford: Clarendon Press, 1997.

Clifton, Robin. "The Popular Fear of Catholics During the English Revolution." *Past and Present* 52 (August 1971): 23–53.

Coletti, Theresa. *Mary Magdalene and the Drama of the Saints: Theater, Gender, and Religion in Late Medieval England.* Philadelphia: University of Pennsylvania Press, 2004.

Collins, Christopher. *Reading the Written Image: Verbal Play, Interpretation, and the Roots of Iconophobia.* University Park: Pennsylvania State University Press, 1991.

Collinson, Patrick. *From Iconoclasm to Iconophobia: The Cultural Impact of the Second English Reformation.* Reading: University of Reading Press, 1985.

———. *The Religion of Protestants: The Church in English Society, 1559–1625.* Oxford: Oxford University Press, 1995.

Corns, Thomas N. *Uncloistered Virtue: English Political Literature, 1640–1660.* Oxford: Clarendon Press, 1992.

Crawford, Patricia. *Women and Religion in England, 1500–1720.* New York: Routledge, 1996.

Crawford, Patricia, and Laura Gowing, eds. *Women's Worlds in Seventeenth-Century England: A Sourcebook.* London: Routledge, 2000.

Cunnington, Cecil Willett, and Phillis Cunnington. *Handbook of English Costume in the Sixteenth Century.* London: Faber and Faber, 1970.

———. *The History of Underclothes.* London: Faber and Faber, 1981.

Dawson, Anthony B., and Paul Yachnin. *The Culture of Playgoing in Shakespeare's England: A Collaborative Debate.* Cambridge: Cambridge University Press, 2001.

Delasanta, Rodney K., and Constance M. Rousseau. "Chaucer's *Orygenes upon the Maudeleyne:* A Translation." *Chaucer Review* 30:4 (1996): 319–42.

De Leeuw, Patricia Allwin. "Gregory the Great's 'Homilies on the Gospels' in the Early Middle Ages." *Studi Medievali* 26, fasc. 2 (1985): 855–69.

Dethloff, Diana. "Portraiture and Concepts of Beauty in Restoration Painting." In *Painted Ladies: Women at the Court of Charles II,* edited by Catherine

MacLeod and Julia Marciari Alexander, 26–34. London: National Portrait Gallery Publications, 2001.

Devlin, Christopher. *The Life of Robert Southwell, Poet and Martyr.* London: Longmans, Green, 1956.

Diamond, Elin. "*Gestus* and Signature in Aphra Behn's *The Rover.*" *ELH* 56 (1998): 519–41.

———. *Unmaking Mimesis: Essays on Feminism and Theater.* London: Routledge, 1997.

Dickens, A. G. *The English Reformation.* 2nd ed. London: B. T. Batsford, 1989.

Diehl, Huston. *Staging Reform, Reforming the Stage: Protestantism and Popular Theater in Early Modern England.* Ithaca: Cornell University Press, 1997.

Dimmick, Jeremy, James Simpson, and Nicolette Zeeman, eds. *Images, Idolatry, and Iconoclasm in Late Medieval England: Textuality and the Visual Image.* Oxford: Oxford University Press, 2002.

Doebler, Bettie Anne, and Retha M. Warnicke. "Magdalen Herbert Danvers and Donne's Vision of Comfort." *George Herbert Journal* 10 (1986–87): 5–22.

Doerksen, Daniel W. *Conforming to the Word: Herbert, Donne, and the English Church Before Laud.* Lewisburg, Pa.: Bucknell University Press, 1997.

Doerksen, Daniel W., and Christopher Hodgkins, eds. *Centered on the Word: Literature, Scripture, and the Tudor-Stuart Middle Way.* Newark: University of Delaware Press, 2004.

Dolan, Frances E. *Whores of Babylon: Catholicism, Gender, and Seventeenth-Century Print Culture.* Ithaca: Cornell University Press, 1999.

Douglass, E. Jane Dempsey. *Women, Freedom and Calvin.* Philadelphia: Westminster Press, 1985.

Driver, Martha W. "Mirrors of a Collective Past: Re-Considering Images of Medieval Women." In *Women and the Book: Assessing the Visual Evidence,* edited by Lesley Smith and Jane H. M. Taylor, 75–93. London: British Library; Toronto: University of Toronto Press, 1997.

Duffy, Eamon. *The Stripping of the Altars: Traditional Religion in England, 1400–1580.* New Haven: Yale University Press, 1992.

Duffy, Maureen. *The Passionate Shepherdess: Aphra Behn, 1640–89.* London: Jonathan Cape, 1977.

Dyck, Paul. " 'So rare a use': Scissors, Reading, and Devotion at Little Gidding." *George Herbert Journal* 27:2 (2003–4): 67–81.

Eire, Carlos. *War Against the Idols: The Reformation of Worship from Erasmus to Calvin.* Cambridge: Cambridge University Press, 1986.

Edmond, Mary. "Oliver, Isaac (c. 1565–1617)." *ODNB.* Oxford: Oxford University Press, 2004. Available at http://www.oxforddnb.com/view/article/20723.

Ewing, Elizabeth. *Dress and Undress: A History of Women's Underwear.* London: B. T. Batsford, 1978.

———. *Fashion in Underwear.* London: B. T. Batsford, 1971.

Fisher, Nicholas. "Whitehall, Robert (bap. 1624, d. 1685)." *ODNB.* Oxford: Oxford University Press, 2004. Available at http://www.oxforddnb.com/view/article/29284.

Forsyth, Ilene Haering. "Magi and Majesty: A Study of Romanesque Sculpture and Liturgical Drama." *Art Bulletin* 50:3 (1968): 215–22.

Freedburg, S. J. "Observations on the Painting of the Maniera." *Art Bulletin* 47:3–4 (1965): 187–97.

Gallagher, Catherine, and Stephen Greenblatt. *Practicing New Historicism.* Chicago: University of Chicago Press, 2001.

Gaunt, William. *Court Painting in England from Tudor to Victorian Times.* London: Constable, 1980.

Gellrich, Jesse M. *The Idea of the Book in the Middle Ages: Language Theory, Mythology, and Fiction.* Ithaca: Cornell University Press, 1985.

Genest, John. *Some Account of the English Stage, from the Restoration in 1660 to 1830* [1832]. New York: Burt Franklin, 1965.

Gilman, Ernest B. *Iconoclasm and Poetry in the English Reformation: Down Went Dagon.* Chicago: University of Chicago Press, 1986.

Goreau, Angeline. *Reconstructing Aphra: A Social Biography of Aphra Behn.* New York: Dial Press, 1980.

Greenblatt, Stephen. *Hamlet in Purgatory.* Princeton: Princeton University Press, 2001.

Gregerson, Linda. *The Reformation of the Subject: Spenser, Milton, and the English Protestant Epic.* Cambridge: Cambridge University Press, 2006.

Griffiths, Antony. *The Print in Stuart Britain, 1603–1689.* London: British Museum Press, 1998.

Grosz, Elizabeth, *Volatile Bodies: Toward a Corporeal Feminism.* Bloomington: Indiana University Press, 1994.

Guibbory, Achsah. *Ceremony and Community from Herbert to Milton: Literature, Religion, and Cultural Conflict in Seventeenth-Century England.* Cambridge: Cambridge University Press, 1998.

Haigh, Christopher. *English Reformations: Religion, Politics, and Society Under the Tudors.* Oxford: Clarendon Press, 1993.

Hamilton, Anthony. *Memoirs of the Comte de Gramont.* Translated by Peter Quennell. London: Routledge and Sons, 1930.

Hammond, Gerald. *The Making of the English Bible.* Manchester: Carcanet New Press, 1982.

Happé, Peter. "The Protestant Adaptation of the Saint Play." In *The Saint Play in Medieval Europe,* edited by Clifford Davidson and Clyde Waring Brockett, 205–40. Kalamazoo, Mich.: Medieval Institute Publications, 1986.

Hartwig, Joan. "Tears as a Way of Seeing." In *On the Celebrated and Neglected Poems of Andrew Marvell*, edited by Claude J. Summers and Ted-Larry Pebworth, 70–85. Columbia: University of Missouri Press, 1992.

Harvey, Elizabeth D. "Introduction: 'The Sense of All Senses.'" In *Sensible Flesh: On Touch in Early Modern Culture*, edited by Elizabeth D. Harvey. Philadelphia: University of Pennsylvania Press, 2003.

Haskins, Susan. *Mary Magdalen: Myth and Metaphor*. New York: Harcourt Brace, 1993.

Hearon, Holly E. *The Mary Magdalene Tradition: Witness and Counter Witness in Early Christian Communities*. Collegeville, Minn.: Liturgical Press, 2004.

Heffernan, James A. "Ekphrasis and Representation." *New Literary History* 22:2 (1991): 297–316.

Henderson, George. "Bible Illustration in the Age of Laud." *Transactions of the Cambridge Bibliographical Society* 8 (1982): 176.

Herbert, Arthur Sumner, T. H. Darlow, H. F. Moule, and the British & Foreign Bible Society Library. *Historical Catalogue of Printed Editions of the English Bible: 1525–1961*. London: British & Foreign Bible Society, 1968.

Highfill, Philip H. *A Biographical Dictionary of Actors, Actresses, Musicians, Dancers, Managers and Other Stage Personnel in London, 1660–1800*. Carbondale: Southern Illinois University Press, 1973.

Hill, Christopher. *The English Bible and the Seventeenth-Century Revolution*. London: Allen Lane, 1993.

Hill-Vásquez, Heather. *Sacred Players: The Politics of Response in the Middle English Religious Drama*. Washington, D.C.: Catholic University of America Press, 2007.

Hodgkins, Christopher. *Authority, Church, and Society in George Herbert: A Return to the Middle Way*. Columbia: University of Missouri Press, 1993.

Hodgson, Elizabeth. "Prophecy and Gendered Mourning in Lanyer's *Salve Deus Rex Judeorum*." *Studies in English Literature* 43:1 (2003): 101–16.

Hollander, Anne. *Seeing Through Clothes*. Berkeley: University of California Press, 1993.

Holmes, Richard R. "The English Miniature Painters Illustrated in the Royal and Other Collections. Article III—Isaac Oliver." *Burlington Magazine* 9:37 (1906): 22–29.

Howarth, David. "The Arrival of van Dyck in England." *Burlington Magazine* 132:1051 (1990): 709–10.

Howarth, David, ed. *Art and Patronage in the Caroline Courts: Essays in Honour of Sir Oliver Millar*. Cambridge: Cambridge University Press, 1993.

Hufstader, Anselm. "Lefèvre d'Étaples and the Magdalen." *Studies in the Renaissance* 16 (1969): 31–60.

Hurley, Ann Hollinshead. *John Donne's Poetry and Early Modern Visual Culture*. Selinsgrove, Pa.: Susquehanna University Press, 2005.

Jackson, Ken, and Arthur F. Marotti. "The Turn to Religion in Early Modern Studies." *Criticism* 46:1 (2004): 167–90.

Jacobovici, Simcha, and Charles R. Pellegrino. *The Jesus Family Tomb: The Discovery, the Investigation, and the Evidence That Could Change History.* New York: HarperCollins, 2007.

Janelle, Pierre. *Robert Southwell, the Writer: A Study in Religious Inspiration.* New York: Sheed & Ward, 1935.

Jansen, Katherine Ludwig. *The Making of the Magdalen: Preaching and Popular Devotion in the Later Middle Ages.* Princeton: Princeton University Press, 2000.

Jenkins, Gary W. "Smith, Henry (ca. 1560–1591)." *ODNB.* Oxford: Oxford University Press, 2004. Available at http://www.oxforddnb.com/view/article/25811.

Kendall, Ritchie. *The Drama of Dissent.* Chapel Hill: University of North Carolina Press, 1986.

Kessler, Herbert L. *Spiritual Seeing: Picturing God's Invisibility in Medieval Art.* Philadelphia: University of Pennsylvania Press, 2000.

King, John. *English Reformation Literature: The Tudor Origins of the Protestant Tradition.* Princeton: Princeton University Press, 1982.

King, Karen L. *The Gospel of Mary of Magdala: Jesus and the First Woman Apostle.* Santa Rosa, Calif.: Polebridge Press, 2003.

King, Laura. "Sacred Eroticism, Rapturous Anguish: Christianity's Penitent Prostitutes and the Vexation of Allegory, 1370–1608." Ph.D. diss., University of California, Berkeley, 1993.

Kobialka, Michal. *This Is My Body: Representational Practices in the Early Middle Ages.* Ann Arbor: University of Michigan Press, 1999.

Koerner, Joseph Leo. *The Reformation of the Image.* Chicago: University of Chicago Press, 2004.

Krieger, Murray. "*Ekphrasis* and the Still Movement of Poetry." In *The Poet as Critic*, edited by Frederick P. W. McDowell, 3–36. Evanston, Ill.: Northwestern University Press, 1967.

Kronenfeld, Judy. *King Lear and the Naked Truth: Rethinking the Language of Religion and Resistance.* Durham, N.C.: Duke University Press, 1998.

Kuchar, Gary. "Aemilia Lanyer and the Virgin's Swoon: Theology and Iconography in *Salve Deus Rex Judaeorum.*" *English Literary Renaissance* 37:1 (2007): 47–73.

———. "Andrew Marvell's Anamorphic Tears." *Studies in Philology* 103:3 (2006): 345–81.

———. *Divine Subjection: The Rhetoric of Sacramental Devotion in Early Modern England.* Pittsburgh, Pa.: Duquesne University Press, 2005.

———. "Gender and Recusant Melancholia in Robert Southwell's *Mary Magdalene's Funeral Tears.*" In *Catholic Culture in Early Modern England*, edited by Ronald Corthell, Frances E. Dolan, Christopher Highley, and Arthur F. Marotti, 135–57. Notre Dame, Ind.: University of Notre Dame Press, 2007.

———. "Henry Constable and the Question of Catholic Poetics: Affective Piety and Erotic Identification in the *Spirituall Sonnettes.*" *Philological Quarterly* 85:1–2 (2006): 69–90.

———. *The Poetry of Religious Sorrow in Early Modern England.* Cambridge: Cambridge University Press, 2008.

Kunzle, David. "Dress Reform and Antifeminism: A Response to Helene E. Robert's 'The Exquisite Slave: The Role of Clothes in the Making of the Victorian Woman." *Signs* 2:3 (1977): 570–79.

Lake, Peter. *Anglicans and Puritans? Presbyterianism and English Conformist Thought from Whitgift to Hooker.* London: Unwin Hyman, 1988.

———. "Anti-Popery: The Structure of a Prejudice." In *Conflict in Early Stuart England: Studies in Religion and Politics, 1603–1642*, edited by Richard Cust and Ann Hughes, 72–106. London: Longman, 1989.

———. "Business as Usual? The Immediate Reception of Hooker's *Ecclesiastical Polity.*" *Journal of Ecclesiastical History* 52:3 (2001): 456–86.

———. "Lancelot Andrewes, John Buckeridge, and Avant-Guarde Conformity at the Court of James I." In *The Mental World of the Jacobean Court*, edited by Linda Levy Peck, 113–33. Cambridge: Cambridge University Press, 1991.

Lake, Peter, with Michael Questier. *The Anti-Christ's Lewd Hat: Protestants, Papists and Players in Post-Reformation England.* New Haven: Yale University Press, 2002.

Levi, Peter. *The English Bible, 1534–1859.* Grand Rapids, Mich.: Eerdmans, 1974.

Levine, Laura. *Men in Women's Clothing: Antitheatricality and Effeminization, 1579–1642.* Cambridge: Cambridge University Press, 1994.

Lewalski, Barbara Kiefer. *Protestant Poetics and the Seventeenth-Century Religious Lyric.* Princeton: Princeton University Press, 1979.

Lupton, Julia Reinhard. *Afterlives of the Saints: Hagiography, Typology, and Renaissance Literature.* Stanford: Stanford University Press, 1996.

Luxon, Thomas H. *Literal Figures: Puritan Allegory and the Reformation Crisis in Representation.* Chicago: University of Chicago Press, 1995.

MacCulloch, Diarmaid. *The Reformation: A History.* New York: Viking Penguin, 2003.

MacLeod, Catherine, and Julia Marciari Alexander, eds. *Painted Ladies: Women at the Court of Charles II.* London: National Portrait Gallery Publications, 2001.

Malcolmson, Cristina. *Heart-Work: George Herbert and the Protestant Ethic.* Stanford: Stanford University Press, 1999.

Maltby, Judith. *Prayer Book and People in Elizabethan and Early Stuart England.* Cambridge: Cambridge University Press, 1998.

Malvern, Marjorie M. *Venus in a Sackcloth: The Magdalen's Origins and Meta-morphoses.* Carbondale: Southern Illinois University Press, 1975.

Mandelbrote, Scott. "The Authority of the Word: Manuscript, Print, and the Text of the Bible in Seventeenth-Century England." In *The Uses of Script and Print, 1300–1700,* edited by Julia Crick and Alexandra Walsham, 135–53. Cambridge: Cambridge University Press, 2004.

Marotti, Arthur F., ed. *Catholicism and Anti-Catholicism in Early Modern English Texts.* New York: St. Martin's Press, 1999.

———. *Religious Ideology and Cultural Fantasy: Catholic and Anti-Catholic Discourses in Early Modern England.* Notre Dame, Ind.: University of Notre Dame Press, 2005.

Marshall, Bruce D. "The Divided Church and Its Theology." *Modern Theology* 16:3 (2000): 377–95.

Marshall, Peter. *Reformation England, 1480–1642.* London: Arnold, 2003.

Martz, Louis Lohr. *From Renaissance to Baroque: Essays on Literature and Art.* Columbia: University of Missouri Press, 1991.

———. *The Poetry of Meditation: A Study in English Religious Literature of the Seventeenth Century.* 2nd ed. New Haven: Yale University Press, 1962.

Mateer, David. "Marbeck, John (ca. 1505–1585?)." *ODNB.* Oxford: Oxford University Press, 2004. Available at http://www.oxforddnb.com/view/article/18026.

Matthew, H. C. G., and Brian Harrison, eds. *Oxford Dictionary of National Biography.* In Association with the British Academy. From the Earliest Times to the Year 2000. Oxford: Oxford University Press, 2004. Available at http://www.oxforddnb.com.

Maus, Katharine Eisaman. *Inwardness and Theater in the English Renaissance.* Chicago: University of Chicago Press, 1995.

Mazzola, Elizabeth. *The Pathology of the English Renaissance: Sacred Remains and Holy Ghosts.* Leiden: Brill, 1998.

McCall, John P. "Chaucer and the Pseudo Origen *de Maria Magdalena*: A Preliminary Study." *Speculum* 46:3 (1971): 491–509.

McClain, Lisa. "'They have taken away my Lord': Mary Magdalene, Christ's Missing Body, and the Mass in Reformation England." *Sixteenth Century Journal* 38:1 (2007): 77–96.

McClendon, Muriel C., Joseph P. Ward, and Michael MacDonald, eds. *Protestant Identities: Religion, Society, and Self-Fashioning in Post-Reformation England.* Stanford: Stanford University Press, 2000.

McCullough, Peter. "Making Dead Men Speak: Laudianism, Print, and the Works of Lancelot Andrewes, 1626–1642." *Historical Journal* 41:2 (1998): 401–24.

McMullan, Gordon, and David Matthews, eds. *Reading the Medieval in Early Modern England.* Cambridge: Cambridge University Press, 2007.

Merleau-Ponty, Maurice. *The Visible and the Invisible.* Translated by Alphonso Lingus. Evanston, Ill.: Northwestern University Press, 1968.

Meyer, Marvin. *The Gnostic Discoveries: The Impact of the Nag Hammadi Library.* San Francisco: Harper, 2005.

Meyer, Marvin, and Esther A. De Boer. *The Gospels of Mary: The Secret Tradition of Mary Magdalene, the Companion of Jesus.* San Francisco: Harper, 2004.

Michalski, Sergiusz. *The Reformation and the Visual Arts: The Protestant Image Question in Western and Eastern Europe.* London: Routledge, 1993.

Millar, Oliver. *Tudor, Stuart, and Early Georgian Pictures in the Collection of Her Majesty the Queen.* London: Phaidon, 1963.

Miller, Greg. "Scribal and Print Publication: The Case of George Herbert's English Poems." *George Herbert Journal* 23 (1999–2000): 14–34.

Mitchell, W. J. T. *Iconology: Image, Text, Ideology.* Chicago: University of Chicago Press, 1986.

———. *Picture Theory: Essays on Verbal and Visual Representation.* Chicago: University of Chicago Press, 1994.

Most, Glenn W. *Doubting Thomas.* Cambridge, Mass.: Harvard University Press, 2005.

Nead, Lynda. *The Female Nude: Art, Obscenity, and Sexuality.* New York: Routledge, 1992.

Netzley, Ryan. "Oral Devotion: Eucharistic Theology and Richard Crashaw's Religious Lyrics." *Texas Studies in Literature and Language* 44:3 (2002): 247–72.

———. " 'Take and Taste': Sacramental Physiology, Eucharistic Experience, and George Herbert's *The Temple.*" In *Varieties of Devotion in the Middle Ages and Renaissance,* edited by Susan S. Karant-Nunn, 179–206. Turnhout, Belgium: Brepols, 2003.

Nicolson, Adam. *God's Secretaries: The Making of the King James Bible.* New York: HarperCollins, 2003.

Nora, Pierre. *Realms of Memory: Rethinking the French Past.* Edited by Lawrence D. Kritzman. Translated by Arthur Goldhammer. New York: Columbia University Press, 1996.

O'Connell, Michael. *The Idolatrous Eye: Iconoclasm and Theater in Early-Modern England.* New York: Oxford University Press, 2000.

O'Connell, Sheila. *The Popular Print in England.* London: British Museum Press, 1999.

Orgel, Stephen. "Idols of the Gallery: Becoming a Connoisseur in Renaissance England." In *Early Modern Visual Culture: Representation, Race, and Empire in Renaissance England,* edited by Peter Erickson and Clark Hulse, 251–83. Philadelphia: University of Pennsylvania Press, 2000.

———. *Impersonations: The Performance of Gender in Shakespeare's England.* Cambridge: Cambridge University Press, 1996.

Orlin, Lena Cowen. *Private Matters and Public Culture in Post-Reformation England.* Ithaca: Cornell University Press, 1994.

O'Sullivan, Orlaith, ed. *The Bible as Book: The Reformation.* New Castle, Del.: Oak Knoll Press, 2000.

Pagels, Elaine. *The Gnostic Gospels.* New York: Random House, 1979.

Parish, H. L. "Robinson, Thomas (fl. c. 1520–1561)." *ODNB.* Oxford: Oxford University Press, 2004. Available at http://www.oxforddnb.com/view/article/23811.

Parrish, Paul. "Crashaw's Two Weepers." *Concerning Poetry* 10 (1977): 47–59.

———. "Moderate Sorrow and Immoderate Tears: Mourning in Crashaw." In *Speaking Grief in English Literary Culture: Shakespeare to Milton,* edited by Margo Swiss and David A. Kent, 217–41. Pittsburgh, Pa.: Duquesne University Press, 2002.

———. "'O Sweet Contest': Gender and Value in 'The Weeper.'" In *New Perspectives on the Life and Art of Richard Crashaw,* edited by John R. Roberts, 127–39. Columbia: University of Missouri Press, 1990.

———. "Richard Crashaw, Mary Collet, and the 'Arminian Nunnery' of Little Gidding." In *Representing Women in Renaissance England,* edited by Claude J. Summers and Ted-Larry Pebworth, 187–200. Columbia: University of Missouri Press, 1997.

Parry, Graham. *The Arts of the Anglican Counter-Reformation: Glory, Laud and Honour.* Woodbridge, Suffolk: Boydell, 2006.

Paster, Gail Kern. "The Body and Its Passions." *Shakespeare Studies* 29 (2001): 44–50.

———. *The Body Embarrassed: Drama and the Disciplines of Shame in Early Modern England.* Ithaca: Cornell University Press, 1993.

———. *Humoring the Body: Emotions and the Shakespearean Stage.* Chicago: University of Chicago Press, 2004.

Peck, Linda Levy. *Consuming Splendor: Society and Culture in Seventeenth-Century England.* Cambridge: Cambridge University Press, 2005.

Pelikan, Jaroslav, Valerie R. Hotchkiss, and David Price. *The Reformation of the Bible/The Bible of the Reformation.* New Haven: Yale University Press, 1996.

Penketh, Sandra. "Women and Books of Hours." In *Women and the Book: Assessing the Visual Evidence,* edited by Lesley Smith and Jane H. M. Taylor, 266–81. London: British Library; Toronto: University of Toronto Press, 1997.

Peter, Arthur Granville. *The Story of the Church of St. Mary Magdalene Launceston.* Gloucester: British Publishing Company, 1936.

Peters, Christine. *Patterns of Piety: Women, Gender and Religion in Late Medieval and Reformation England.* Cambridge: Cambridge University Press, 2003.

Pettegree, Andrew. *Reformation and the Culture of Persuasion.* Cambridge: Cambridge University Press, 2005.

Phillippy, Patricia. *Women, Death, and Literature in Post-Reformation England.* Cambridge: Cambridge University Press, 2002.

Phillips, John. *The Reformation of Images: Destruction of Art in England, 1535–1660.* Berkeley: University of California Press, 1973.

Picknett, Lynn. *Mary Magdalene: Christianity's Hidden Goddess.* New York: Carroll and Graf, 2003.

Pinkus, Karen. *Picturing Silence: Emblem Language, Counter-Reformation Materiality.* Ann Arbor: University of Michigan Press, 1996.

Poynter, F. N. L. *A Bibliography of Gervase Markham.* Oxford: Oxford Bibliographical Society Publications, 1962.

Praz, Mario. *The Flaming Heart: Essays on Crashaw, Machiavelli, and Other Studies in the Relations Between Italian and English Literature from Chaucer to T. S. Eliot* (1958). Gloucester, Mass.: Peter Smith, 1966.

Questier, Michael. *Conversion, Politics, and Religion in England, 1580–1621.* Cambridge: Cambridge University Press, 1996.

Radner, Ephraim. *The End of the Church: A Pneumatology of Christian Division in the West.* Grand Rapids, Mich.: Eerdmans, 1998.

Rambuss, Richard. *Closet Devotions.* Durham, N.C.: Duke University Press, 1998.

———. "Sacred Subjects and the Aversive Metaphysical Conceit: Crashaw, Serrano, Ofili." *ELH* 72 (2004): 497–501.

Ransome, Joyce. "Monotessaron: The Harmonies of Little Gidding." *Seventeenth Century* 20:1 (2005): 22–52.

Reed, Jonathan L., and John Dominic Crossan. *Excavating Jesus: Beneath the Stones, Behind the Texts: Revised and Updated.* San Francisco: HarperOne, 2003.

Rex, Richard. *The Theology of John Fisher.* Cambridge: Cambridge University Press, 1991.

Roberts, Lorraine M. and John R. Roberts. "Crashavian Criticism: A Brief Interpretive History." In *New Perspectives on the Life and Art of Richard Crashaw*, edited by John R. Roberts, 1–29. Columbia: University of Missouri Press, 1990.

Roston, Murray. *Renaissance Perspectives in Literature and the Visual Arts.* Princeton: Princeton University Press, 1987.

Rubin, Miri. *Corpus Christi: The Eucharist in Late Medieval Culture.* Cambridge: Cambridge University Press, 1992.

Russell, Anne, ed. *The Rover; or, The Banished Cavaliers*, by Aphra Behn. Peterborough, Ont.: Broadview Press, 1998.

Sanok, Catherine. *Her Life Historical: Exemplarity and Female Saints' Lives in Late Medieval England.* Philadelphia: University of Pennsylvania Press, 2007.

Saxer, Victor. *Le culte de Marie Magdaleine en Occident des origines à la fin du moyen-âge.* 2 vols. Cahiers d'archéologie et d'histoire 3. Auxerre-Paris: Publications de la Société de Fouilles Archéologiques et des Monuments Historiques de l'Yvonne; Paris: Librairie Clavreuil, 1959.

———. "L'homilie latine du Pseudo-Origène sur Jean 20, 11–r18: Tradition manuscrite et origine historique." *Studi Medievali* 3d ser., 26 (1985): 667–76.

Scarry, Elaine. *Dreaming by the Book.* Princeton: Princeton University Press, 2001.

Schaberg, Jane. *The Resurrection of Mary Magdalene: Legends, Apocrypha, and the Christian Testament.* New York: Continuum, 2004.

Schoenfledt, Michael Carl. *Bodies and Selves in Early Modern England: Physiology and Inwardness in Spenser, Shakespeare, Herbert, and Milton.* Cambridge: Cambridge University Press, 1999.

———. *Prayer and Power: George Herbert and Renaissance Courtship.* Chicago: University of Chicago Press, 1991.

———. "'That Spectacle of Too Much Weight': The Poetics of Sacrifice in Donne, Herbert, and Milton." *Journal of Medieval and Early Modern Studies* 31:3 (2001): 561–84.

Schwenger, Peter. "Crashaw's Perspectivist Metaphor." *Comparative Literature* 28:1 (1976): 65–74.

Semler, L. E. *The English Mannerist Poets and the Visual Arts.* Madison, N.J.: Fairleigh Dickinson University Press, 1998.

Sheils, William Joseph. "Robinson, Thomas (fl. 1622)." *ODNB.* Oxford: Oxford University Press, 2004. Available at http://www.oxforddnb.com/view/article/23875.

Shell, Alison. *Catholicism, Controversy, and the English Literary Imagination: 1558–1660.* Cambridge: Cambridge University Press, 1999.

Shuger, Debora Kuller. *The Renaissance Bible: Scholarship, Sacrifice, and Subjectivity.* Berkeley: University of California Press, 1994.

Simpson, James. "The Rule of Medieval Imagination." In *Images, Idolatry, and Iconoclasm in Late Medieval England: Textuality and the Visual Image*, edited by Jeremy Dimmick, James Simpson, and Nicolette Zeeman, 4–24. Oxford: Oxford University Press, 2002.

Sinfield, Alan. *Literature and Protestant England.* London: Barnes and Noble, 1983.

Skerpan-Wheeler, Elizabeth. *The Rhetoric of Politics in the English Revolution.* Columbia: University of Missouri Press, 1992.

Slater, Ann Pasternak, ed. *The Complete English Works: George Herbert.* New York: Alfred A. Knopf, 1995.

Smith, Lesley. "*Scriba, Femina:* Medieval Depictions of Women Writing." In *Women and the Book: Assessing the Visual Evidence*, edited by Lesley Smith and Jane H. M. Taylor, 21–44. London: British Library; Toronto: University of Toronto Press, 1997.

Smith, Lesley, and Jane H. M. Taylor, eds. *Women and the Book: Assessing the Visual Evidence*. London: British Library, 1997.

Smith, Nigel, ed. *The Poems of Andrew Marvell*. London: Pearson Longman, 2007.

Stallybrass, Peter. "Worn Worlds: Clothes and Identity on the Renaissance Stage." In *Subject and Object in Renaissance Culture*, edited by Margreta de Grazia, Maureen Quilligan, and Peter Stallybrass, 289–320. Cambridge: Cambridge University Press, 1996.

Steggle, Matthew. "Markham, Gervase (1568?–1637)." *ODNB*. Oxford: Oxford University Press, 2004. Available at http://www.oxforddnb.com/view/article/18065.

Stewart, Stanley. "Herbert and the 'Harmonies' of Little Gidding." *Cythara* 24 (1984): 3–26.

Stewart, Susan A. *Poetry and the Fate of the Senses*. Chicago: University of Chicago Press, 2002.

Stoker, David. "Thomason, George (ca. 1602–1666)." *ODNB*. Oxford: Oxford University Press, 2004. Available at http://www.oxforddnb.com/view/article/27250.

Strier, Richard. "Changing the Object: Herbert and Excess." *George Herbert Journal* 2 (1978): 24–37.

———. "George Herbert and Tears." *ELH* 46:2 (1979): 221–47.

———. *Love Known: Theology and Experience in George Herbert's Poetry*. Chicago: University of Chicago Press, 1983.

Strong, Roy. *The Cult of Elizabeth*. London: Thames and Hudson, 1977.

Strong, Roy, and Brian Allen. *The British Portrait, 1660–1960*. Woodbridge, Suffolk: Antique Collectors' Club, 1991.

Sullivan, Ceri. "Constable, Henry (1562–1613)." *ODNB*. Oxford: Oxford University Press, 2004. Available at http://www.oxforddnb.com/view/article/6103.

———. *Dismembered Rhetoric: English Recusant Writing, 1580–1603*. Madison, N.J.: Fairleigh Dickinson University Press; London: Associated University Presses, 1995.

———. "The Physiology of Penitence in 1590s Weeping Texts." *Cahiers élisabéthains* 57 (2000): 31–47.

———. *The Rhetoric of Conscience in Donne, Herbert and Vaughan*. Oxford: Oxford University Press, 2008.

Surtz, Edward L. *The Works and Days of John Fisher*. Cambridge, Mass.: Harvard University Press, 1967.

Swann, Marjorie. *Curiosities and Texts: The Culture of Collecting in Early Modern England*. Philadelphia: University of Pennsylvania Press, 2001.

Targoff, Ramie. *Common Prayer: The Language of Public Devotion in Early Modern England.* Chicago: University of Chicago Press, 2001.

Tassi, Marguerite A. *The Scandal of Images: Iconoclasm, Eroticism, and Painting in Early Modern English Drama.* Selinsgrove, Pa.: Susquehanna University Press, 2005.

Thimmes, Pamela. "Memory and Revision: Mary Magdalene Research Since 1975." *Currents in Research* 6 (1988): 193–226.

Thomas, Keith. "Cleanliness and Godliness in Early Modern England." In *Religion, Culture and Society in Early Modern Britain,* edited by Anthony Fletcher and Peter Roberts, 66–67. Cambridge: Cambridge University Press, 1994.

Thompson, John Lee. *John Calvin and the Daughters of Sarah: Women in Regular and Exceptional Roles in the Exegesis of Calvin, His Predecessors, and His Contemporaries.* Durham, N.C.: Duke University Press, 1989.

Todd, Janet M. *The Secret Life of Aphra Behn.* New Brunswick, N.J.: Rutgers University Press, 1997.

Trill, Suzanne. "Engendering Penitence: Nicholas Breton and the 'Countesse of Penbrooke.'" In *Voicing Women: Gender and Sexuality in Early Modern Writing,* edited by Kate Chedgzoy, Melanie Hansen, and Suzanne Trill, 25–44. Liverpool: Liverpool University Press, 1998.

Tumbleson, Raymond D. *Catholicism in the English Protestant Imagination: Nationalism, Religion, and Literature, 1600–1745.* Cambridge: Cambridge University Press, 1998.

Tyacke, Nicholas, ed. *England's Long Reformation, 1500–1800.* London: Routledge, 1998.

Veith, Gene Edward. *Reformation Spirituality: The Religion of George Herbert.* Lewisburg, Pa.: Bucknell University Press, 1985.

Vendler, Helen. *The Poetry of George Herbert.* Cambridge, Mass.: Harvard University Press, 1975.

Wall, Wendy. "Our Bodies/Our Texts? Renaissance Women and the Trials of Authorship." In *Anxious Power: Reading, Writing, and Ambivalence in Narrative by Women,* edited by Carol J. Singley and Susan Elizabeth Sweeney, 51–71. Albany: State University of New York Press, 1993.

———. "Renaissance National Husbandry: Gervase Markham and the Publication of England." *Sixteenth Century Journal* 27:3 (1996): 767–85.

Walsham, Alexandra. "'Domme preachers'? Post-Reformation English Catholicism and the Culture of Print." *Past and Present* 168 (2000): 72–123.

———. "Jewels for Gentlewomen: Religious Books as Artefacts in Late Medieval and Early Modern England." *Studies in Church History* 38 (2004): 123–42.

———. "Unclasping the Book? Post-Reformation English Catholicism and the Vernacular Bible." *Journal of British Studies* 42:2 (2003): 141–66.

Watt, Tessa. *Cheap Print and Popular Piety, 1550–1640*. Cambridge: Cambridge University Press, 1991.

Weil, Rachel. "Sometimes a Scepter Is Only a Scepter: Pornography and Politics in Restoration England." In *The Invention of Pornography: Obscenity and the Origins of Modernity, 1500–1800*, edited by Lynn Hunt, 125–53. New York: Zone Books, 1996.

Welborn, Amy. *De-Coding Mary Magdalene: Truth, Legend and Lies*. Huntington, Ind.: Our Sunday Visitor, 2006.

Wells-Cole, Anthony. *Art and Decoration in Elizabethan and Jacobean England: The Influence of Continental Prints, 1558–1625*. New Haven: Yale University Press, 1997.

Whalen, Robert. "George Herbert's Sacramental Puritanism." *Renaissance Quarterly* 54:4 (2001): 1273–1307.

White, Paul Whitfield. "Lewis Wager's *Life and Repentaunce of Mary Magdalene* and John Calvin." *Notes and Queries* 28:6 (1981): 508–12.

———. *Reformation Biblical Drama in England: An Old Spelling Critical Edition*. New York: Garland, 1992.

———. *Theatre and Reformation: Protestantism, Patronage, and Playing in Tudor England*. Cambridge: Cambridge University Press, 1993.

Wickes, George. "Henry Constable, Poet and Courtier 1562–1613." No. 272 in Catholic Record Society *Biographical Studies* 2:4 (1953): 272–300.

Wiener, Carol. "The Beleaguered Isle: A Study of Elizabethan and Early Jacobean Anti-Catholicism." *Past and Present* 51 (1971): 27–62.

Wolfe, Heather. "Elizabeth (Tanfield) Cary, Viscountess Falkland, to Susan (Villiers) Fielding, Countess of Denbigh (c. December 1626)." In *Reading Early Modern Women: An Anthology of Texts in Manuscript and Print*, edited by Helen Ostovich and Elizabeth Sauer, 211–14. London: Routledge, 2004.

Womack, Peter. "Shakespeare and the Sea of Stories." *Journal of Medieval and Early Modern Studies* 29:1 (1999): 169–87.

Wynne, S. M. "Gwyn, Eleanor (1651?–1687)." *ODNB*. Oxford: Oxford University Press, 2004. Available at http://www.oxforddnb.com/view/article/11816.

———. "Palmer, Barbara, Countess of Castlemaine and Suo Jure Duchess of Cleveland (bap. 1640, d. 1709)." *ODNB*. Oxford: Oxford University Press, 2004. Available at http://www.oxforddnb.com/view/article/28285.

Young, R. V. *Doctrine and Devotion in Seventeenth-Century Poetry: Studies in Donne, Herbert, Crashaw, and Vaughan*. Cambridge: D. S. Brewer, 2000.

INDEX

PATRICIA BADIR
is associate professor of English literature
at the University of British Columbia.